Briefcase on Constitutional and Administrative Law

David Herling, D Phil (Oxon), BA, Barrister
Lecturer in Law
City University, London

First published in Great Britain 1995 by Cavendish Publishing Limited, The Glass House, Wharton Street, London WC1X 9PX.

Telephone: 0171-278 8000 Facsimile: 0171-278 8080

E-mail: info@cavendishpublishing.com

Visit our Home Page on http://www.cavendishpublishing.com

© Herling, D 1997

First edition 1995

Herling, David
Briefcase on constitutional and administrative law – 2nd ed
1. Administrative law – England 2. Administrative law – Wales
3. England – Constitutional law 4. Wales – Constitutional law
I Title
342.4'2

ISBN 1 85941 254 8

Printed and bound in Great Britain

Preface

The revision and expansion of the first edition have not altered its aims. Despite the resources of law libraries, textbook discussions and lecture notes, there remains a place for a systematic, straightforward and portable account of the leading cases in constitutional and administrative law.

Of the book's three sections, the administrative law division has received the greatest number of additions. In part, this reflects the rapidity with which juridical review develops (or, in the area of the legitimate expectations, the persistence of an inclination towards doctrinal campaigning among certain judges); as a counterweight to the principled part of the litigation, adding new cases on time limits and the availability of alternative remedies.

The constitutional and civil liberties sections continue to provide, respectively, a fairly full account of major cases and an insight into the rights in the common law. The chapter on parliamentary privilege has been substantially updated, and the cases on particular prerogative powers now include the Privy Council's decision in *Reckley*, as unfortunate as it was diplomatic. The comments of the Court of Appeal in *R v Morrisey, R v Staines* now stands in interesting juxtaposition to the opinions of their Lordships in the *Brind* and *Derbyshire* cases, as the new government contemplates the incorporation of the European Convention into domestic law.

It is a pleasure to have the opportunity to thank the production team at Cavendish for the friendly and relaxed professionalism. I am also grateful to the students at City University and readers from further afield whose comments on the book were very much borne in mind as I prepared the second edition.

David Herling
August 1997

Contents

Part 3 Civil liberties and the common law

Table of Cases

Table of Statutes

Part 1 Constitutional law

1 Conventions distinguished from laws

1.1 The nature of constitutional conventions

Dicey, AV, *An Introduction to the Study of the Law of the Constitution*
(1965, 10th edn) pp 23–24

The rules which make up constitutional law, as the term is used in England, include two sets of principles or maxims of a totally different character.

The one set of rules are in the strictest sense 'laws', since they are rules which (either written or unwritten, whether enacted by statute or derived from the mass of custom, tradition, or judge-made maxims known as the common law) are enforced by the courts; these rules constitute 'constitutional law' in the proper sense of that term, and may for the sake of convenience be called collectively 'the law of the constitution'.

The other set of rules consist of conventions, understandings, habits, or practices which, though they may regulate the conduct of the several members of the sovereign power, of the Ministry, or of other officials, are not in reality laws at all since they are not enforced by the courts. This portion of constitutional law may, for the sake of distinction, be termed the 'conventions of the constitution', or 'constitutional morality'.

1.2 The distinction between laws and conventions

Madzimbamuto v Lardner-Burke (1969) PC
The appellant's husband was detained under regulations made by the new regime in Rhodesia which had assumed power upon the Rhodesian Prime Minister's Unilateral Declaration of Independence. Six days after the Declaration, the UK Parliament had passed the Southern Rhodesia Act 1965 which declared that Rhodesia was still part of Her Majesty's Dominions, and that the UK government and Parliament still had responsibility for and jurisdiction over it. The Southern Rhodesia (Constitution Order 1965), made under the Act, declared that no laws might be made by the Legislature of

Southern Rhodesia. The Rhodesian courts held that although the new regime was unlawful it was necessary to give effect to its laws as it was the only effective government in Rhodesia. Mrs Madzimbamuto appealed to the Privy Council.

Held, allowing the appeal (by a majority), that it was for Parliament alone to determine whether the maintenance of law and order would justify giving effect to laws made by the usurping government. In the absence of any such determination, the UK Parliament's laws should continue to be regarded as binding by the courts, whatever the political reality of the situation. *Per* Lord Reid:

> It is often said that it would be unconstitutional for the United Kingdom Parliament to do certain things, meaning that the moral, political and other reasons against doing them are so strong that most people would regard it as highly improper if Parliament did these things. But that does not mean that it is beyond the power of Parliament to do such things. If Parliament chose to do any of them the courts could not hold the Act of Parliament invalid. It may be that it would be unconstitutional to disregard this convention. But it may also be that the unilateral Declaration of Independence released the United Kingdom from any obligation to observe the convention. Their Lordships in declaring the law are not concerned with these matters. They are only concerned with the legal powers of Parliament.

1.3 The courts will admit evidence of conventions to establish a cause of action

Attorney General v Jonathan Cape Ltd (1976)

The Secretary to the Cabinet had refused to approve publication of extracts from the Cabinet diaries of Richard Crossman on the ground that it would be contrary to the public interest. He argued that revelation of discussions in Cabinet would breach the convention of collective ministerial responsibility. The Attorney General sought injunctions to prevent the publication of the diaries in *The Sunday Times*. He submitted that the confidential character of the information contained in the diaries could be derived, *inter alia*, from the fact that publication would tend to undermine the future operation of the convention. The defendants contended that the evidence did not prove the existence of a convention of collective cabinet responsibility, and that if it did, the convention was binding in conscience only.

Held, refusing the injunctions, that the general effect of the evidence was that the convention was an established feature of the English form of government. However, although the maintenance of the convention of collective responsibility in cabinet was in the public interest, and the court would therefore intervene in a clear case to uphold it by injunction where the public interest demanded, the information in the present case was nearly 10 years old and its publication would not inhibit the continued freedom of discussion in cabinet.

1.4 Conventions cannot crystallise into law

Reference Re Amendment of the Constitution of Canada (1982) Supreme Court of Canada

Among a number of questions put to the court was the following:

Does the Canadian Constitution empower, whether by statute, convention or otherwise, the Senate and the House of Commons of Canada to cause the Canadian Constitution to be amended without the consent of the provinces and in spite of the objection of several of them ...?

The Attorney General of Manitoba submitted that the amendment before the court was contrary to convention, that a convention may crystallise into law, and that in consequence the federal government could not legally request the amendment.

Held (by the majority) that the question was to be answered in the affirmative as to the legal position, and in the negative as far as convention was concerned. The majority stated:

No instance of an explicit recognition of a convention as having matured into a rule of law was produced. The very nature of a convention, as political in inception and as depending on a consistent course of political recognition by those for whose benefit and to whose detriment (if any) the convention developed over a considerable period of time is inconsistent with its legal enforcement.

The attempted assimilation of the growth of a convention to the growth of the common law is misconceived. The latter is the product of judicial effort, based on justiciable issues which have attained legal formulation and are subject to modification and even reversal by the courts which gave them birth when acting within their role in the State in obedience to statutes or constitutional directives. No such parental role is played by the courts with respect to conventions ...

The main purpose of constitutional conventions is to ensure that the legal framework of the Constitution will be operated in accordance with the prevailing constitutional values or principles of the period ... perhaps the main reason why conventional rules cannot be enforced by the courts is that they are generally in conflict with the legal rules which they postulate and the courts are bound to enforce the legal rules. The conflict is not of a type which would entail the commission of any illegality. It results from the fact that legal rules create wide powers, discretions and rights which conventions prescribe should be exercised only in a certain limited manner, if at all ...

This conflict between convention and law which prevents the courts from enforcing conventions also prevents conventions crystallising into laws, unless it be by statutory adoption ...

It should be borne in mind, however, that while they are not laws, some conventions may be more important than some laws. Their importance depends on that of the value or principle which they are meant to safeguard. Also they form an integral part of the Constitution and of the constitutional system ...

That is why it is perfectly appropriate to say that to violate a convention is to do something which is unconstitutional although it entails no direct legal consequence.

2 The rule of law

2.1 Government according to the law

Dicey, AV, *An Introduction to the Study of the Law of the Constitution*
(1965, 10th edn) pp 188, 202

We mean, in the first place, that no man is punishable or can be lawfully made
to suffer in body or goods except for a distinct breach of law established in the
ordinary legal manner before the ordinary courts of the land. In this sense the
rule of law is contrasted with every system of government based on the exercise
by persons in authority of wide, arbitrary, or discretionary powers of constraint
... It means ... the absolute supremacy or predominance of regular law as
opposed to the influence of arbitrary power, and excludes the existence of arbi-
trariness, of prerogative, or even of wide discretionary authority on the part of
the government. Englishmen are ruled by the law, and by the law alone; a man
may with us be punished for a breach of the law, but he can be punished for
nothing else.

R v Coventry City Council, *ex parte* **Phoenix Aviation (and other
applications) (1995)**

During 1994 and 1995, protesters sought to draw public attention to and/or
to disrupt and prevent the export of live animals through British ports and
airports. This trade was lawful; those demonstrating against it had regularly exceeded their lawful right of protest. The Divisional Court heard
and determined three separate applications for judicial review together,
each arising in connection with the response of transport authorities to the
disruption caused by these demonstrations. The first and second applications were brought by businesses involved in the livestock export trade
against decisions to close (i) Coventry City Airport and (ii) Dover Harbour
to that trade. In the third application, a local authority challenged the failure of a statutory port authority to ban the export of live animals through
Millbay Docks at Plymouth. Each application called for consideration of
the relevant transport authority's statutory duties, the extent of its statutory discretions (if any) in the discharge of such duties, and the factors which
might properly influence the exercise of discretion.

Held, that the first two applications would be granted, and the third
refused. In each case, the transport authority enjoyed no general discretion

5

to distinguish between lawful trades. Even were this incorrect, discretion could not properly be exercised to ban the livestock trade on the ground that it would cause unlawful disruption. *Per* Simon Brown LJ:

> One thread runs consistently through the case law: the recognition that public authorities must beware of surrendering to the dictates of unlawful pressure groups. The implications of such surrender for the rule of law can hardly be exaggerated ... Tempting though it may sometimes be for public authorities to yield too readily to threats of disruption, they must expect the courts to review any such decision with particular rigour – this is not an area where they can be permitted a wide measure of discretion. As when fundamental rights are in play, the courts will adopt a more interventionist role.

> Turning briefly to the present cases, all of them to our mind have one thing in common, a consideration which brings small credit to any of the three authorities concerned to bar this trade. None of them, it appears, gave the least thought to the awesome implications for the rule of law of doing what they propose.

2.1.1 The courts are independent of the executive in the administration of justice

Prohibitions del Roy (Case of Prohibitions) (1607)

The king purported to hear and decide a case himself. On appeal, it was argued that in matters which were not covered by express legal authority, the monarch himself 'may take what causes he shall please to determine, from the determination of the judges, and may determine them himself'. This right was divinely given to the king, and the judges were merely his delegates to exercise it during his pleasure.

Held, annulling the king's determination, that matters concerning the administration of justice were solely determined in the Courts of Justice, and that no king after the Norman Conquest had assumed the right to judge any case himself. *Per* Lord Coke CJ:

> ... then the King said that he thought the law was founded on reason, and that he and others had reason, as well as the judges: to which it was answered by me, that true it was, that God had endowed His Majesty with excellent science, and great endowments of nature: but His Majesty was not learned in the laws of his realm of England, and causes which concern the life, or inheritance, or goods, or fortunes of his subjects, are not to be decided by natural reason but by the artificial reason and judgment of the law, which law is an art which requires long study and experience, before that a man can attain to the cognizance of it: that the law was the golden metwand and measure to try the causes of the subjects; and which protected His Majesty in safety and peace: with which the King was greatly offended, and said, that then he should be under the law, which was treason to affirm, as he said: to which I said, that Bracton saith, *quod Rex non debet esse sub homine, sed sub Deo et lege.*

Liversidge v Anderson (1941) (HL)

The appellant was detained in prison under the Defence (General) Regulations 1939. Regulation 18B provided as follows: 'If the Secretary of State has reasonable cause to believe any person to be of hostile origin or associations ... and that by reason thereof it is necessary to exercise control over him, he may make an order against that person directing that he be detained.' In the course of an action for a declaration that his detention was unlawful, and damages for false imprisonment, the appellant sought particulars of the grounds on which the Secretary of State believed him to be of hostile associations, and the grounds on which he believed it necessary to exercise control over him. Having failed at first instance and before the Court of Appeal, the appellant appealed to the House of Lords.

Held, by a majority, that the appeal would be dismissed. On their true construction, the words 'has reasonable cause to believe' meant no more than that the Secretary of State should, in good faith, himself consider that he had reasonable cause.

Lord Atkin, dissenting, stated that the relevant words were capable only of meaning that the Secretary of State should objectively have good cause, and observed that for generations this meaning had consistently been attributed to similar expressions in the area of police powers and the wider criminal law. With regard to the opinion of the majority of their Lordships, he said:

> I view with apprehension the attitude of judges who, on a mere question of construction, when face to face with claims involving the liberty of the subject, show themselves more executive-minded than the executive. Their function is to give words their natural meaning ... In England amidst the clash of arms the laws are not silent. They may be changed, but they speak the same language in war as in peace. It has always been one of the pillars of freedom, one of the principles of liberty for which, on recent authority, we are now fighting, that the judges are no respecters of persons, and stand between the subject and any attempted encroachments on his liberty by the executive, alert to see that any coercive action is justified in law. In this case I have listened to arguments which might have been addressed acceptably to the Court of King's Bench in the time of Charles I.

2.1.2 The powers of the executive do not exceed those known to the courts

Entick v Carrington (1765)

Entick was alleged to be the author of seditious writings. Two king's messengers, purporting to act under the authority of a warrant issued not by a court but by the Secretary of State, broke into Entick's house and carried away his papers. Entick sued the messengers for trespass. The Secretary of State argued that he had the power to issue warrants because it was essential to government that he should have it.

Held that the warrant was illegal and void. It was incumbent upon the Secretary of State to establish what law authorised his invasion of another's rights. He had been unable to show any statute or common law to sanction the issue of the warrant. The arguments of State necessity, or of a claimed distinction between State offences and others, were of no validity. *Per* Lord Camden CJ:

> By the laws of England, every invasion of private property, be it ever so minute, is a trespass. No man can set his foot upon my ground without my licence, but he is liable to an action, though the damage be nothing ... If he admits the fact, he is bound to shew by way of justification, that some positive law has empowered or excused him. The justification is submitted to the judges, who are to look into the books; and see if such a justification can be maintained by the text of the statute law, or by the principles of common law. If no such excuse can be found or produced, the silence of the books is an authority against the defendant, and the plaintiff must have judgment.

R v Inland Revenue Commissioners, *ex parte* Rossminster Ltd (1980) HL

Rossminster's premises were searched by officers of the Inland Revenue acting pursuant to warrants issued by the appropriate judicial authority. The warrants were drafted in broad and general terms, and did not specify the detail or types of offences which Rossminster was suspected of having committed. The Court of Appeal found in favour of Rossminster. It held that the court was under a duty to construe the legislation to ensure that it encroached as little as possible on the liberties of subjects. Unless a person knew the details of an offence of which he was suspected, he could take no steps to secure himself or his property. The warrant was therefore invalid. The Inland Revenue Commissioners appealed to the House of Lords.

Held, allowing the appeal, that the warrant accorded sufficiently with the provisions of the legislation under which it had been issued. The courts did have a duty to supervise the legality of any exercise of a power which, as here, substantially infringed individual liberties. However, they had no right to impede the working of legislation.

Morris v Beardmore (1980) (HL)

Following an accident in which the appellant's car had been involved police officers wished to interview him. The appellant's son let them into his house, but the appellant refused to come down from his bedroom, and informed the police that they were trespassing. The police did not leave, but asked him to provide a specimen for a breath test. He refused, and was charged with failure to provide the specimen. The Divisional Court, overturning the decision of the justices, held that the request for the specimen was not vitiated by the fact of the trespass. The appellant appealed to the House of Lords.

Held, allowing the appeal, that the appellant had not validly been required to provide the specimen, since the request had come not from a police officer in the execution of his duty, but from an officer who was trespassing. It was correct to state that the relevant statute contained no provision prohibiting the action taken by the officers, but that did not establish its legality; if Parliament intended to authorise the doing of an act which otherwise would constitute a tort actionable at the suit of the person to whom the act was done, that required express provision in the statute.

2.1.3 The rule of law imposes duties upon law-makers

Laws should be clear

Merkur Island Shipping Corp v Laughton (1983) CA, HL

The plaintiffs sought an interlocutory injunction to prevent the 'blacking' of their ship by a trade union. The question arose whether legislation in principle prevented the trade union from being liable for loss caused by secondary picketing. The answer involved the court in construing three Acts of Parliament together.

In judgment, Lord Donaldson referred to the difficulty which the court had experienced and the time which had been spent in seeking to understand the statutory provisions. It was necessary to the efficacy and maintenance of the rule of law that people should be able to discover what the law required of them. When Parliament's legislation directly affected individuals, clarity and simplicity of expression ought to be given as high a priority as refinements of policy. *Per* Lord Diplock:

> Absence of clarity is destructive of the rule of law; it is unfair to those who wish to preserve the rule of law; it encourages those who wish to undermine it. The statutory provisions which it became necessary to piece together into a coherent whole in order to decide the stage three point are drafted in a manner which, having regard to their subject matter and the persons who will be called upon to apply them, can, in my view, only be characterised as most regrettably lacking in the requisite degree of clarity.

The presumption against the retroactive effect of legislation

Phillips v Eyre (1870)

Following the suppression of a rebellion in Jamaica, an Indemnity Act was passed. The plaintiff sued for assault and false imprisonment.

Held, *per* Willes J:

> Retrospective laws are, no doubt, *prima facie* of questionable policy, and contrary to the general principle that legislation by which the conduct of mankind is to be regulated ought, when introduced for the first time, to deal with future acts, and ought not to change the character of past transactions carried on upon the faith of the then existing law ... Accordingly, the court will not ascribe

9

retrospective force to new laws affecting rights, unless by express words or necessary implication it appears that such was the intention of the legislature.

Waddington v Miah (1974) (HL)

The respondent had been convicted at Grimsby Crown Court on counts of being an illegal immigrant and being in possession of a false passport, contrary to ss 24 and 26 (respectively) of the Immigration Act 1971. The offences were alleged in the indictment to have been committed on dates before the relevant sections had come into force. The Court of Appeal quashed the convictions on the ground that the language of the 1971 Act was not apt to compel a construction according its provisions retroactive effect. The Crown appealed to the House of Lords.

Held, dismissing the appeal, that the case was a very clear one. The 1971 Act contained no transitional provisions which would allow it to be used to prosecute offences under Acts which it had repealed. In view of the fact that the Universal Declaration of Human Rights approved by the General Assembly of the United Nations and the European Convention on Human Rights each effectively pronounced against the enactment of retroactive criminal legislation, it was scarcely credible that any government department would promote or that Parliament would pass such legislation.

Note ──

For an example of retroactive criminal legislation, see the War Crimes Act 1991.

Retroactivity and the common law

C v Director of Public Prosecutions (1994–95) Divisional Court and HL

A rebuttable presumption of incapacity of harm applied to children aged between 10 and 13. The appellant was convicted of interfering with a motorcycle with the intent to commit theft or of taking and driving away contrary to s 9(1) of the Criminal Attempts Act 1981. The appellant was aged 12 at the time of the offence, and it was therefore necessary for the prosecution to prove, in addition to the *mens rea* for the offence, that he had known that what he was doing was seriously wrong. He appealed by way of case stated on the ground that the prosecution had failed to rebut the presumption. In the Divisional Court, Laws J held that the presumption was no longer part of English law. Laws J recognised that since the common law had not yet developed a practice of prospective rulings, the effect of his decision would be to change the law as at the time of the appellant's offence. In may cases, this would be a powerful inhibition upon the extent to which the common law courts could justly alter the scope of the criminal law. However, this was not such a case, because if the appellant were able to complain that he had ordered his behaviour on the basis that the presumption still existed, he would conclusively have rebutted its application to his case. The appellant appealed to the House of Lords.

Held, allowing the appeal and overturning the Divisional Court's decision, that the presumption continued to be part of English law. Regarding the issue of retroactivity, Lord Lowry conceded that Laws J was correct to consider that it would work no practical injustice in the appellant's case, but objectively, something which when done was not regarded as a crime would, if the Divisional Court were right, ultimately turn out to have been one.

The necessity for the publication of laws

Simmonds v Newell (1953)

Section 3(2) of the Statutory Instruments Act 1946 read as follows:

> In any proceedings against any person for an offence consisting of a contravention of any such statutory instrument, it shall be a defence to prove that the instrument had not been issued by His Majesty's Stationery Office at the date of the alleged contravention unless it is proved that at that date reasonable steps had been taken for the purpose of bringing the purport of the instrument to the notice of the public, or of persons likely to be affected by it, or of the persons charged.

A company and its directors were prosecuted for selling steel above the maximum price permitted by the Iron and Steel Prices Order 1951. The decision was taken in the Ministry of Supply not to print the schedules to the order which specified maximum prices; the schedules were available for inspection at Steel House in London, and copies of some of them were to be distributed by trade associations. The Solicitor General accepted that in this situation the Crown bore the burden of proving that s 3(2) had been satisfied.

Held that since no evidence had been adduced to show that the order had been publicised, the defendants should have been acquitted. *Per* Lord Goddard CJ: '... it is not desirable, in criminal matters, that people should be prosecuted for breaches of orders unless the orders can fairly be said to be known to the public.'

Lim Chin Aik v R (1963) (PC)

An order was made under the Singapore Immigration Ordinance 1952 prohibiting the appellant from entering Singapore. He entered, and was convicted under the Ordinance of entering Singapore while prohibited by an order from so doing. The relevant section of the Ordinance contained no express *mens rea* requirement, and it was conceded by the Crown that the appellant had not been proved to have *mens rea* with regard to his infraction of the order.

Held, allowing the appeal, that the presumption that *mens rea* was required for conviction had not been overcome. In response to the Crown's argument that knowledge of the order did not need to be proved since ignorance of the law was no defence, Lord Evershed stated:

Their Lordships are unable to accept this contention. In their Lordships' opinion, even if the making of the order by the minister be regarded as an exercise of the legislative as distinct from the executive or administrative function (as they do not concede), the maxim cannot apply to such a case as the present where it appears that there is in the State of Singapore no provision, corresponding, for example, to that contained on s 3(2) of the English Statutory Instruments Act 1946, for the publication in any form of an order of the kind made in the present case or any other provision designed to enable a man by appropriate inquiry to find out what 'the law' is.

The principle that laws should be stable

Practice Statement (Judicial precedent) (1966) HL
Per Lord Gardiner LC:

Their Lordships regard the use of precedent as an indispensable foundation upon which to decide what is the law and its application to individual cases. It provides at least some degree of certainty upon which individuals can rely in the conduct of their affairs, as well as a basis for orderly development of legal rules.

Their Lordships nevertheless recognise that too rigid adherence to precedent may lead to injustice in a particular case and also unduly restrict the proper development of the law. They propose, therefore, to modify their present practice and, while treating former decisions of this House as normally binding, to depart from a previous decision when it appears right to do so.

In this connection they will bear in mind the danger of disturbing retrospectively the basis on which contracts, settlements of property, and fiscal arrangements have been entered into and also the especial need for certainty in the criminal law.

This announcement is not intended to affect the use of precedent elsewhere than in this House.

Williams v Fawcett (1986) CA
The appellant had been committed to prison for various breaches of an undertaking not to molest the respondent. He appealed against his committal on the grounds that the order to commit failed to specify the breaches, that an adjournment had wrongly been refused, and that the notice to show cause why he should not be committed had been signed by the respondent's solicitor, and not by the 'proper officer' (as required by rules of court).

Held, that the appeal would be allowed on the first two of these grounds, but not on the third. Sir John Donaldson MR reviewed four decisions of the Court of Appeal (one of them his own) which suggested that the committal should be quashed on the third ground as well. Although the Court of

Appeal was normally obliged to follow its own previous decisions, it was established by *Young v Bristol Aeroplane Co Ltd* (1944) that it might depart from an earlier decision which it was satisfied had been made *per incuriam* (wrongly and carelessly). Such cases would be of the rarest occurrence. The Master of the Rolls continued:

> If we are bound by these decisions, and we are unless they can be treated as having been reached *per incuriam*, they represent a very considerable change in the law for which, so far as I can see, there is absolutely no warrant. The change to which I refer is, of course, a requirement that these notices shall be signed by the proper officer. The rule of *stare decisis* is of the very greatest importance, particularly in an appellate court, such as this, which sits in six or seven divisions simultaneously. But for this rule, the law would not only bifurcate; it would branch off in six or seven different directions.

The *per incuriam* doctrine was to be treated as extending to a series of decisions in which the growth of a manifest slip or error could be clearly detected. That was so here. The earlier four decisions would therefore not be followed.

Judicial creativity and the stability of laws

Duport Steels Ltd v Sirs (1980) HL
Facts: see 3.3 below.
Per Lord Scarman:

> My basic criticism of all three judgments in the Court of Appeal is that in their desire to do justice the court failed to do justice according to law ...
>
> In our society the judges have in some aspects of their work a discretionary power to do justice so wide that they may be regarded as law makers. The common law and equity, both of them in essence systems of private law, are fields where, subject to the increasing intrusion of statute law, society has been content to allow the judges to formulate and develop the law. The judges, even in this, their very own field of creative endeavour, have accepted, in the interests of certainty, the self-denying ordinance of *stare decisis*, the doctrine of binding precedent; and no doubt this judicially imposed limitation on judicial law-making has helped to maintain confidence in the certainty and even-handedness of the law.

2.2 Equality before the law

Dicey, AV, *An Introduction to the Study of the Law of the Constitution* (1965, 10th edn) pp 202–03

> It means ... equality before the law, or the equal subjection of all classes to the ordinary law of the land administered by the ordinary law courts; the 'rule of law' in this sense excludes the idea of any exemption of officials or others from

the duty of obedience to the law which governs other citizens or from the jurisdiction of the ordinary tribunals; there can be with us nothing really corresponding to the 'administrative law' (*droit administratif*) or the 'administrative tribunals' (*tribuneaux administratifs*) of France. The notion which lies at the bottom of the 'administrative law' known to foreign countries is, that affairs or disputes in which the government or its servants are concerned are beyond the sphere of the civil courts and must be dealt with by special and more or less official bodies. This idea is utterly unknown to the law of England, and indeed is fundamentally inconsistent with our traditions and customs.

2.2.1 The law's application to the executive

British Broadcasting Corporation v Johns (Inspector of Taxes) (1964) (CA)

The Corporation was established as a non-profit making body by Royal Charter. It was assessed to income tax on the surplus of its receipts of funds appropriated to it by Parliament over its expenses. The Corporation argued (*inter alia*) that as an emanation of the Crown it enjoyed Crown immunity from taxation because it was a body constituted by the Crown for the purpose of executing functions required and created for the purpose of government.

Held, that the Corporation's contention was incorrect. Diplock LJ explained the basis of Crown immunity as follows:

> Since laws are made by rulers for subjects, a general expression in a law such as 'any person' descriptive of those on whom the law imposes obligations or restraints is not to be read as including the ruler himself. Under our more sophisticated constitution the question of sovereignty has in the course of history come to be treated as comprising three distinct functions of a ruler: executive, legislative and judicial, though the distinction between these functions in the case, for instance, of prerogative powers and administrative tribunals is sometimes blurred. The modern rule of construction of statutes is that the Crown, which today personifies the executive government of the country and is also a party to all the legislation, is not bound by a statute which imposes obligations or restraints on persons or in respect of property, unless the statute says so expressly or by necessary implication.

Rederiaktiebolaget Amphitrite v R (1921)

The suppliants were a Swedish shipping company, and owners of the ship *Amphitrite*. During the First World War they obtained the following undertaking from the British legation in Stockholm: 'I am instructed to say that the steamship *Amphitrite* will earn her own release and be given a coal cargo if she proceed to the United Kingdom with a full cargo consisting of at least 60% approved goods.' In the event the ship was detained. The suppliants submitted a petition of right against the Crown for damages for breach of contract.

Held, that there was no contract between the suppliants and the Crown. The government could bind itself by a commercial contract and, if it did so, it would be bound to perform its undertaking or pay damages for failure to do so. However, the statement by the British legation was merely an expression of intention to act in a particular way in a certain event. *Per* Rowlatt J:

My main reason for so thinking is that it is not competent for the government to fetter its future executive action, which must necessarily be determined by the needs of the community when the question arises. It cannot by contract hamper its freedom of action in matters which concern the welfare of the State.

Q What would be the difference between the 'commercial contract' to which Rowlatt J refers, and the arrangement relied upon by the suppliant?

M v Home Office (1993) HL

Following the rejection of his application for asylum, M was ordered to be removed from the UK by 6.30 pm on 1 May 1991. At 5.20 pm on that day, M made a new application for judicial review of the refusal of asylum, based on new grounds. Garland J, to whom the application was made in chambers, obtained an undertaking from counsel for the Home Office that M's removal would be postponed (counsel understood that he had undertaken to *endeavour* to prevent M's removal). As a result of confusion it was not postponed, and M was not removed from the plane taking him to Zaire during a stopover in Paris. At 11.20 pm, Garland J made an *ex parte* order requiring the Home Secretary to procure M's return to the UK.

On 2 May the Home Secretary cancelled arrangements for M's return on the grounds that the original decision to refuse M's asylum application had been correct, and that the court lacked jurisdiction to make an *ex parte* order against a minister of the Crown. Garland J subsequently set aside his order of 1 May. An action alleging contempt of court for breach of the undertaking and the order was then brought on M's behalf against the Home Office and the Home Secretary. At first instance the action was dismissed on the basis that s 21 of the Crown Proceedings Act 1947 protected government departments and ministers from proceedings for contempt of court. The Court of Appeal held that the order of Garland J, although made without jurisdiction, was binding until set aside. Government departments and ministers were protected from liability by the Act since for these purposes they lacked legal personality but Kenneth Baker, the Home Secretary, was personally guilty of contempt of court.

The Home Secretary appealed, and the applicant cross-appealed on his application against the Home Office.

Held, that the courts below had erred in holding that there was no jurisdiction in these circumstances for the ordering of an injunction or the finding of contempt. Injunctive power was to be inferred from s 31 of the Supreme Court Act 1981. The power to make a finding of contempt existed as a matter of principle and necessity, albeit only against a Minister or department, and not directly against the Crown. *Per* Lord Templeman:

> ... the argument that there is no power to enforce the law by injunction or contempt proceedings against a minister in his personal capacity would, if upheld, establish the proposition that the executive obey the law as a matter of grace and not as a matter of necessity, a proposition which would reverse the result of the Civil War.

Since the Home Secretary had acted throughout on advice, and since his error was understandable, it was not proper to find him personally in contempt of court.

2.3 Rights are declared by the common law

Dicey, AV, *An Introduction to the Study of the Law of the Constitution* (1965, 10th edn) pp 195, 203

> We may say that the constitution is pervaded by the rule of law on the ground that the general principles of the constitution (as for example the right to personal liberty, or the right of public meeting) are with us the result of judicial decisions determining the rights of private persons in particular cases brought before the courts; whereas under many foreign constitutions the security (such as it is) given to the rights of individuals results, or appears to result, from the general principles of the constitution ... in short, the principles of private law have with us been by the action of the courts and Parliament so extended as to determine the position of the Crown and of its servants; thus, the constitution is the result of the ordinary law of the land.

2.3.1 The principle in the keeping of the courts

Malone v Metropolitan Police Commissioner (No 2) (1979)
The plaintiff was charged with handling stolen goods. In the course of his trial, counsel for the prosecution admitted that Malone's telephone had been tapped and his conversations recorded on the authority of a warrant issued by the Home Secretary. Malone brought proceedings against the Metropolitan Police Commissioner claiming declarations, *inter alia*, that the tapping was unlawful.

Held, that the action failed. *Per* Sir Robert Megarry VC:

> England, it may be said, is not a country where everything is forbidden except what is expressly permitted; it is a country where everything is permitted except what is expressly forbidden ... If the tapping of telephones by the Post Office at the request of the police can be carried out without any breach of the law, it does not require any statutory or common law power to justify it; it can lawfully be done simply because there is nothing to make it unlawful. The question, of course, is whether tapping can be carried out without infringing the law

... There is admittedly no statute which in terms authorises the tapping of telephones with or without a warrant. Nevertheless, any conclusion that the tapping of telephones is therefore illegal would plainly be superficial in the extreme. The reason why a search of premises which is not authorised by law is illegal is that it involves the tort of trespass to those premises; and any trespass, whether to land or goods or to the person, that is made without legal authority is *prima facie* illegal. Telephone tapping by the Post Office, on the other hand, involves no act of trespass.

Harman v Secretary of State for the Home Department (1983) HL

The appellant was a solicitor. In the course of an action brought by her client against the Home Office, she obtained discovery of quantities of documents, and gave an undertaking that she would not use them other than for the purposes of the instant action. After extracts from some of the documents had been read out in open court, the appellant allowed a journalist to have access to those documents. The journalist wrote and published an article based on the documents. The Home Office applied for an order that the appellant was in contempt of court.

At first instance and in the Court of Appeal, the contempt was found proved. The appellant appealed to the House of Lords.

Held (by a majority), dismissing the appeal, that the appellant had correctly been held to be in contempt of court.

Per Lord Diplock:

My Lords, in a case which has attracted a good deal of publicity it may assist in clearing up misconceptions if I start by saying what the case is *not* about. It is *not* about freedom of speech, freedom of the press, openness of justice or documents coming into 'the public domain'; nor, with all respect to those of your Lordships who think the contrary, does it in my opinion call for consideration of any of those human rights and fundamental freedoms which in the European Convention on Human Rights are contained in separate articles each starting with a statement in absolute terms but followed immediately by very broadly stated exceptions.

What this case *is* about is an aspect of the law of discovery of documents in civil actions in the High Court.

Per Lord Scarman:

A balance has to be struck between two interests of the law on the one hand, the protection of a litigant's private right to keep his documents to himself notwithstanding his duty to disclose them to the other side in the litigation, and, on the other, the protection of the right, which the law recognises, subject to certain exceptions, as the right of everyone, to speak freely, and to impart information and ideas, upon matters of public knowledge.

Q Of the approaches adopted respectively by Lord Diplock and Lord Scarman, which more closely follows Dicey's account of the means by which judicial decision-making gives rise to the general principles of the constitution?

3 Parliament and the courts

3.1 The relationship of Parliament and the courts

3.1.1 The consequences of conflict

Jay and Topham's Case (1689)

The Serjeant at Arms of the House of Commons, Serjeant Topham, arrested various individuals for breach of privileges of the House. Actions for assault and battery and false imprisonment were brought against him by those whom he had arrested. Before the Court of King's Bench, he pleaded that he had acted in obedience to the House of Commons, and that the Court therefore had no jurisdiction over him. This plea was rejected by the judges, and judgment was given against him. The Committee of Privileges reported to the House that the judgment of the Court was itself a breach of the privileges of Parliament. The House ordered three of the King's Bench judges to attend before it. After hearing an explanation (from the two who in fact attended) for their failure to accede to Serjeant Topham's arguments, the House resolved that they had acted in breach of privilege, and committed them to the custody of the Serjeant at Arms.

3.1.2 The judicial view of parliamentary claims to privilege

R v Paty (1705)

Five inhabitants of the town of Aylesbury began a legal action against the constables of that constituency on the ground that they had wrongly refused to permit them to vote. The Speaker of the House of Commons committed them to Newgate prison for contempt of the jurisdiction and breach of the known privileges of the House of Commons. They applied for writs of *habeas corpus* to the Court of Queen's Bench.

Held, by a majority, that the House of Commons was the proper judge of its own privileges. Dissenting, Holt CJ denied that the commencing and prosecuting of an action was a breach of privilege, and stated that when the House of Commons exceeded its legal bounds and authority, its acts were wrongful and could not be more justified than the acts of ordinary men. The authority of the House of Commons was from the law, and as it was circumscribed, so it might be exceeded.

Stockdale v Hansard (1839)
A report by two inspectors of prisons described a medical book found in the possession of a prisoner in Newgate Prison as 'disgusting and obscene'. By order of the House of Commons, *Hansard* printed and sold the report. The plaintiff, who was the book's publisher, brought an action for libel against *Hansard*. The defendants contended that they had acted solely in obedience to the order of the House, and that the report was to be regarded as part of the proceedings of the Commons (and therefore protected by parliamentary privilege), since it had been presented to and laid before the House. The House had resolved that the power of publishing its proceedings was an essential incident of its constitutional functions. The plaintiff replied that a resolution of the House of Commons could not alter the law of the land.

Held, that the defence pleaded was not known to the law. The defendants were seeking to assert an arbitrary and absolute power overriding the law. The mere resolution of one chamber of Parliament could confer no such power. The House of Commons undoubtedly enjoyed necessary and important privileges, but the courts and not the Commons were the arbiters of the extent of such privileges. The judgment of the House of Commons on a matter within its jurisdiction would be beyond the scrutiny of the courts, but the courts were bound to inquire whether a matter before them did indeed fall within the jurisdiction of the House. The defendants had argued on the grounds of necessity, custom and universal acquiescence for the existence of a privilege to protect the publication of libellous material. The defendants had failed to establish the first two grounds, and the third was irrelevant to the legality of the privilege claimed.

Note ───

Section 1 of the Parliamentary Papers Act 1840 stays either criminal or civil proceedings against persons for the publication of papers or reports certified to have been printed by the authority of either House of Parliament.

3.1.3 The judicial view of Parliament's right to punish contempt

The Sheriff of Middlesex's Case (1840)
Hansard failed to put in a defence to a further action arising from the same facts as *Stockdale v Hansard* (1839). Acting pursuant to a writ of the Court of Queen's Bench, the Sheriff of Middlesex levied execution upon *Hansard's* property. The House of Commons committed the sheriff for contempt of the House. In response to a writ of *habeas corpus*, the sergeant at arms of the House produced the Speaker's warrant of commitment. The warrant did not specify the contempt alleged. A motion was brought for the sheriff's discharge from custody.

Held, that the court had no jurisdiction to interfere in the sheriff's detainment. A warrant for commitment which alleged a general contempt of the House could be inquired into no further by the court. It constituted a complete answer to the writ of *habeas corpus*. Conversely, the court would act as justice might require where a warrant had been issued which purported to commit not for contempt, but for some arbitrary and unjust cause.

3.1.4 The courts and the proceedings of the House

Bradlaugh v Gossett (1884)

The plaintiff, an atheist, was duly elected as Member of Parliament for Northampton. The House took the view that as an atheist he could not sit or vote in the Commons, since he could not properly take the oath as required by statute. He was therefore prevented by a resolution of the House of Commons from taking the oath. The defendant was sergeant at arms in the Commons, and had forcibly ejected the plaintiff when he sought to enter the House. The plaintiff sought an injunction to prevent the defendant from enforcing the order of the House, and a declaration that the order was void. The defendant asserted that the statement of claim disclosed no cause of action.

Held, dismissing the plaintiff's action, that even if the House had misinterpreted the provisions of the Parliamentary Oaths Act 1866 the matter remained outside the jurisdiction of the court. Where statute determined rights to be exercised within the House, the House alone had jurisdiction to interpret the statute. Statutory rights exercisable out of the House were in the sole keeping of the courts. The officers of the House would be subject to the sanctions of the ordinary law for crimes committed in the House, and Parliament had never sought to suggest otherwise. However, the sergeant at arms had the right to use reasonable force to eject the plaintiff from the House.

3.2 Privileges of Parliament

3.2.1 Freedom from civil arrest

Stourton v Stourton (1963)

Baron Mowbray, Segrave and Stourton was a peer of the realm, and entitled to sit in the House of Lords. In the course of proceedings brought against him by his wife under the Married Women's Property Act 1882, he breached an order made by the court. His wife applied for a writ of attachment with a power of arrest against him. Baron Mowbray claimed parliamentary privilege against civil arrest. The matter was heard at a time when Parliament was sitting.

Held, that since the parliamentary privilege from arrest clearly applied only to arrest in connection with civil matters and not to criminal arrest, it was necessary in each case to ascertain whether the arrest in question was merely designed to compel compliance with civil law or was truly punitive in nature. The power of arrest sought in the present case was civil, not criminal. To grant it would lead the court and the court's officers into an invasion of the privilege of Parliament.

3.2.2 Freedom of speech in Parliament

Church of Scientology of California v Johnson-Smith (1972)

In the course of a defamation action against the defendant, a Member of Parliament, for remarks made by him in a television interview, the plaintiffs sought to prove the defendant's actual malice by adducing evidence of what he had said in Parliament. Counsel for the defendant suggested that admission of the evidence might involve the court in a breach of parliamentary privilege, and the court heard argument on the point from the Attorney General as *amicus curiae*.

Held, that the evidence would be excluded. It was clear that no action for defamation could be maintained on the basis of what was said in Parliament. It would equally be a breach of privilege to permit reference to *Hansard's* reports of parliamentary proceedings as evidence to support a cause of action arising outside Parliament. Extracts from *Hansard* could be read in court without further comment in order to establish matters of fact, but it was not proper to draw further inferences from them. The law on this aspect of parliamentary privilege derived from Article 9 of the Bill of Rights (1688), which provided:

> That the freedome of speech and debates or proceedings in Parlyament ought not to be impeached or questioned in any court or place out of Parlyament.

Rost v Edwards (1990)

The plaintiff sought damages for libel in respect of an article said to allege that he had misused his position as a member of the House of Commons Select Committee on Energy for personal gain. At the trial of the action, he wished to call evidence to establish that the article had adversely affected his chances of being appointed chairman of the Select Committee, and had resulted in his deselection from the standing committee on the Energy Bill. When it became clear that questions of parliamentary privilege might be involved, the case was adjourned pending the court's resolution of possible conflict between the privilege secured by Article 9 of the Bill of Rights and the plaintiff's right freely to present his case in court.

Held, that if the plaintiff wished to call evidence to support his account of the consequences of the alleged libel, it would be necessary for him to petition the House of Commons for its consent. This was so because the common law established that the use intended by the plaintiff to be made

21

of the material which he sought to adduce would amount to a questioning of parliamentary proceedings. Had the authorities been less insistent, Popplewell J stated that the court might have been prepared to hold that the 'questioning' forbidden by the Bill of Rights was only that which involved some allegation of improper motive. After observing the constitutional need for comity between Parliament and the courts, Popplewell J continued:

> I hope ... I may be permitted to say this, that the effect of this judgment if the House declines the petition *may* (and I emphasise the word *may*) be to deprive a litigant of his proper rights. This has particular importance in a case where, as far as one can see, neither freedom of speech nor the dignity of the House will have been affected. No question, as I understand it, arises of questioning the validity of any decision of the House or its committee or making any suggestion of improper motive. Accordingly, in so far as it is appropriate for me to make any comment on the exercise of the House's judgment about a matter over which they have exclusive jurisdiction, as I have ruled, I express the hope that they will approach the matter sympathetically.

Prebble v Television New Zealand Ltd (1994) (PC)
The defendant company broadcast a television programme in which it alleged that the plaintiff, a Minister in the government of New Zealand, had abused his position by conspiring to assist certain business interests during a privatisation in return for party political donations. In response to the plaintiff's action for libel, the defendant pleaded (*inter alia*) justification, relying on particulars of proceedings in the New Zealand Parliament. The plaintiff applied to strike out these particulars on the ground that they infringed parliamentary privilege. The plaintiff succeeded at first instance. The New Zealand Court of Appeal upheld the judge's ruling, and additionally held that in light of the defendant's resulting disadvantage in the litigation, the action should be stayed pending the waiver of privilege by the House of Representatives. The plaintiff appealed against the stay of proceedings to the Privy Council, which addressed the questions whether the defendant's particulars infringed Article 9 of the Bill of Rights and, if so, whether the New Zealand Court of Appeal had been correct to order a stay. The defendant submitted either that privilege only operated to prevent examination of a statement which was itself said to give rise to legal liability, or alternatively that privilege did not operate to protect the maker himself of a parliamentary statement against a defendant's challenge to his veracity or *bona fides*.

Held, allowing the appeal in part, that the defendant's case did involve a breach of Article 9, but that since the greater part of it rested on matters not subject to privilege, there had been insufficient reason to grant a stay effectively preventing the plaintiff from vindicating his reputation. Such a stay was to be granted only in extreme circumstances. Both the defendant's submissions were rejected. The defendant had relied on the Australian case of *Wright and Advertiser Newspapers Ltd v Lewis* (1990) in support of the second submission. Lord Browne-Wilkinson cited that case and continued:

Although their Lordships are sympathetic with the concern felt by the South Australian Supreme Court, they cannot accept that the fact that the maker of the statement is the initiator of the court proceedings can affect the question whether Article 9 is infringed. The privilege protected by Article 9 is the privilege of Parliament itself. The actions of any individual member of Parliament, even if he has an individual privilege of his own, cannot determine whether or not the privilege of Parliament is to apply.

Note ——
Section 13 of the Defamation Act 1996 overrules this aspect of *Prebble's* case, allowing individual members of Parliament to waive parliamentary privilege.

Beswick v Beswick (1967) (HL)

The respondent argued that s 56(1) of the Law of Property Act 1925 allowed her to sue in her personal capacity on a contract to which she was not party.

Held, that the contention was incorrect (though the respondent was permitted to maintain an action as administratrix of her late husband's estate). The 1925 Act was a consolidating Act, and it was quite certain that those responsible for the legislation must have believed and intended that s 56 would make no substantial change in earlier law. *Per* Lord Reid:

In construing any Act of Parliament we are seeking the intention of Parliament, and it is quite true that we must deduce that intention from the words of the Act. If the words of the Act are capable only of one meaning, we must give them that meaning no matter how they got there. If, however, they are capable of having more than one meaning we are, in my view, well entitled to see how they got there. For purely practical reasons, we do not permit debates in either House to be cited: it would add greatly to the time and expense involved in preparing cases involving the construction of a statute if counsel were expected to read all the debates in *Hansard,* and it would often be impractical for counsel to get access to at least the older reports of debates in select committees of the House of Commons; moreover, in a very large proportion of cases such a search, even if practicable, would throw no light on the question before the court ...

Davis v Johnson (1978) (HL)

On appeal from the grant of an ouster injunction, the question arose whether s 1 of the Domestic Violence and Matrimonial Proceedings Act 1976 did or did not confer jurisdiction on a county court to exclude a person from premises in which he had a proprietory interest.

Held, dismissing the appeal, that the power conferred by s 1 was exercisable irrespective of the proprietory rights with which it might conflict. The House of Lords reached this conclusion without reference to *Hansard*. *Per* Lord Scarman:

> There are two good reasons why the courts should refuse to have regard to what is said in Parliament or by Ministers as aids to the interpretation of a statute. First, such material is an unreliable guide to the meaning of what is enacted. It promotes confusion, not clarity. The cut and thrust of debate and the pressures of executive responsibility, essential features of open and responsible government, are not always conducive to a clear and unbiased explanation of the meaning of statutory language. And the volume of parliamentary and ministerial utterances can confuse by its very size. Secondly, counsel are not permitted to refer to *Hansard* in argument. So long as this rule is maintained by Parliament (it is not the creation of the judges), it must be wrong for the judge to make any judicial use of proceedings in Parliament for the purpose of interpreting statutes ... It may be that, since membership of the European Communities has introduced into our law a style of legislation (regulations having direct effect) which by means of the lengthy recital (or preamble) identifies material to which resort may be had in construing its provisions, Parliament will consider doing likewise in statutes where it would be appropriate, eg those based on a report by the Law Commission, a royal commission, departmental committee or some other law reform body.

Pepper (Inspector of Taxes) v Hart (1993) (HL)

The appellants, who were members of staff at an independent school, had received a taxable benefit – the education of their sons at concessionary fees at that school. Under s 61(1) of the Finance Act 1976, they were to be taxed on the 'cash equivalent' of that benefit. Section 63 of the Act defined 'cash equivalent' as 'an amount equal to the cost of the benefit', and defined that amount as 'the amount of any expense incurred in or in connection with its provision'. The Crown contended that the amount in question was the ordinary cost of an education at the school (the 'average cost'). The appellants argued that the cost of the benefit was to be regarded as the actual cost of its provision to the school, which was negligible (the 'marginal cost'). To support their contention, the appellants sought to refer the House to *Hansard's* report of the proceedings in Parliament which had led to the passage of the 1976 Act.

Held (by a majority) that the rule prohibiting reference to *Hansard* in the construction of legislation should be relaxed. The arguments against so doing were these: (a) that the rule reflected and preserved the proper roles of Parliament and the courts; (b) that relaxation of the rule would expose litigants to the practical difficulty of the expense involved in researching parliamentary material; (c) that the citizen ought to have access to a known and defined legal text which regulated his legal rights, and (d) that

Hansard was an improbable source of helpful guidance as to the proper construction of legislation. In favour of relaxation, it was desirable that where ambiguity or obscurity attended the legislatively expressed will of Parliament the courts should not blind themselves to a clear indication of what Parliament intended by its choice of words. The Attorney General (for the Crown) had submitted that the courts' use of parliamentary material would infringe Article 9 of the Bill of Rights, but consultation of such material in the view of the House would not amount to the 'impeachment' or 'questioning' of the freedom of speech or debate in Parliament. Reference to parliamentary material would therefore be permitted where legislation was ambiguous or obscure, or tended to lead to an absurdity; where the material relied upon consisted of one or more statements by a Minister or other promoter of the Bill together if necessary with such other parliamentary material as was necessary to understand such statements and their effect; and the statements relied on were clear. These requirements were satisfied in the present case, and statements made to Parliament by the Financial Secretary to the Treasury made it clear that s 63 of the Act was intended to have the meaning argued for by the appellants.

3.2.3 Publications of either House are absolutely privileged
See the note following *Stockdale v Hansard* (1839), 3.1.1 above.

3.2.4 Unauthorised reports of proceedings in Parliament and common law qualified privilege

Wason v Walter (1868)
The plaintiff sued one of the proprietors of *The Times* for libel. The newspaper had published a report of a debate in the House of Lords in which the plaintiff considered himself to have been defamed.

Held, that the English law of defamation was based upon the concept of malice. In the majority of cases, it was not necessary to prove actual malice; it would be presumed as a matter of law to have accompanied the defendant's wrongful act. However, there were circumstances in which the presumption of malice would not arise, and in such a case it would be necessary for the plaintiff to prove actual malice, if he could. Reports of proceedings in Parliament were such an example. The rationale for extending qualified privilege to them was explained by Cockburn CJ to be the same as that which underlay the privileged status of the reports of the proceedings of courts of justice:

> The presumption of malice is negatived in the one case, as in the other, by the fact that the publication has in view the instruction and advantage of the public, and has no particular reference to the party concerned. There is in the one case, as in the other, a preponderance of general good over partial and occasional evil.

3.2.5 The right to control internal proceedings

Bradlaugh v Gossett (1884)

Facts: see 3.1.3 above.

Per Stephen J:

The House of Commons is not a court of justice, but the effect of its privilege to regulate its own internal concerns practically invests it with a judicial character when it has to apply to particular cases the provisions of Acts of Parliament. We must presume that it discharges this function properly and with due regard to the laws, in the making of which it has so great a share. If its determination is not in accordance with the law, this resembles the case of an error by a judge whose decision is not subject to appeal.

Rost v Edwards (1990)

Facts: see 3.2.2 above. Among the matters which the plaintiff wished to put before the jury, he wanted to explain what the Register of Members' Interests was, what the criteria for registration were, what he was therefore required to disclose, and what in fact he did disclose. Counsel for the defendants concurred with the plaintiff in submitting that the Register was not a 'proceeding in Parliament', but the Solicitor General argued that it was.

Held, that the Register was not a 'proceeding in Parliament'. The plaintiff and defendants would therefore be permitted to make use of it in the trial. *Per* Popplewell J:

The Solicitor General observed that the expression 'proceedings in Parliament' has not yet been defined either by statute or by case law in this jurisdiction, though he referred me to s 16(2) of the Australian Parliamentary Privileges Act 1987. However, he submitted that it embraced the various forms of business in which either House takes action and the whole process by which either House reaches a decision in a particular debate. He also submitted that it embraced things said or done by a member of Parliament in the exercise of his function as a member in a committee in either House, and everything said or done in either House in the transaction of parliamentary business, whether by a member of either House or by an official of either House. In particular, he said it embraced the regulation by either House of its proceedings, for example, the practice and procedure relating to the Register of Members' Interests ...

The approach I have to this aspect of the case is this. There are clearly cases where Parliament is to be the sole judge of its affairs. Equally, there are clear cases where the courts are to have exclusive jurisdiction. In a case which may be described as a grey area a court, while giving full attention to the necessity for comity between the courts and Parliament, should not be astute to find a reason for ousting the jurisdiction of the courts or even defeating a proper claim by a party to litigation before it. If Parliament wishes to cover a particular area with privilege it has the ability to do so by passing an Act of Parliament giving itself the right to exclusive jurisdiction. Ousting the jurisdiction of the courts has always been regarded as requiring the clearest possible words. Nothing in the authorities, as I have indicated, in any way covers the instant situation ... It is clearly not possible to arrive at an exhaustive definition.

3.2.6 The right to punish for contempt of Parliament

The Sheriff of Middlesex's Case (1840)
See 3.1.3 above.

3.3 Maintaining the constitutional balance between legislature and judicature

Duport Steels Ltd v Sirs (1980) HL
In the course of an industrial dispute, and in order to put pressure on the government to provide the British Steel Corporation with the funds necessary for it to make an increased pay award to its employees, a trade union called out on strike those of its members who worked for British Steel, and those who worked for private employers. The private employers sought injunctions against the union. Section 13(1) of the Trade Union and Labour Relations Act 1974 conferred immunity from liability in tort for an act done by a person 'in contemplation or furtherance of a trade dispute'. The Court of Appeal construed the relevant provisions of the Act narrowly and found for the employers. The union appealed to the House of Lords.

Held, reversing the decision of the Court of Appeal, that the duty of the courts was to apply the laws made by Parliament, and not to adapt them to the judicial view of what they ought to be. *Per* Lord Diplock:

My Lords, at a time when more and more cases involve the application of legislation which gives effect to policies that are the subject of bitter public and parliamentary controversy, it cannot be too strongly emphasised that the British Constitution, though largely unwritten, is firmly based upon the separation of powers; Parliament makes the laws, the judiciary interpret them ...

It endangers continued public confidence in the political impartiality of the judiciary, which is essential to the continuance of the rule of law, if judges, under the guise of interpretation, provide their own preferred amendments to statutes, which experience of their operation has shown to have had consequences that members of the court before whom the matter comes consider to be injurious to the public interest.

R v Her Majesty's Treasury, *ex parte* Smedley (1985) CA
The appellant sought an order of *certiorari* to quash the decision of the Chancellor of the Exchequer to operate a procedure provided by s 1(2) of the European Communities Act 1972, in order to confer the status of Community Treaty on a financial undertaking given by the government to

27

the Community. The procedure entitled the Treasury to give effect to the undertaking upon an affirmative resolution of both Houses of Parliament without needing to introduce legislation for the purpose.

Held, that the legitimacy of the proposed action by the Treasury depended upon there being a sufficiently close connection between the undertaking and the Treaties. Here, sufficient connection did exist, and the appeal would therefore be dismissed. Where an administrative order or regulation was required by statute to be approved by resolution of both Houses of Parliament, the court could, in an appropriate case, intervene by using judicial review to examine the governmental exercise of the discretion to operate that procedure before both Houses had given their approval. However, the jurisdiction to do so was to be exercised with great circumspection in order to avoid encroaching on the functions of Parliament. *Per* Sir John Donaldson MR:

> Before considering Mr Smedley's objections ... I think that I should say a word about the respective roles of Parliament and the courts. Although the UK has no written constitution, it is a constitutional convention of the highest importance that the legislature and the judicature are separate and independent of one another, subject to certain ultimate rights of Parliament over the judicature which are immaterial for present purposes. It therefore behoves the courts to be ever sensitive to the paramount need to refrain from trespassing upon the province of Parliament or, so far as this can be avoided, even appearing to do so. Although it is not a matter for me, I would hope and expect that Parliament would be similarly sensitive to the need to refrain from trespassing upon the province of the courts.
>
> Against that background, it would clearly be a breach of the constitutional conventions for this court, or any court, to express a view, let alone take any action, concerning the decision to lay this draft Order in Council before Parliament or concerning the wisdom or otherwise of Parliament approving that draft.

R v Secretary of State for the Home Department, *ex parte* **Fire Brigades Union (1995) HL**
See 5.5.3 below.

4 The legislative sovereignty of Parliament

4.1 Statute overrides international law

Mortensen v Peters (1906)

The appellant was the captain of a Norwegian trawler. He was convicted by the sheriff court of fishing with an otter trawl within the Moray Firth, contrary to a by-law made under the Herring Fishery (Scotland) Act 1889. He appealed on the ground that, since he was not a British subject and had not been fishing within British territorial waters, he was not subject to the jurisdiction of the Scottish court.

Held, dismissing the appeal, that the question for the court was purely one of construction. If the appellant's conduct fell within the terms of the Act, the court was bound to give effect to its terms. There was a presumption that Parliament would not seek to exceed what an international tribunal might hold to be its proper sphere of legislative competence, but if by express words or plain implication Parliament had done so, the presumption would have no further effect.

Cheney v Conn (1968)

The plaintiff, a taxpayer, challenged assessments of income tax and surtax raised under the Finance Act 1964 on the ground that a part of the tax raised was used to fund the construction of nuclear weapons. He contended, *inter alia*, that the construction of nuclear weapons was contrary to international law, which was part of the law of England.

Held, dismissing the appeal by way of case stated, that while it was correct that international law formed part of the law of England, where a statute is unambiguous its provisions must be followed even if they are contrary to international law. *Per* Ungoed-Thomas J:

> What the statute itself enacts cannot be unlawful, because what the statute says and provides is itself the law, and the highest form of law that is known to this country. It is the law which prevails over every other form of law, and it is not for the court to say that a parliamentary enactment, the highest law in this country, is illegal.

4.2   Statute overrides political fact

Madzimbamuto v Lardner-Burke (1969)
See 1.2 above.

4.3   The courts and the legislative sovereignty of Parliament

4.3.1   Challenge to the content of Acts of Parliament

Dr Bonham's Case (1610)
The censors of the College of Physicians imposed various sanctions, including imprisonment, upon a doctor whom they considered to have practised without their authority.

Held that the censors had wrongly acted as judges and parties in the matter. Although there was statutory sanction for this, Lord Coke CJ stated that the common law would prevail over any such denial of natural justice. *Per* Lord Coke CJ:

> And it appears in our books, that in many cases, the common law will control Acts of Parliament, and sometimes adjudge them to be utterly void: for when an Act of Parliament is against common right and reason, or repugnant, or impossible to be performed, the common law will control it and adjudge such Act to be void.

City of London v Wood (1702)
An action on a debt was brought by the Mayor and Commonalty of London in the Mayor's Court. One of the grounds of appeal from the judgment was that the Mayor had been – technically at least – both judge and plaintiff in his own court.

Held, that this objection was correct.
Per Holt CJ:

> And what my Lord Coke says in Dr Bonham's case ... is far from any extravagancy; for it is a very reasonable and true saying, that if an Act of Parliament should ordain that the same person should be party and judge, or, which is the same thing, judge in his own cause, it would be a void Act of Parliament; for it is impossible that one should be judge and party, for the judge is to determine between party and party, or between the government and the party; and an Act of Parliament can do no wrong, though it may do several things that look pretty odd ... An Act of Parliament may not make adultery lawful, that is, cannot make it lawful for A to lie with the wife of B but it may make the wife of A to be the wife of B and dissolve her marriage with A.

Q Why, in the context of this argument, does Holt CJ declare that 'an Act of Parliament can do no wrong'?

R v Jordan (1967)

The defendant was sentenced to 18 months' imprisonment for offences under the Race Relations Act 1965. He applied for legal aid to seek a writ of *habeas corpus* on the ground that the Act was invalid as being a curtailment of his rights of free speech.

Held, dismissing the application, that Parliament was supreme and there was no power in the courts to question the validity of an Act of Parliament. The ground of the application was completely unarguable.

4.3.2 Challenge to the manner in which an Act has been passed

The Westminster Parliament

Edinburgh & Dalkeith Railway Co v Wauchope (1842) (HL)

The respondent, a landowner, had argued in the Court of Session that a private Act of Parliament authorising the construction of a railway should be disapplied because its promoters had failed to give notice as required by House of Commons standing orders to persons affected by its provisions. The argument was abandoned in the House of Lords, but Lord Campbell commented:

> My Lords, I think it right to say a word or two before I sit down, upon the point that has been raised with regard to an Act of Parliament being held inoperative by a court of justice because the forms, in respect of an Act of Parliament, have not been complied with. There seems great reason to believe that notion has prevailed to a considerable extent in Scotland ... It seems to me there is no foundation for it whatever; all that a court of justice can look to is the parliamentary roll; they see that an Act has passed both Houses of Parliament, and that it has received the royal assent, and no court of justice can inquire into the manner in which it was introduced into Parliament, what was done previously to its being introduced, or what passed in Parliament during the various stages of its progress through both Houses of Parliament. I therefore trust that no such inquiry will hereafter be entered into in Scotland, and that due effect will be given to every Act of Parliament, both private as well as public, upon the just construction which appears to arise upon it.

Lee v Bude and Torrington Junction Railway Co (1871)

(The facts, so far as they are material, are sufficiently given in the passage cited below.) *Per* Willes J:

> It is further urged that the company was a mere nonentity, and that there never were any shares or shareholders. That resolves itself into this, that Parliament was induced by fraudulent recitals (introduced, it is said, by the plaintiffs) to pass the Act which formed the company. I would observe, as to these Acts of Parliament, that they are the law of this land; and we do not sit here as a court

of appeal from Parliament. It was once said ... that, if an Act of Parliament were to create a man judge in his own cause, the court might disregard it. That dictum, however, stands as a warning, rather than an authority to be followed. We sit here as the servants of the Queen and the legislature. Are we to act as regents over what is done by Parliament with the consent of the Queen, Lords and Commons? I deny that any such authority exists. If an Act of Parliament has been obtained improperly, it is for the legislature to correct it by repealing it: but, so long as it exists as law, the courts are bound to obey it. The proceedings here are judicial, not autocratic, which they would be if we could make laws instead of administering them.

Pickin v British Railways Board (1974) HL

The respondent, a railway enthusiast, owned land adjoining an abandoned railway line. Relying on a private Act of Parliament of 1836, he argued that the strip of land over which an abandoned track passed vested in the owners of the land to either side of the track. The Board claimed that by a further private Act, the British Railways Act 1968, it retained ownership of the land. In reply, Pickin alleged that the 1968 Act was invalid, since its passage through Parliament had been obtained by fraud. The Bill had been represented as unopposed, whereas notice had not been given to affected landowners as the rules of parliamentary procedure required. Furthermore, the Bill had falsely stated that a list of landowners was deposited with the clerk of the County Council.

Held, allowing the Board's appeal, that *Pickin's* case depended upon proof that the Board's fraud caused the passing of the 1968 Act. Proof of that, in turn, required examination of the manner in which the officers of Parliament dealt with the Bill's passage. There was no authority to permit such an investigation. If an Act had been obtained in breach of parliamentary procedure, it was for Parliament, and not the courts, to investigate the matter.

Manuel v Attorney General (1983) Chancery Division and CA

At the request of the Senate and the House of Commons of Canada, the UK Parliament passed the Canada Act 1982, whereby it terminated its competence to legislate for Canada. The plaintiffs, who were Indian chiefs, argued that the Act was *ultra vires* Parliament. They submitted that by the Statute of Westminster 1931, Parliament had deprived itself of all power to legislate for Canada save in accordance with s 4 of that Act which required the prior consent of the Canadian Parliament, the provincial legislatures and the Indian nations. They claimed that the proper consents had not been obtained. The Attorney General moved that the statement of claim be struck out as disclosing no reasonable cause of action.

Held (Chancery Division), that the case was covered by the authority of *Pickin v British Railways Board* (1973) (4.3.2 above). It made no difference that the Act in that case had been purely domestic legislation, while the present Act purported to apply outside the UK. *Per* Megarry VC: 'The Canada Act 1982 is an Act of Parliament, and sitting as a judge in an English court I owe full and dutiful obedience to that Act.'

Held (Court of Appeal), dismissing the appeal, that on the true construction of the 1931 Act all that was required was a declaration of the Dominion's request for and consent to the legislation. Actual consent was not required. If compliance with s 4 was legally required, then it was present by reason of the conforming declaration contained in the preamble to the 1982 Act. For the purposes of the appeal, it was assumed that Parliament could restrict the form of subsequent legislation, although the proposition appeared to be contrary to *Ellen Street Estates Ltd v Minister of Health* (1934) (see 4.3.2 below). The court emphasised that it was not purporting to decide the issue.

Comparison: the Israeli Knesset

Tnuat Le'or v Speaker of the Knesset (1992) (Israeli Supreme Court)

The Knesset is the sovereign Parliament of the State of Israel and, in common with the Parliaments of the UK and New Zealand, is subject to no limiting instrument. A law passed by the Knesset (*Basic Law: The Knesset*) provided (*inter alia*) that certain of its provisions could be varied only by laws enacted by a special majority consisting of more than half of all Knesset members. The special majority requirement applied to every stage of the law-making process save a debate on a motion for the Knesset agenda. The applicants alleged that the effect of the Political Parties (Financing) (Amendment No 8) Law 1988 was to contravene substantive provisions of the *Basic Law: The Knesset*, and that only a simple majority had voted in favour of the 1988 Law at an early stage of its passage through the Knesset. In three earlier cases in which similar points had arisen the government, as respondent, had invited the court to adjudicate on the merits of the challenge, and had taken no issue on the court's authority to conduct a review of legislation on the ground of its non-conformity with special majority entrenchment provisions.

Held, that the court's power to review primary legislation on this ground had become an established part of Israeli jurisprudence. Where legislation contravened the content of entrenched laws the Knesset was under a self-imposed obligation to enact the contravening law in the manner laid down by the basic law in question. The power of review equally existed where legislation failed to comply with qualitative norms imposed by entrenched laws. In either case the court was empowered to declare the non-conforming legislation null and void. In the judgment of Elon DP, these were the only circumstances in which the power of judicial review over primary legislation existed. Barak J was of the opinion that judicial review of the content of primary legislation violating fundamental principles was in theory possible whether or not such principles were expressed in entrenched law. This power of review was consistent with the democratic character of the Israeli system, but in deference of the socio-legal conceptions prevailing in Israel, the court would not regard itself as authorised to exercise such power. On the facts of the present case, the 1988 Law did contravene substantive provisions of the *Basic Law: The Knesset*, and (in the opinion of the majority) it had not been passed in accordance with the special majority requirement. The 1988 Law was therefore void.

Q Does Article 9 of the Bill of Rights effectively prohibit a British court from adopting this approach to an Act of Parliament?

The doctrine of implied repeal: conflicting Acts of Parliament

Ellen Street Estates Ltd v Minister of Health (1934) CA
Section 2 of the Acquisition of Land (Assessment of Compensation) Act 1919 enacted rules governing the quantum of compensation to be paid in respect of land compulsorily acquired. Section 46 of the Housing Act 1925 created rules for the assessment of compensation which differed from those of the earlier Act, and were less favourable to the appellant. Section 7(1) of the 1919 Act stated:

> The provisions of the Act or order by which the land is authorised to be acquired, or of any Act incorporated herewith, shall in relation to the matters dealt with in this Act, have effect subject to this Act, and so far as inconsistent with this Act those provisions shall cease to have or shall not have effect ...

Section 46 of the 1925 Act included the words:

> Subject as aforesaid, the compensation to be paid for such land shall be assessed in accordance with [the 1919 Act].

The appellant argued that compensation should be assessed in accordance with the 1919 provisions.

Held, that in so far as the 1925 provisions were inconsistent with the 1919 provisions, the 1925 provisions alone applied. Parliament could alter an Act previously passed either by expressly modifying or repealing it, or, as here, by enacting provisions inconsistent with it. The latter provisions would impliedly repeal inconsistent previous enactments. *Per* Maugham LJ:

> The Legislature cannot, according to our constitution, bind itself as to the form of subsequent legislation, and it is impossible for Parliament to enact that in a subsequent statute dealing with the same subject matter there can be no implied repeal.

Manuel v Attorney General (1983) CA
See 4.3.2 above.

The doctrine of implied repeal and the European Communities Act 1972

Macarthys v Smith (1979) CA

See 4.5.2 below.

Derivative legislatures

Attorney General for New South Wales v Trethowan and Others (1932) PC

Section 5 of the Colonial Laws Validity Act 1865 (an Act of the Westminster Parliament) gave the legislature of New South Wales (NSW) power to make laws altering its constitution 'provided that such laws shall have been passed in such manner and form as may from time to time be required by any Act of Parliament ... or colonial law ...'. Section 7A of the Constitution Act (an Act of the NSW legislature) provided that no Bill abolishing the Legislative Council should be presented to the governor for the royal assent unless approved by a majority of electors voting in a referendum, and s 7A was protected from repeal by an equivalent provision. In 1930, the NSW government intended to present to the governor a Bill to abolish the Legislative Council and another Bill to repeal s 7A. Neither measure had been approved in a referendum. The plaintiffs, who were members of the Legislative Council, sought a declaration that presentation of the bills would be unlawful, and injunctions restraining the presentation of the bills.

Held, that s 7A was a colonial law within the meaning of s 5 of the 1865 Act. The procedural condition created by s 7A (the referendum requirement) was binding on the NSW legislature by virtue of s 5 of the 1865 Act. It would therefore be unlawful to present the bills to the governor unless they had first received the referendum approval required by s 7A. If the bills received the royal assent, but did not have referendum approval, they would not be valid Acts of the NSW legislature.

In the High Court of Australia, Dixon J gave the following consideration (*obiter*) to the effect of entrenchment in UK law:

An Act of the British Parliament which contained a provision that no Bill repealing any part of the Act including the part so restraining its own repeal should be presented for the royal assent unless the Bill were first approved by the electors, would have the force of law until the Sovereign actually did assent to a Bill for its repeal. In strictness, it would be an unlawful proceeding to present such a Bill for the royal assent before it had been approved by the electors. If, before the Bill received the assent of the Crown, it was found possible ... to raise for judicial decision the question whether it was lawful to present the Bill for that assent, the courts would be bound to pronounce it unlawful to do so. Moreover, if it happened that, notwithstanding the statutory inhibition, the Bill did receive the royal assent although it was not submitted to the electors, the courts might be called upon to consider whether the supreme legislative power in respect of the matter had in truth been exercised in the manner required for its authentic expression and by the elements in which it had come to reside. But the answer to this question, whether evident or obscure, would be deduced from the principle of parliamentary supremacy over the law.

Q Is the last sentence of this passage reconcilable with what precedes it?

Q Is the principle of parliamentary supremacy over the law a matter of statute or of common law?

Bribery Commissioner v Ranasinghe (1965) PC

By virtue of the Constitution of Ceylon, the Ceylon Parliament had power to amend or repeal the Constitution provided that a Bill for that purpose was certified by the Speaker as having obtained the requisite parliamentary majority. A provision of the Ceylon Bribery Amendment Act 1958, governing the appointment of tribunal members, conflicted with the Constitution of Ceylon. The 1958 Act had not been certified by the Speaker. The Supreme Court of Ceylon held the respondent's conviction for a bribery offence to be null and void on the ground that the appointment of members of the bribery tribunal was unlawful since the enabling provision of the 1958 Act had not been properly enacted. The Bribery Commissioner appealed to the Privy Council.

Held, dismissing the appeal, that in the case of amendment and repeal of the constitution the Speaker's certificate was a necessary part of the legislative process. A Bill which did not bear the certificate would be invalid, even after it had received the royal assent. The court would inquire whether the Speaker's certificate was endorsed on the original copy of the Bill. It was true that a narrow view had been taken in England of the court's power to look behind an authentic copy of an Act. However, there had never been any need in the UK for courts to look into the law-making process, since there was never a governing instrument which prescribed law-making powers. *Per* Lord Pearce:

> The court has a duty to see that the constitution is not infringed and to preserve it inviolate. Unless, therefore, there is some very cogent reason for doing so, the court must not decline to open its eyes to the truth.

Q Can Lord Pearce's view be reconciled with the decision in *Pickin v British Railways Board* (4.3.2 above)?

4.3.3 The status and powers of Parliament under the 1707 Union legislation

MacCormick v The Lord Advocate (1953) Court of Session

The petitioners sought a declarator that a proclamation by which the Queen took the title 'Elizabeth the Second of the United Kingdom of Great Britain' was contrary to Article I of the Treaty and Acts of Union of 1707.

The Acts, which had been passed by the Parliaments of England and Scotland, had extinguished those Parliaments and established the Parliament of Great Britain as their successor. The petitioners argued, *inter alia*, that Parliament had no power to alter those provisions in the Treaty and Acts of Union which were declared to be fundamental and unalterable, since the legislative authority from which they derived was anterior to Parliament.

Held, dismissing the appeal, that the petitioners had raised no issue which they could show to be justiciable by the court. *Per* Lord President Cooper:

> The Treaty and the associated legislation ... contain some clauses which expressly reserve to the Parliament of Great Britain powers of subsequent modification, and other clauses which either contain no such power or emphatically exclude subsequent alteration ... I have never been able to understand how it is possible to reconcile with elementary canons of construction the adoption by the English constitutional theorists of the same attitude to these markedly different types of provisions ...
>
> I have not found in the Union legislation any provision that the Parliament of Great Britain should be 'absolutely sovereign' in the sense that Parliament should be free to alter the Treaty at will ...
>
> [I]t is of little avail to ask whether the Parliament of Great Britain 'can' do this thing or that, without going on to inquire who can stop them if they do ... This at least is plain, that there is neither precedent nor authority of any kind for the view that the domestic courts of either Scotland or England have jurisdiction to determine whether a governmental act of the type here in controversy is or is not conform to the provisions of a treaty ...

Gibson v The Lord Advocate (1975) Court of Session

Article XVIII of the Act of Union 1707 authorised Parliament to alter certain aspects of Scots law, but provided 'that no alteration be made in laws which concern private right except for evident utility of the subjects within Scotland'. A Scots fisherman sought a declarator that the opening of Scottish coastal waters to nationals of other Community states under EEC Regulations (directly applicable by the European Communities Act 1972) was contrary to Article XVIII.

Held, dismissing the appeal, that the issue was outside the sphere of private rights. *Per* Lord Keith (*obiter*):

> ... the question whether a particular Act of the UK Parliament altering a particular aspect of Scots private law is or is not 'for the evident utility' of the subjects within Scotland is not a justiciable issue in this court.

Lord Keith added, however, that he expressed no view on what the position would be:

... if the UK Parliament passed an Act purporting to abolish the Court of Session or the Church of Scotland or to substitute English law for the whole body of Scots private law.

Pringle (1991)

The Abolition of Domestic Rates, etc (Scotland) Act 1987 introduced the Community Charge legislation in Scotland one year earlier than it was due to be introduced in England and Wales. The petitioner argued that it accordingly infringed Article IV of the Scots Act of Union which, he claimed, required that there should be no difference in the rights, privileges and advantages enjoyed by citizens in Great Britain unless expressly provided for in the Treaty of Union. The petitioner did not directly allege that the 1987 Act was invalid, but sought relief from his own liability to pay the Community Charge.

Held, dismissing the petition, that the court had no jurisdiction to grant the remedy claimed. Reaching no conclusion on the compatibility of the 1987 Act and Article IV of the Act of Union, the Lord President Lord Hope rejected the respondent's submission that the issue as a whole was not justiciable, but stated that much more detailed inquiry would be needed before he would be persuaded of the alleged incompatibility.

4.4 Challenge in the courts to subordinate legislation

4.4.1 By-laws

Kruse v Johnson (1898)

Kruse, a Minister of religion, was conducting an open-air service within 50 yards of a dwelling house in a village in Kent. He continued to sing a hymn after he had been asked by a police constable to stop. A by-law made by Kent County Council read as follows:

> No person shall sound or play upon any musical or noisy instrument or sing in any public place or highway within 50 yards of any dwelling-house after being required by a constable or by an inmate of such house personally or by his or her servant, to desist.

Johnson, a police superintendent, preferred an information against Kruse, who was convicted by the magistrates under the by-law. He appealed by way of a case stated to the Divisional Court, contending that the by-law was invalid for unreasonableness since it was not on its face limited to acts which were a nuisance, and because it might be put into operation by a policeman independently of judicial process.

Held (by a majority), that the conviction would be confirmed. Lord Russell of Killowen CJ considered the nature of a by-law, and said:

A by-law of the class we are considering I take to be an ordinance affecting the public or some portion of the public, imposed by some authority clothed with statutory powers, ordering something to be done or not to be done, and accompanied by some sanction or penalty for its non-observance. It necessarily involves restriction of liberty of action by persons who come under its operation as to acts which, but for the by-law, they would be free to do or not to do as they pleased. Further, it involves this consequence – that, if validly made, it has the force of law within the sphere of its legitimate operation – see *Edmund v Watermen's Co* (1855) ... We thus find that Parliament has thought fit to delegate to representative public bodies ... the power of exercising their own judgment as to what are the by-laws which to them seem proper to be made for good rule and government in their own localities. But that power is accompanied by certain safeguards; there must be antecedent publication of the by-law, with a view, I presume, of eliciting the public opinion of the locality upon it, and such by-laws shall have no force until after they have been forwarded to the Secretary of State.

However, the presence of the safeguards did not prevent the court from examining the validity of by-laws when they were brought into question. The court would be less vigilant to examine the by-laws of representative public bodies than it would be in the case of by-laws made by railway companies and similar undertakings. They ought to be 'benevolently' interpreted, and credit given to those who were to administer them that they would be reasonably administered. The court might find by-laws to be unreasonable if they were partial in their operation, as between different classes, manifestly unjust, made in bad faith, or oppressive. In any of these cases it would be possible to say that Parliament never intended to give authority to make such rules.

The by-law in the present case could not be said to be unreasonable; annoyance was a subjective concept, and a policeman was a responsible person in whom it was not improper to vest the power of putting the by-law into operation against an individual.

Q In the opinion of Lord Russell the publication of by-laws is intended to elicit public comment in the locality. Is there any other explanation for the requirement of antecedent publication?

Q Does the power vested by the by-law in a policeman to curtail the individual's freedom to sing infringe the first limb of the rule of law? If not, why not?

4.4.2 Statutory Instruments

R v Sheer Metalcraft Ltd (1954)

Facts as in *Simmonds v Newell* (1953) (2.1.2 above). The defendants argued at trial that the Iron and Steel Prices Order was not a valid statutory instrument, since the schedules setting out the maximum prices had not been printed with it and the Minister had not certified under Regulation 7 of the 1947 Statutory Instruments Regulations that this was unnecessary.

Held that the order was valid. The making of a statutory instrument and its issue were different procedures. The making of a valid instrument was complete when it had been made by the Minister concerned and laid before Parliament. At that stage it entered into force and was capable of being contravened. Where the remaining procedures relating to its issue had not been complied with, the burden was upon the Crown to prove that the instrument had nevertheless been brought to the attention of the public or of persons likely to be affected by it, or of the defendants themselves.

Hoffman-La Roche AG v Secretary of State for Trade and Industry (1975) HL

The Secretary of State applied for an injunction to compel certain pharmaceutical companies to reduce the price of various products in accordance with a statutory instrument made for that purpose. The companies alleged that the statutory instrument had been made in breach of aspects of natural justice required by statute to be observed as a precondition to the valid making of subordinate legislation in the area. They refused to reduce their prices, and issued a writ claiming that the statutory instrument was *ultra vires* and void.

Held, granting the injunction sought by the Secretary of State, that the companies had failed to show a sufficiently strong *prima facie* case that the statutory instrument was *ultra vires*. *Per* Lord Diplock:

> My Lords, in constitutional law a clear distinction can be drawn between an Act of Parliament and subordinate legislation, even though the latter is contained in an order made by statutory instrument approved by resolutions of both Houses of Parliament. Despite this indication that the majority of members of both houses of the contemporary Parliament regard the order as being for the common weal, I entertain no doubt that the courts have jurisdiction to declare it to be invalid if they are satisfied that that in making it the Minister who did so acted outwith the legislative powers conferred on him by the previous Act of Parliament under which the order purported to be made; and this is so whether the order is *ultra vires* by reason of its contents (patent defects) or by reason of defects in the procedure followed prior to its being made (latent defects).

4.5 The consequences of membership of the European Union for the legislative sovereignty of Parliament

4.5.1 EC law overrides subsequent inconsistent domestic legislation

The European view

Costa v ENEL Case 6/64 (1964) European Court of Justice
The plaintiff sought to avoid paying his electricity bill on the basis that Italian legislation nationalising the Italian electricity industry breached Articles 102, 93, 53 and 37 of the EC Treaty. The magistrate sought a preliminary ruling from the European Court of Justice (ECJ) under Article 177. The Italian government argued that the magistrate's request for a preliminary ruling under Article 177 was 'absolutely inadmissible', since the Italian court was bound to apply Italian domestic law.

Held, that subsequent national laws could not override EC legislation, and that the request for a preliminary ruling on the interpretation of EC Treaty law was therefore appropriate. On the relative status of EC and domestic law, the court said as follows:

> The precedence of Community law is confirmed by Article 189, whereby a regulation 'shall be binding' and 'directly applicable in all Member States'. This provision, which is subject to no reservation, would be quite meaningless if a State could unilaterally nullify its effects by means of a legislative measure which could prevail over Community law.
>
> It follows from all these observations that the law stemming from the Treaty, an independent source of law, could not, because of its special and original nature, be overridden by domestic legal provisions, however framed, without being deprived of its character as Community law and without the legal basis of the Community itself being called into question.
>
> The transfer by the States from their domestic legal system to the Community legal system of the rights and obligations arising under the Treaty carries with it a permanent limitation of their sovereign rights, against which a subsequent unilateral act incompatible with the concept of the Community cannot prevail.

The view of the English courts

Felixstowe Dock and Railway Co v British Transport Docks Board (1976) CA
By an agreement between the appellants and respondents, the latter were to take over the former, and were to obtain the consent of Parliament to the takeover by promoting the passage of a private Bill. The appellants argued that the proposed takeover would be void as an abuse of a dominant position contrary to Article 86 of the EC Treaty.

Held, that the appeal would be dismissed. Lord Denning MR, after considering Article 86, continued (*obiter*):

It seems to me that once the Bill is passed by Parliament and becomes a Statute that will dispose of all this discussion about the Treaty. These courts will have to abide by the Statute without regard to the Treaty at all.

R v Secretary of State for Transport, *ex parte* Factortame Ltd (No 2) (1990) European Court of Justice and HL

The applicants, which were companies incorporated under UK law, owned deep-sea fishing vessels registered as British under the Merchant Shipping Act 1894. Most of the applicants' directors and shareholders were Spanish nationals. The Merchant Shipping Act 1988 required all vessels to be re-registered. Under the 1988 Act and regulations issued pursuant to it, the applicants' connections with Spain would disqualify their vessels from registration as British. The applicants sought to challenge the legality of the relevant provisions of the Act and the regulations by judicial review on the grounds that the legislation contravened the EC Treaty and the European Communities Act 1972 by depriving them of enforceable Community rights.

The Divisional Court sought a preliminary ruling from the ECJ on the nature and extent of the Community rights said to be infringed by the Act, and granted interim relief in the form of an injunction to disapply the Act pending final judgment in the case. The Court of Appeal set aside the Divisional Court's order. The House of Lords upheld the ruling of the Court of Appeal, holding that the English courts had no jurisdiction to grant an injunction against the Crown, or to disapply an English Act of Parliament in advance of any decision of the ECJ that the Act contravened Community law.

Held (European Court of Justice):

... the reply to the question raised should be that Community law must be interpreted as meaning that a national court which, in a case before it concerning Community law, considers that the sole obstacle which precludes it from granting interim relief is a rule of national law must set aside that rule.

Held (House of Lords), *per* Lord Bridge:

... whatever limitation of its sovereignty Parliament accepted when it enacted the European Communities Act 1972 was entirely voluntary. Under the terms of the Act of 1972, it has always been clear that it was the duty of a UK court, when delivering final judgment, to override any rule of national law found to be in conflict with any directly enforceable rule of Community law ... there is nothing in any way novel in according supremacy to rules of Community law in those areas to which they apply and to insist that, in the protection of rights under Community law, national courts must not be inhibited by rules of national law from granting interim relief in appropriate cases is no more than a logical recognition of that supremacy.

4.5.2 The obligation to construe domestic legislation to achieve conformity with the EC Treaty

The original European view

Von Colson and Kamann v Land Nordrhein-Westfalen Case 14/83 (1984) European Court of Justice

The applicants established before a German court that they had been refused jobs on the grounds of their sex. The only remedy available under German law was the reimbursement of travel expenses incurred by the applicants in attending the job interviews. The applicants claimed that this was contrary to Article 6 of the Equal Treatment Directive 76/207/EEC. The directive left it to Member States to put in place effective remedies in order to achieve the object of the directive. An Article 177 preliminary reference was made to the European Court.

Held, that the directive, although it left Member States free to choose remedies for breach of the prohibition against sex discrimination, required that remedies chosen should constitute an effective deterrent, and that compensation should therefore be adequate in relation to the damage sustained. The national court therefore came under a duty

> to interpret and apply the legislation *adopted for the implementation of the directive* in conformity with the requirements of Community law, in so far as it is given discretion to do so under national law. (Emphasis added.)

Q Compare this statement with the formulation in *Marleasing SA v La Commercial Internacional de Alimentacion SA* (see 4.5.2 below). Can they be reconciled?

The view of the English courts

Macarthys v Smith (1979) CA

The respondent, Mrs Smith, was appointed to a position formerly occupied by a male employee. Her duties were the same as his had been, but she received less pay. She claimed that she was entitled to be paid at the same rate for the same work. Her claim succeeded before the industrial tribunal and the Employment Appeal Tribunal. The Equal Pay Act appeared to be restricted in its operation to a case where the male and the female employees were employed at the same time. Her employer appealed.

Held (by a majority), that an Article 177 reference to the European Court was appropriate. *Per* Lord Denning MR (in whose dissenting view a purposive construction should be given to the Act to permit comparison of successive employments of male and female employees and thereby give effect to the object of Article 119 of the Treaty):

> In construing our statute, we are entitled to look to the Treaty as an aid to its construction, and even more, not only as an aid but as an overriding force. If in close investigation it should appear that our legislation is deficient – or is inconsistent with Community law – by some oversight of our draftsmen – then it is

our bounden duty to give priority to Community law. Such is the result of s 2(1) and (4) of the European Communities Act 1972.

I pause here, however, to make one observation on a constitutional point. Thus far I have assumed that our Parliament, whenever it passes legislation, intends to fulfil its obligations under the Treaty. If the time should come when our Parliament deliberately passes an Act – with the intention of repudiating the Treaty or any provision in it – or intentionally of acting inconsistently with it – and says so in express terms – then I should have thought it would be the duty of our courts to follow the statute of our Parliament. I do not, however, envisage any such situation. As I said in *Blackburn v Attorney General* (1971): 'But, if Parliament should happen to do so, then I say we will consider that event when it happens.' Unless there is an intentional and express repudiation of the Treaty, it is our duty to give priority to the Treaty. In the present case I assume that the UK intended to fulfil its obligations under Article 119.

Purposive construction not applicable to legislation not introduced in order to comply with Treaty obligations

Duke v GEC Reliance Systems Ltd (1988) HL

The appellant was dismissed by her employer when she was between the ages of 60 and 65 pursuant to the employer's policy that female employees were to be retired at 60 and male employees at 65. The appellant alleged that this constituted sex discrimination. She sought to bring an action under s 6(4) of the Sex Discrimination Act 1975. She argued, in the alternative, that if on a plain reading s 6(4) preserved the lawfulness of discriminatory retirement ages for men and women, it should nevertheless be construed in a manner to give effect to the Equal Treatment Directive (76/207/EEC) adopted by the Council of Ministers on 9 February 1976.

Held, dismissing the appeal, that the Sex Discrimination Act 1975 was not passed in order to give effect to the Equal Treatment Directive, but had been intended (until its amendment in 1986) to preserve discriminatory retirement ages. Section 2(4) of the European Communities Act 1972 did not enable or constrain a British court to distort the meaning of a British statute to achieve an equivalent to direct effect between individuals.

Per Lord Templeman:

> The *Von Colson* case is no authority for the proposition that the German court was bound to invent a German law of adequate compensation if no such law existed and no authority for the proposition that a court of a Member State must distort the meaning of a domestic statute so as to conform with Community law which is not directly applicable.

Purposive construction applicable to legislation introduced in order to comply with Treaty obligations

Litster v Forth Dry Dock & Engineering Co Ltd (1990) HL

Directive 77/187/EEC provided safeguards for employees where a business was transferred between owners. The Transfer of Undertakings (Protection of Employment) Regulations 1981 were made to implement the directive. The Regulations permitted employees to pursue actions against the new employer provided they had been in the employment of the former owner immediately before the transfer. A company became insolvent and went into receivership. The employees were made redundant one hour before the transfer of the business. An appeal by the employer to the Court of Session from tribunal judgments favourable to the employees was successful. The employees appealed to the House of Lords, contending that the relevant part of the Regulations should not be interpreted narrowly, but should be given a purposive construction in order to conform to the object of the directive.

Held, allowing the appeal, that the UK courts were under a duty to follow the practice of the European Court of Justice by giving a purposive construction to directives and to regulations issued for the purpose of complying with directives. *Per* Lord Oliver:

> The critical question, it seems to me, is whether, even allowing for the greater latitude in construction permissible in the case of legislation introduced to give effect to this country's Community obligations, it is possible to attribute to Regulation 8(1) when read in conjunction with Regulation 5, the same result as that attributed to Article 4 in the *Bork* case (1989) IRLR 41. Purely as a matter of language, it clearly is not ... If this provision fell to be construed by reference to the ordinary rules of construction applicable to a purely domestic statute and without reference to Treaty obligations, it would, I think, be quite impermissible to regard it as having the same prohibitory effect ... *Pickstone v Freemans plc* [1989] AC 66, has established that the greater flexibility available to the court in applying a purposive construction to legislation designed to give effect to the UK's Treaty obligations to the Community enables the court, where necessary, to supply by implication words appropriate to comply with those obligations ... Having regard to the manifest purpose of the regulations, I do not, for my part, feel inhibited from making such an implication in the instant case.

The current European view

Marleasing SA v La Comercial Internacional Case C-196/89 (1992)

Marleasing sought a declaration that the contracts setting up the defendant companies were void as sham transactions intended for the defrauding of creditors, and that the companies were therefore nullities. This involved pleading 'lack of cause'. Directive 68/151/EEC listed the exclusive grounds on which nullity could be invoked, but did not include lack of cause. The directive was unimplemented in Spain and the deadline for implementation had passed. The Spanish court made an Article 177 reference on the status of the directive.

Held, that although a directive could not impose obligations on individuals (and consequently a provision of a directive could not be relied upon against a private party) the Spanish court was nevertheless under an obligation to interpret national law in the light of the wording and the purpose of the directive. In so stating, the court broadened the doctrine of *Von Colson*:

> in applying national law, *whether the provisions in question were adopted before or after the directive*, the national court called upon to interpret it is required to do so, as far as possible, in the light of the wording and the purpose of the directive in order to achieve the result pursued by the latter and thereby comply with the third para of Article 189 of the Treaty. (Emphasis added.)

Q In the light of this decision should *Duke v GEC Reliance Ltd* (1988) (see 4.5.2 above) continue to be regarded as good law?

Fundamental principles of Community law in the domestic courts

R v Ministry of Agriculture, Fisheries and Food, *ex parte* **First City Trading (1996)**

The applicant sought to review the beef stocks transfer scheme which had been designed by the Ministry to give financial aid to certain exporters affected by the European Community's decision to prohibit the export of beef slaughtered in the UK. The applicant argued that the scheme discriminated without objective justification in favour of exporters with slaughtering and cutting-up facilities, and against exporters who lacked those facilities, and that it therefore breached the fundamental Community law principles of equal treatment or non-discrimination.

Held, that in deciding whether fundamental principles of Community law applied to a domestic measure, distinctions were to be drawn between (a) those measures taken solely by virtue of domestic law, and those authorised or obliged to be taken by virtue of substantive Community law (for instance, the passing of domestic legislation in order to give effect to a directive); and (b) between principles of law developed by the European Court within its limited jurisdiction, and Community Treaty provisions, which had sovereign legislative force. The principles of Community law as developed by the European Court applied only to measures taken pursuant to powers or duties conferred or imposed by substantive Community law. The government's scheme was within the first category of measure. It could not therefore be challenged by reference to the Community principle of equal treatment, and the application accordingly failed.

5 The prerogative powers of the Crown

5.1 Definitions

Blackstone, *Commentaries on the Laws of England* (1778, 8th edn) Book 1, p 239

By the word prerogative we usually understand that special pre-eminence, which the king hath, over and above all other persons, and out of the ordinary course of the common law, in right of his regal dignity. It signifies, in its etymology (from *prae* and *rogo*), something which is required or demanded before, or in preference to, all others. And hence it follows, that it must be in its nature singular and eccentrical; that it can only be applied to those rights and capacities which the king enjoys alone, in contradistinction to others, and not to those which he enjoys in common with any of his subjects: for if once any prerogative of the crown could be held in common with the subject, it would cease to be prerogative any longer. And therefore Finch [*Law*, 1627, p 85] lays it down as a maxim, that the prerogative is that law in case of the king, which is law in no case of the subject.

Dicey, AV, *An Introduction to the Study of the Law of the Constitution* (1959, 10th edn) pp 424–25

The prerogative appears to be both historically and as a matter of actual fact nothing else than the residue of discretionary or arbitrary authority, which at any given time is legally left in the hands of the Crown ... From the time of the Norman Conquest down to the Revolution of 1688, the Crown possessed in reality many of the attributes of sovereignty. The prerogative is the name for the remaining portion of the Crown's original authority ... Every act which the executive government can lawfully do without the authority of the Act of Parliament is done in virtue of this prerogative.

5.2 Prerogative powers conflicting with law

Case of Monopolies (Darcy v Allein) (1602)

The plaintiff had received from Queen Elizabeth I the grant of a sole licence for 21 years to import and sell playing cards, and to manufacture playing cards. In return for the monopoly the plaintiff had paid 100 marks to the Queen. The plaintiff brought an action against the defendant for infringement of the monopoly.

Held, that the grant of the monopoly to the plaintiff was contrary to common law and statute, and therefore void.

5.3 Prerogative powers unauthorised by law

Case of Proclamations (1610)

The King sought, by proclamation, to declare the building of new houses in London and the making of wheat starch to be offences (in order that he could levy fines upon offenders).

Held that the King had no prerogative power to declare new offences by proclamation. The law of England was divided into three parts – common law, statute and custom – but the King's proclamation was no part of the law. The King enjoyed no prerogative powers except those which the law of the land allowed him. The most he might do by proclamation to prevent offending was to admonish his subjects to keep the law upon pain of punishment inflicted according to the law.

British Broadcasting Corporation v Johns (Inspector of Taxes) (1964) (CA)

Facts: see 2.2.1 above. Counsel for the Corporation also argued that the Crown had a prerogative right to a monopoly of the use of wireless telegraphy and telephony, since they were (at the relevant time) new inventions, and that it had chosen to exercise this monopoly through the Corporation. Rejecting this submission, Diplock LJ said:

This contention involves adopting what [counsel for the BBC] describes as a modern, and I as a 17th century, view, of the scope of the prerogative. But it is 350 years and a civil war too late for the Queen's courts to broaden the prerogative. The limits within which the executive government may impose obligations or restraints on citizens of the United Kingdom without any statutory authority are now well settled and incapable of extension.

5.4 Legal challenge to the exercise of prerogative powers

Council of Civil Service Unions v Minister for the Civil Service (1985) HL

Facts: see 15.5.1 below.

Per Lord Roskill:

If the executive instead of acting under a statutory power acts under a prerogative power and in particular ... so as to affect the rights of the citizen, I am unable to see, subject to what I shall say later, that there is any logical reason why the fact that the source of the power is the prerogative and not statute

should today deprive the citizen of that right of challenge to the manner of its exercise which he would possess were the source of the power statutory ...
But I do not think that that right of challenge can be unqualified. It must, I think, depend upon the subject matter of the prerogative power which is exercised. Many examples were given during the argument of prerogative powers which as at present advised I do not think could properly be made the subject of judicial review. Prerogative powers such as those relating to the making of treaties, the defence of the realm, the prerogative of mercy, the grant of honours, the dissolution of Parliament and the appointment of ministers as well as others are not, I think, subject to judicial review because their nature and subject matter are not such as to be amenable to the judicial process. The courts are not the place where to determine whether a treaty should be concluded or the armed forces disposed in a particular manner or Parliament dissolved on one date rather than another.

5.5 The relationship between prerogative and statute

5.5.1 The prerogative is abridged by statute

Attorney General v De Keyser's Royal Hotel Ltd (1920) HL
The Army Council took possession of De Keyser's Royal Hotel. The premises were used for the purposes of the War Office. The lessees of the hotel claimed compensation as of right. The Crown argued that the hotel had been possessed under the Defence of the Realm Regulations or by a *de facto* exercise of the prerogative, and that the exercise of neither power obliged the Crown to pay compensation. The lessees argued that the taking of the hotel was authorised by the Defence Act 1842 which made the payment of compensation mandatory.

Held, dismissing the Crown's appeal, that where power was conferred on the Crown by legislation, the Crown would be taken to act under those powers, and not under equivalent pre-existing prerogative powers. *Per* Lord Atkinson:

... when such a statute expressing the will and intention of the King and of the three estates of the realm is passed, it abridges the royal prerogative while it is in force to the extent that the Crown can only do the particular thing under and in accordance with the statutory provisions, and that its prerogative power to do that thing is in abeyance.

Per Lord Moulton:

There can be no excuse for reverting to prerogative powers ... when the Legislature has given to the Crown statutory powers ... which cover all that can be necessary for the defence of the nation, and are moreover accompanied by safeguards to the individual, which are in agreement with the demands of justice.

Per Lord Sumner:

> ... if there is adequate power to do all that is required by proceeding under the statute, where is the emergency and public necessity which is the foundation for resort to the prerogative?

Laker Airways v Department of Trade (1977) CA

In 1972 the Civil Aviation Authority granted Laker Airways a licence pursuant to statute to enable it to operate a cut-price service between London and New York. The following year the government designated Laker Airways as a scheduled carrier under the Bermuda Agreement with the result that the US authorities then became bound to give Laker landing rights in New York. Following a change of government in the UK and the institution of a policy calculated to protect British Airways from competition on the London – New York route, a new Secretary of State issued guidance causing the Civil Aviation Authority to withdraw Laker's licence. The Secretary of State also revoked Laker's designation under the Bermuda Agreement. Laker challenged both actions. The Secretary of State claimed that the revocation of the designation was a prerogative act relating to the government's conduct of international affairs which was not justiciable by the courts.

Held, that the Secretary of State was effectively claiming the right to frustrate the statutory grant of the licence to Laker by prerogative powers. The question for the court was whether he might withdraw the designation while the licence remained in force. The Attorney General had argued that the Secretary of State was free to do so because the Civil Aviation Act 1971 under which the licence had been granted did not curb the prerogative powers of the Crown. However, *Walker v Baird* (1892) (see 5.7.2 below) made it clear that prerogative powers could not be used in this way to take away the rights of citizens. The 1971 Act was intended by Parliament to govern the rights and duties of British citizens in all aspects of civil aviation. The Act made provision for revocation of a licence and should be taken to regulate all aspects of revocation. The Secretary of State had used the prerogative power unlawfully.

5.5.2 Prerogative powers directed towards the protection of the individual

R v Secretary of State for the Home Department, *ex parte* Northumbria Police Authority (1989) CA
Facts: see 5.6.2 below.
Per Purchas LJ:

> It is well established that the courts will intervene to prevent executive action under prerogative powers in violation of property or other rights of the individual where this is inconsistent with statutory provisions providing for the same executive action. Where the executive action is directed towards the

benefit or protection of the individual, it is unlikely that its use will attract the intervention of the courts. In my judgment, before the courts will hold that such executive action is contrary to legislation, express and unequivocal terms must be found in the statute which deprive the individual from receiving the benefit or protection intended by the exercise of prerogative power ...

5.5.3 The prerogative may not be used to frustrate the will of Parliament

R v Secretary of State for the Home Department, *ex parte* Fire Brigades Union (1995) HL

The Criminal Injuries Compensation Board was set up in 1964 under prerogative powers in order to compensate the victims of crime. Compensation under the scheme was assessed on the same basis as damages at common law. Sections 108–17 and Schedules 6 and 7 of the 1988 Criminal Justice Act substantially gave statutory enactment to the scheme. Section 171 provided that '... this Act shall come into force on such day as the Secretary of State may by order made by statutory instrument appoint and different days may be appointed ... for different provisions'.

No order had been made under the section to bring the statutory scheme into force and the original scheme was still in operation. In a white paper published in December 1993, the government proposed to introduce a tariff system of compensation for criminal injuries, using prerogative powers. It was common ground that in several cases payments under the tariff scheme would be less than those under the old or the statutory systems of compensation. Paragraph 38 of the white paper read: '... With the demise of the current scheme the provisions in the 1988 Act will not now be implemented. They will accordingly be repealed when a suitable legislative opportunity occurs.' The applicants argued that although s 177 gave the Secretary of State a discretion as to when the statutory scheme might be implemented, it equally imposed on him a duty to implement it at some time. The Court of Appeal upheld the application by a majority.

Held (by a majority), that the Secretary of State's appeal should be dismissed. Although the court could not intervene in the legislative process by requiring the Secretary of State to introduce the statutory scheme, it did not follow that he had an absolute and unfettered discretion whether or not to bring it into effect. He was under a duty to keep its introduction under consideration, and not to procure events to take place and then rely on those events as grounds for not introducing the statutory scheme. In claiming that the introduction of the tariff scheme under the prerogative rendered undesirable the implementation of the statutory scheme, the Secretary of State had abused his discretion and had acted unlawfully.

In the view of the minority, the Secretary of State was answerable to Parliament for any failure in his responsibilities, and that was the only place for any possible failure to be called in question. In the absence of a written constitution sensitivity was required of the parliamentarian, the administrator and the judge alike if the delicate balance of the unwritten rules of the constitution was not to be disturbed and all recent advances undone. The Secretary of State's decision in the present case was quite unsuitable to be the subject of review by a court of law.

5.6   Particular prerogative powers

5.6.1 The war prerogative

Burmah Oil Co Ltd v Lord Advocate (1965) HL
During the Japanese invasion of Burma in 1942 the appellant's oil installations were destroyed on the order of the commander of the British forces in order to prevent them coming into the possession of the invading forces. The respondent had originally argued that this did not amount to an exercise of prerogative power, but the point was not relied upon in the House of Lords. The appellant sought compensation, and appealed to the House of Lords on the preliminary finding in the lower courts that in the circumstances compensation was not payable.

Held, allowing the appeal (by a majority), that although the prerogative power to wage war had been recognised for centuries, the authorities disclosed no rule that private property might be taken by the Crown, even in times of war or imminent danger, without any payment being made for it.

Note ───
The effect of this decision was reversed by the passing of the War Damage Act 1965, which retrospectively cancelled the Crown's liability to pay compensation for war damage lawfully caused.

5.6.2 The prerogative power of keeping the peace

R v Secretary of State for the Home Department, *ex parte* Northumbria Police Authority (1989) CA
The Home Secretary issued a circular stating that all police requirements for plastic baton rounds and CS gas were to be met from a central store. Local police authorities were to be notified of the provision of such equipment. The Northumbria Police Authority sought a declaration that the Home Secretary had no power to issue the equipment without the consent of the local police authority, save in a grave emergency. The Authority contended that the Police Act 1964 constituted a complete and comprehensive code defining and limiting the functions of local police authorities, chief constables and the Home Secretary with regard to the provision of equipment to police forces. The Act gave the Home Secretary no power to provide equipment without the consent of the local police authorities. The Home

Secretary argued that he enjoyed further prerogative powers to supply equipment without the consent of local police authorities. The Divisional Court accepted both arguments. The Authority appealed, and the Home Secretary cross appealed.

Held, allowing the cross appeal, that the 1964 Act imposed no requirement on the Home Secretary to supply equipment only with the consent of local police authorities. Therefore, the supply as made was lawful under the Act. The appeal would therefore be dismissed. Further, although it had been the invariable practice to leave the maintenance of public order to the police, the Crown retained a prerogative power to keep the peace. *Per* Nourse LJ:

> At all events, there being no decision to the contrary, I decline to hold that a power so valuable to the common good no longer exists ... I therefore conclude that, if the necessary power had not been available under s 41 of the 1964 Act, the terms and implementation of para 4 of the Home Office circular would have been within the prerogative powers of the Crown.

Q Can this case be reconciled with *Attorney General v De Keyser's Royal Hotel* (1920) (see 5.5.1 above)?

5.6.3 The treaty-making power of the Crown

Blackburn v Attorney General (1971) CA

The appellant applied for declarations that by signing the Treaty of Rome, the government would permanently surrender in part the sovereignty of the Crown in Parliament and in so doing would act contrary to the law. At first instance the appellant's statement of claim was struck out as disclosing no reasonable cause of action.

Held, dismissing the appeal, that when ministers of the Crown negotiate and sign a treaty, their actions cannot be challenged or questioned in the courts. Lord Denning MR added that no treaty had yet been signed. If a treaty was to be signed, and incorporated into English law, the courts would take such notice of it as Parliament instructed.

Ex parte **Molyneaux and others (1986)**

The Anglo-Irish agreement concluded by the governments of the Irish Republic and the UK in 1985 provided for the establishment of an Intergovernmental Conference concerned with Northern Ireland and its relations with the Irish Republic. The applicants were members and officers of the Ulster Unionist Council. They sought a declaration by way of judicial review that it would be contrary to law for the UK government to implement the agreement by use of the prerogative without the authority of new legislation. In support of this they argued: (1) that the agreement and its implementation would impose fetters on the statutory powers and duties of the Secretary of State for Northern Ireland; (2) that the agreement would contravene Article 6 of the Union with Ireland Act 1800 since it would remove parity of privilege and status as between the people of Northern Ireland and those of Great Britain; and (3) that the prerogative power on which the government had purported to rely in entering the agreement had in fact been delegated in its entirety to the Northern Ireland executive authority by the Northern Ireland Constitution Act 1973.

Held, that the application disclosed no arguable case and would accordingly be dismissed. The applicants' second contention was wrong, because there could be no contravention of Article 6 save by a treaty with a foreign power, and the Ireland Act 1949 provided that the Republic was not to have that status in law. The third argument failed because the delegation of the prerogative by the 1973 Act had been only partial, and an Act of the following year had in any event returned the delegated power to the Secretary of State. With respect to the first contention the court denied that the agreement would constitute a fetter on the discretion of the Secretary of State. The establishment of the Intergovernmental Conference would not therefore contravene any statute, any rule of common law or any constitutional convention. Nor would it amount, as the applicants had originally claimed, to the establishment in the UK of a new standing body for the purpose of influencing the conduct of the government without the authority of the Queen in Parliament. It would establish nothing in the UK because it existed only in the field of international relations. Taylor J concluded:

> It is akin to a treaty. It concerns relations between the UK and another sovereign state and it is not the function of this court to inquire into the exercise of the prerogative in entering into such an agreement or by way of anticipation to decide whether the method proposed of implementing the agreement is appropriate.

R v Secretary of State for Foreign and Commonwealth Affairs, *ex parte* Rees-Mogg (1994)

The applicant sought, *inter alia*, a declaration that by ratifying Title V of the Treaty on European Union signed at Maastricht on 7 February 1992, the government would be transferring part of the prerogative powers to conduct foreign and security policy to Community Institutions without statutory authority.

Held, dismissing the application, that Title V did not entail a transfer of prerogative powers but an exercise of them. The applicant's arguments would be rejected either on the grounds that the questions raised were not justiciable, or, if they were, that they failed on the merits. After citing *Blackburn v Attorney General* and *Ex parte Molyneaux* as authorities for the proposition that the court had no jurisdiction to consider the question raised by the applicant, Lloyd LJ stated that it would be possible for the court to accept that argument and to go no further. However, counsel for the applicant had pointed out that the principle of non-justiciability was not universal and absolute, but subject to exceptions. Section 6 of the European Parliamentary Elections Act 1978 created such an exception, obliging a court, if so required, to consider whether any treaty which the government proposed to ratify involved an increase in the powers of the European Parliament. Lloyd LJ stated that although that exception was not in issue in the present case, he was prepared to assume that he was entitled to consider the applicant's assertions.

Q Is this case any authority for the proposition that the court may assume jurisdiction to give a declaratory judgment on the propriety of an exercise of prerogative powers in relation to treaties?

5.6.4 The prerogative of mercy

de Freitas v Benny (1975) (PC)
The appellant was convicted of murder and sentenced to death by the Supreme Court of Trinidad and Tobago. After exhausting all his rights of appeal against conviction, he applied to court claiming (a) that the execution upon him of the death sentence would infringe his rights to life as secured by the Constitution of Trinidad and Tobago since it amounted either *per se* or because of delay to 'cruel and unusual punishment', prohibited by the Constitution; and (b) that before advice was tendered to the Governor General regarding the exercise of the prerogative of mercy, the appellant was entitled to be shown the material placed before the Advisory Committee on the prerogative of mercy, and entitled to be heard and legally represented before the Committee.

Held, dismissing the appeal, that death was made a mandatory penalty for murder by the law of Trinidad and Tobago so that the prohibition against cruel and unusual punishment did not apply to it. The appellant's arguments concerning delay were rejected. The claimed rights to notice and a hearing in connection with the decision on the prerogative of mercy did not exist. *Per* Lord Diplock:

Except in so far as it may have been altered by the Constitution the legal nature of the exercise of the royal prerogative of mercy in Trinidad and Tobago remains the same as it was in England at common law. At common law this has always been a matter which lies solely in the discretion of the sovereign, who by constitutional convention exercises it in respect of England on the advice of the Home Secretary to whom Her Majesty delegates the discretion. Mercy is not the subject of legal rights. It begins where legal rights end. A convicted person has no legal right even to have his case considered by the Home Secretary in connection with the exercise of the prerogative of mercy. In tendering his advice to the sovereign the Home Secretary is doing something that is often cited as the exemplar of a purely discretionary act as contrasted with the exercise of a quasi-judicial foundation.

The Advisory Committee was a purely consultative body without any decision-making power. No provisions of the Constitution of Trinidad and Tobago had the effect of converting the purely discretionary functions of the Minister, on whose advice the Governor General acted, into quasi-judicial functions. The appellant therefore had no legal right to disclosure of material provided to the Advisory Committee and the Minister.

R v Secretary of State for the Home Department, *ex parte* Bentley (1994)

The applicant was the sister of Derek Bentley, who had been hanged in 1953 for his part in the murder of a police officer. The fatal shot had been fired by Bentley's accomplice but he, being too young to be subject to the death penalty, was sentenced instead to life imprisonment. Despite a recommendation from the jury and the advice of Home Office officials that Bentley should not be subject to capital punishment in these circumstances, the then Home Secretary, Sir David Maxwell Fyfe, refused to commute his sentence. In 1992 the Home Secretary declined to recommend a posthumous pardon for Bentley on the grounds that, although he personally agreed that Bentley should not have been hanged, it had been the policy of successive Home Secretaries not to recommend the exercise of the royal prerogative for the grant of a free pardon unless satisfied that the person concerned was both morally and technically innocent of any crime. The applicant alleged that the grant of a free pardon did not entail recognition that Bentley was wrongly convicted, and that the Home Secretary had erred in law in considering that it did.

Held, making no order but inviting the Home Secretary to reconsider his decision, that the *GCHQ* case made it clear that the powers of the court could not be ousted merely by invoking the word 'prerogative'. The question in each case was whether the nature and subject matter of the decision was amenable to the judicial process. The formulation of criteria for the exercise of the prerogative a free pardon was a matter of policy which was not justiciable. However, the prerogative might have been exercised by the grant of a conditional pardon, whereby the penalty first imposed would be (notionally) replaced by a lesser sentence. The Home Secretary had not properly considered that possibility, and should now do so.

Reckley v Minister of Public Safety (No 2) (1996) (PC)

The appellant was convicted of murder and sentenced to death by a Bahamian court. Articles 91 and 92 of the Constitution of The Bahamas provided for non-binding advice on the exercise of the prerogative of mercy to be given by an Advisory Committee to a designated Minister. The decision to grant or withhold mercy would be taken by the Governor General, acting on the Minister's advice. The appellant, having exhausted all other forms of recourse, argued (*inter alia*) that the execution upon him of the death sentence would contravene his constitutional rights since he had not been permitted either to see material placed before the Advisory Committee, or to make representations to the Committee.

Held, dismissing the appeal, that Lord Diplock's analysis of the position in *de Freitas v Benny* (above) was determinative of the point. It was reinforced by the facts (a) that the Advisory Committee's consideration of death sentence cases was legally enjoined and was not dependent on the taking of any initiative by the prisoner; (b) that the Minister was not bound to accept the Committee's advice, so that the discretion he retained was clearly of a purely personal character; and (c) that the Minister's constitutional discretion to determine the material placed before the Committee was inconsistent with the appellant's claimed right to make representations to the Committee. Thus, the exercise of the prerogative of mercy under the Bahamian Constitution was not justiciable. The decision in *Bentley's* case (above) was based on exceptional facts and had no bearing on the present appeal, since it had not been directly concerned with the prerogative of mercy in a death sentence case. The appellant had relied on *Doody's* case (see 16.2 below) as the source of a right in fairness to make representations, but there Lord Mustill had distinguished the situation before him from one in which, as here the prisoner was 'essentially in mercy' so that there was 'no ground to ascribe to him the rights which fairness might otherwise demand'. Lord Goff, having earlier described the Advisory Committee as 'a reputable and impartial source', stated:

... their Lordships wish to stress the nature of the constitutional safeguard which the introduction of the advisory committee has created. On the committee, the designated Minister and the Attorney General will be joined by a group of people nominated by the Governor General. These will, their Lordships are confident, be men and women of distinction, whose presence, and contribution, at the heart of the process will ensure that the condemned man's case is given, and is seen to be given, full and fair consideration ... It is plain to their Lordships that those who drew the Constitution of The Bahamas were well aware of the personal nature of the discretion to be exercised by the Minister and the consequent absence of any supervisory role by the courts, but also considered that, by introducing an advisory committee with the constitution and functions specified in the Constitution, they were providing a safeguard both appropriate and adequate for the situation.

Q If there were evidence that the Advisory Committee's recommendation to the Minister were vitiated by actual bias, would its advice be subject to review?

5.6.5 The issue of a passport

R v Secretary of State for Foreign and Commonwealth Affairs, *ex parte* Everett (1989) CA

The applicant, a British passport holder living in Spain, applied to the British Embassy for a new passport. His request was refused on the grounds that a warrant for his arrest had been issued in the UK and it was the policy of the Secretary of State not to issue new passports to persons who were wanted by the police in connection with serious crime. The applicant sought an order of *certiorari* to quash the decision on the basis that no details of the warrant had been given to him. Details were provided to him before the date of the hearing. At first instance, the court held that the Secretary of State had failed to consider whether the applicant's case was one in which an exception should be made to the policy governing the issue of passports. The Secretary of State appealed, claiming that passports were issued pursuant to prerogative powers which were not justiciable by the courts.

Held, that the appeal would be allowed. The Secretary of State was under a duty to give reasons where he refused a passport, to give details of the warrant extant, and to consider whether an exception to his policy relating to the issue of passports should be made in the circumstances of the applicant's case. Since the information had become available to the applicant, and since there were no exceptional factors in his case, there were no grounds for granting relief. The court accepted the Secretary of State's submission that the issue of passports was an exercise of prerogative power, but rejected his contention that it was therefore not justiciable. As a matter of common sense, the court should be able to inquire into a refusal to issue a passport. The power was not to be compared with plainly non-justiciable exercises of prerogative powers, such as the conduct of foreign affairs or the signing of treaties.

5.7 Acts of State

5.7.1 The attitude of the courts to acts of State

Salaman v Secretary of State for India (1906) PC

The Secretary of State was appointed the successor to the East India Company by the Government of India Act 1858. The company had entered into an agreement with the regents of the infant Maharajah of the Punjab, by which the company assumed sovereignty over the Punjab, took possession of all State property, and in return was to pay a pension to the Maharajah. The appellant was the trustee in bankruptcy of the Maharajah's residuary legatee. He alleged that the company, and subsequently the

Secretary of State, was trustee of the pension, and therefore liable to account to the appellant for arrears.

Held, dismissing the appeal, that the company's actions amounted to acts of State done by the company as trustees for the Crown. *Per* Fletcher Moulton LJ:

> An act of State is essentially an exercise of sovereign power, and hence cannot be challenged, controlled, or interfered with by municipal courts. Its sanction is not that of law, but that of sovereign power, and, whatever it may be, municipal courts must accept it without question. But it may and often must be part of their duty to take cognisance of it. For instance, if an act is relied upon as being an act of State, and thus as affording an answer to claims made by a subject, the courts must decide whether it was in truth an act of State, and what was its nature and extent ... But in such an inquiry the court must confine itself to ascertaining what the act of State in fact was, and not what in their opinion it ought to have been ... Acts of State are not all of one kind; their nature and consequences may differ in an infinite variety of ways, and thus may profoundly affect the position of municipal courts with regard to them ... An act of State need not rest upon or be expressed in documents. It may be evidenced by the nature of the acts done and the circumstances under which they were done; and, if an act is in this way actually shown to have been actually done in such a way as to constitute it an act of State, it is no answer to say that it was in excess of previous or contemporary acts of State to which it might be expected to conform.

5.7.2 British subjects on British territory and the defence of act of State

Walker v Baird (1892) PC

With the authority of the government officers of the Crown seized a lobster fishery in Newfoundland. They claimed to be acting under instruction to enforce an agreement on lobster fishing made between the Crown and the French government. An action was begun against the officers in the Newfoundland courts. The Superior Court of Newfoundland held that the defence of act of State could not be pleaded against British subjects for a trespass within British territory in time of peace. The officers appealed to the Privy Council.

Held, that the appeal would be dismissed. The suggestions that the appellants' acts could be justified as acts of State, or that the court was not competent to inquire into the construction of treaties or other acts of State, were wholly untenable.

5.7.3 Aliens on British territory and the defence of act of State

Johnstone v Pedlar (1921) HL

The respondent, Pedlar, was a naturalised citizen of the US. He was arrested and convicted of an offence in Dublin. He brought an action against Johnstone, the Chief Commissioner of the Dublin Metropolitan Police, claiming for the return of a cheque and sums of money which had been found in his possession at the time of his arrest. Johnstone maintained that these items were the property of an illegal association, and were in the respondent's possession for the illegal purposes of that association. He further maintained that the respondent was an alien, and that the property had been taken from him and detained by an officer of the Crown at the direction of the Crown as an act of State for the defence of the realm and the prevention of crime. In support of this claim he produced a certificate signed by the Chief Secretary for Ireland. The Irish Court of Appeal found for the respondent. The allegations concerning the illegal purpose for which the respondent had had the property were held not to have been proved. Pedlar appealed to the House of Lords.

Held, dismissing the appeal, that the respondent had been in British territory at the time of his arrest. He was not a subject of the British Crown, but it was correct to say that for the purposes of the present case he had to be treated as if he were. The subject of a State at peace with the Crown, while permitted to reside in this country, was under the Crown's protection and owed the Crown a duty of local allegiance. It was for this reason that in cases dealing with the defence of act of State it had been said that the act should have been carried out abroad as well as against a foreigner in order that the defence should succeed. If it were otherwise (*per* Viscount Finlay):

> ... aliens in this country, instead of having the protection of British law, would be at the mercy of any department entitled to use the name of the Crown for an 'act of State'. It would have effects upon aliens in the country of a far-reaching nature as to person and property.

5.7.4 British subjects outside British territory and the defence of act of State

Nissan v Attorney General (1970) HL

Nissan, a citizen of the UK and Colonies, brought an action against the Crown claiming a declaration that he was entitled to compensation in respect of damage by British forces to his hotel, and the destruction of stores. The hotel had been occupied by the British forces in Cyprus in the course of an attempt to restore peace between the opposing Greek and Turkish communities on the island. The involvement of the British forces was pursuant to an agreement between the Crown and the government of Cyprus. Nissan claimed that the occupation of the hotel was a lawful exercise of the prerogative and that compensation was accordingly payable. The Court of Appeal held that compensation was payable. The Attorney General appealed to the House of Lords.

Held, that the appeal would be dismissed. In the opinion of the majority, the occupation of the hotel did not have the character of an act of State. The agreement between the Crown and the government of Cyprus was an act of State, but the occupation of the hotel was not sufficiently closely connected with it to qualify for the same description. Lord Wilberforce, Lord Morris and Lord Pearson declined to decide the question whether there were circumstances in which an act done outside the realm could ever be an act of State in relation to a British subject. *Walker v Baird* (1892) was inconclusive on this point, since the plaintiff had not only been a British subject, but had been on British territory. In the opinion of Lord Reid, the authorities contained *dicta* favouring both views, but His Lordship was not prepared to hold that the description 'act of State' would in any event oust the jurisdiction of the court:

If I thought that any act done against the person or property of a British subject wherever situated could be an act of State in the sense that he was deprived of all right to apply to an English court for redress, then I would think that the taking of this hotel was an act of State. But for the reasons which I have already given I am of opinion that a British subject – at least if he is also a citizen of the UK and Colonies – can never be deprived of his legal right to redress by any assertion by the Crown or decision of the court that the acts of which he complains were acts of State. It seems to me that no useful purpose is served by inquiring whether an act in respect of which a British subject claims legal redress is or is not an act of state, because a decision of that question can make no difference to the result.

6 The Crown and its subjects

6.1 Reciprocal duties

Calvin's Case (1608)

The case concerned the consequences of the union of the Crowns of England and Scotland. The following observation was made:

> As the subject owes to the King his true and faithful allegiance and obedience, so the Sovereign is to govern and protect his subjects ... Allegiance is the mutual bond and obligation between the King and his subjects, whereby subjects are called his liege subjects, because they are bound to obey and serve him; and he is called their liege lord, because he should maintain and defend them.

6.2 The duties of the Crown are not enforceable

China Navigation Co Ltd v Attorney General (1932)

An English shipping company which traded in the China seas requested the Crown to station armed guards aboard its ships as a protection against piracy which was at that time a serious danger in the area. Armed guards were provided in return for payment. The company sought a declaration that the Crown was under a duty to protect British subjects on the high seas.

Held, that there was no duty on the Crown to provide military protection to its subjects in foreign parts and if it chose to do so, it might properly charge for its services. The plaintiffs had misunderstood the nature of the Crown's duty of protection and wrongly sought to assimilate it to the duty of officers of the Crown. *Per* Rowlatt J:

> It seems to me ... that the analogy fails because the word 'duty' in the two cases is made to describe two totally different things. In the case of the officers, they have the duty to perform the duties confided to them by the statutes in question, ie a duty in the eye of the courts of law. But in the case of the Crown and the use of its forces, what is called the duty is not that sort of thing at all. It has not any obligation, as I understand it, which comes within the purview of the courts of law ... It is merely what I venture to call a political duty, using the word 'political' in its proper and original sense. It is what any government would be

expected to do for its people, but the court cannot examine it. Nobody could come to the court and say whether the government of any country did or did not perform its duty in that respect. That confusion with the double use of the word 'duty' lies at the bottom of the whole argument in this case. The case for the plaintiffs is on a complete fallacy.

7 The administration of justice

7.1 The characteristics of a court

Attorney General v BBC (1981) HL

The Attorney General sought an injunction to prevent the BBC from broadcasting a television programme about a sect known as the Exclusive Brethren on the grounds that it would be a contempt of court. The programme asserted, *inter alia*, that the sect was not entitled to an exemption from liability for rates by virtue of s 39 of the General Rate Act 1967, since their meeting rooms were not open to the public and therefore were not 'places of public religious worship' within the meaning of the Act. This question was due to come before a local valuation court at Andover. The question for the court's consideration was whether the local valuation court was a court coming within the rules of the Supreme Court Ord 52, r 1, so that the broadcast might be prejudicial to its proceedings. At first instance and in the Court of Appeal, it was held that it was.

Held, that although a local valuation court was a court, it was not a court of law but a court which discharged administrative functions and therefore the contempt jurisdiction of the Divisional Court did not extend to it. *Per* Lord Scarman:

> I would identify a court in (or 'of') law, ie a court of judicature, as a body established by the law to exercise, either generally or subject to defined limits, the judicial power of the State. In this context, judicial power is to be contrasted with legislative and executive (ie administrative) power. If the body under review is established for a purely legislative or administrative purpose, it is part of the legislative or administrative system of the State, even though it has to perform duties which are judicial in character. Though the ubiquitous presence of the State makes itself felt in all sorts of situations never envisaged when our law was in its formative stage, the judicial power of the State exercised through judges appointed by the State remains an independent, and recognisably separate, function of government.

The local valuation courts resembled in several respects the inferior courts (which were protected by the power of the Divisional Court to punish for contempt of court), but there was no unmistakable hallmark by which a 'court' or 'inferior court' could unerringly be recognised. To extend the scope of contempt of court to the local valuation courts would have the effect of diminishing freedom of speech and freedom of the press.

7.2 Judicial immunity for acts done within jurisdiction

In Re McC (A Minor) (1985) HL

The minor issued a writ claiming damages for false imprisonment against a bench of magistrates which had sentenced him to a period of custody in a training school. The Treatment of Offenders (Northern Ireland) Order 1976 laid down conditions precedent to the passing of a custodial sentence in these circumstances. The conditions were not satisfied in the present case. Section 15 of the Northern Ireland Act 1964 stated:

> No action shall lie against any person by reason of any matter arising in the execution or purported execution of his office of resident magistrate or justice of the peace, unless the court before which the action is brought is satisfied that he acted without jurisdiction or in excess of jurisdiction.

The magistrates appealed to the House of Lords from the finding of the Court of Appeal that they had acted without or in excess of jurisdiction.

Held, that the finding of the Court of Appeal was correct and the appeal would therefore be dismissed. With regard to the issue of judicial immunity, Lord Bridge emphasised that it was confined to acts done within jurisdiction. Thus:

> If the Lord Chief Justice himself, on the acquittal of a defendant charged before him with a criminal offence, were to say: 'That is a perverse verdict', and thereupon proceed to pass a sentence of imprisonment, he could be sued for trespass. But, as Lord Esher MR said in *Anderson v Gorrie* [1895] 1 QB 668, 670: 'the question arises whether there can be an action against a judge of a court of record for doing something within his jurisdiction, but doing it maliciously and contrary to good faith. By the common law of England it is the law that no such action will lie.'
>
> The principle underlying this rule is clear. If one judge in a thousand acts dishonestly within his jurisdiction to the detriment of a party before him, it is less harmful to the health of society to leave that party without a remedy than that nine hundred and ninety honest judges should be harassed by vexatious litigation alleging malice in the exercise of their proper jurisdiction.

Lord Templeman approved the following statement of Buckley LJ in *Sirros v Moore* (1975):

> ... it should now be taken as settled both on authority and on principle that a judge of the High Court is absolutely immune from personal civil liability in respect of any judicial act which he does in his capacity as a judge of that court. He enjoys no such immunity, however, in respect of any act not done in his capacity as a judge.

7.3 Contempt of court

Attorney General v Newspaper Publishing plc (1988) CA

The Attorney General had been granted injunctions to prevent two national newspapers from publishing excerpts from Peter Wright's book *Spycatcher*. Three other newspapers subsequently published passages from the book. The Attorney General applied to commit the newspapers for contempt of court. At first instance it was held, refusing the application, that the injunctions were not applicable to publication other than by the two newspapers against which they had been granted. The Attorney General appealed to the Court of Appeal.

Held, allowing the appeal, that both the judge at first instance and the Court of Appeal had made it clear in the proceedings at which the injunctions were granted that any publication of the book or parts of it, whether by the two defendant newspapers or others, would permanently deprive the Attorney General of his rights before the trial of the matter, and make it impossible for the court to do justice between the parties. The situation was not covered by previous authority, and it was therefore necessary to return to the first principles of the law of contempt of court. *Per* Sir John Donaldson MR:

> Despite its protean nature, contempt has been classified under two heads, namely 'civil contempt' and 'criminal contempt'. Whatever the value of this classification in earlier times, I venture to think that it now tends to mislead rather than assist, because the standard of proof is the same, namely the criminal standard, and there are now common rights of appeal. Of greater assistance is a re-classification as (a) conduct which involves a breach, or assisting in the breach, of a court order and (b) any other conduct which involves an interference with the due administration of justice, either in a particular case or, more generally, as a continuing process, the first category being a special form of the latter, such interference being a characteristic common to all contempts: *per* Lord Diplock in *Attorney General v Leveller Magazine* [1979] AC 440, 440. What distinguishes the two categories is that in general conduct which involves a breach, or assisting in a breach, of a court order is treated as a matter for the parties to raise by complaint to the court, whereas other forms of contempt are in general considered to be a matter for the Attorney General to raise. In doing so, he acts not as a government minister or legal adviser, but as the guardian of the public interest in the due administration of justice.

7.4 The Attorney General and the enforcement of the law

Gouriet v Union of Post Office Workers (1978) HL

Two trades unions proposed to call on their members to refuse to handle post for delivery to South Africa for a week, in protest against the South

African government's apartheid policy. The intended boycott would amount to the commission of offences under the Telegraph Act 1863 and the Post Office Act 1953. Gouriet sought the Attorney General's consent to relator proceedings for an injunction against the unions. The Attorney General, stating that he had considered all the circumstances including the public interest, refused his consent. Gouriet then claimed a declaration against the Attorney General, and final injunctions against the unions. The Court of Appeal held (by a majority) that the court had no power to review the decision of the Attorney General's refusal of consent to relator proceedings, and (also by a majority) that Gouriet was not entitled to a permanent injunction. An interim injunction was, however, granted, pending a claim for declarations against the unions.

The Attorney General and the unions appealed to the House of Lords arguing that the Court of Appeal had no jurisdiction to grant the interim injunctions since Gouriet was not qualified to act on the public behalf to prevent injury to public rights. Gouriet appealed on the basis that the Attorney General could only refuse his consent to the institution of a relator action if it was frivolous, vexatious or oppressive, and that since the intended action fell under none of those heads, the Attorney General had acted improperly.

Held, that the Attorney General's and the unions' appeals would be allowed, and that of Gouriet dismissed. Viscount Dilhorne observed that Gouriet had withdrawn his contention that the Attorney General's refusal of consent to relator proceedings was reviewable, but commented on the proposition as follows:

> The Attorney General has many powers and duties. He may stop any prosecution on indictment by entering a *nolle prosequi*. He merely has to sign a piece of paper saying that he does not wish the prosecution to continue. He need not give any reasons. He can direct the institution of a prosecution and direct the Director of Public Prosecutions to take over the conduct of any criminal proceedings and he may tell him to offer no evidence. In the exercise of these powers, he is not subject to direction by his ministerial colleagues or to control and supervision by the courts. If the court can review his refusal of consent to a relator action, it is an exception to the general rule. No authority was cited which supports the conclusion that the courts can do so. Indeed, such authority as there is points strongly in the opposite direction.

There were no *prima facie* reasons to criticise the Attorney General for refusing to enforce the law. To seek an injunction against a threatened breach of the criminal law was not to enforce the law but to impose liability to a fine or imprisonment for contempt of court additional to the maximum sentence which Parliament had made available as punishment for the offence. Further, it could very well be against the public interest, since the prior issue of an injunction could prejudice a subsequent criminal trial.

Q In the Court of Appeal, Lord Denning MR (dissenting) considered that the Attorney General's refusal to institute the relator action to restrain a threatened breach of the law constituted 'a direct challenge to the rule of law'. In the House of Lords, Viscount Dilhorne expressed his complete dissent from this view. Lord Edmund-Davies observed that the disagreement highlighted the undesirability of making the matter one of disputation in the courts, instead of in Parliament. Which judge is right?

8 The police

8.1 The police are servants of the Crown, not of local government

Fisher v Oldham Corporation (1930)

A warrant for the arrest of Russell, who was suspected of obtaining money on false pretences, was issued by a magistrate in the Borough of Oldham. Russell could not be found in Oldham. A London police officer arrested the plaintiff, who was thought to be Russell. The plaintiff was detained overnight at a London police station, handed over to the Oldham police, and detained for several more hours before the mistake was discovered. The plaintiff brought an action against Oldham Corporation for wrongful arrest and detention. His statement of claim alleged that the defendant Corporation 'acting through their watch committee, are the police authority for the county borough of Oldham and are the employers of the police for the said county borough'. The question for the court was whether the relationship between the corporation and the police was such as to make the corporation liable in law to the plaintiff.

Held, that it was not, and that the action therefore failed. The police had not acted as the servants or agents of the corporation, but had been fulfilling their duties as public servants holding office under the Crown. This appeared from a review of the relevant common law authorities and of statute. However, were it otherwise and local authorities were to be liable in such a case, it would entitle them equally to demand a full measure of control over the arrest and prosecution of all offenders. McCardie J tested the correct view of the police's statutes by the following example:

> Suppose that a police officer arrested a man for a serious felony. Suppose, too, that the watch committee of the borough at once passed a resolution directing that the felon [sic] should be released. Of what value would such a resolution be? Not only would it be the plain duty of the police officer to disregard the resolution, but it would also be the duty of the chief constable to consider whether an information should not at once be laid against the members of the watch committee for a conspiracy to obstruct the course of criminal justice.

8.2 The courts and the duty of the police to enforce the law

R v Metropolitan Police Commissioner, *ex parte* Blackburn (1968) CA

The Betting, Gaming and Lotteries Act 1963 made certain forms of gaming unlawful. Some gaming clubs in London attempted to avoid compliance with the provisions of the Act. When enforcement of its terms became increasingly difficult, the Metropolitan Police Commissioner issued a secret circular to senior officers stating that in future no actions would be taken against gaming clubs for breaches of part of s 32 of the 1963 Act unless there were complaints of cheating, or clubs had become the haunt of criminals. Blackburn sought an order of *mandamus* to compel the commissioner to carry out his public duty.

Held, that the commissioner owed a duty to the public to enforce the law. If circumstances made it necessary, his performance of that duty would be enforced by the court. Chief officers had a wide discretion as to the means by which they carried out that duty, and provided their actions were directed towards discharging it the courts would not interfere. Judicial review would lie in an extreme case against a policy decision which amounted to an abandonment of that duty. However, since the circular had been withdrawn before the conclusion of the proceedings, no relief was required.

8.3 The police have no general duty to individual members of the public

Hill v Chief Constable of West Yorkshire (1989) HL

A 20 year old student was among the murder victims of Peter Sutcliffe, the so-called Yorkshire Ripper. Sutcliffe had committed a number of similar offences in the area over a period of years. The estate of the deceased brought an action against the police authority alleging that it had been negligent in investigating the previous offences, and had thereby failed to catch Sutcliffe and so to prevent the murder of the deceased.

Held, that no duty of care would be recognised. The deceased had been merely a member of the public at large and any risk the alleged negligence presented to her was no different from the risk to thousands of other young women, any one of whom might equally have been Sutcliffe's victim. Although the imposition of a duty of care might in many cases be for the public benefit in increasing safety, to impose a duty in this area could lead to the police carrying on their investigations in a detrimentally defensive manner. Challenges in the courts would involve adjudication on matters of police policy and discretion which the courts were ill-suited to consider, and would divert police resources to the defending such action.

In reality, the plaintiff estate was seeking to mount an investigation into the efficiency of a police force. That task could be undertaken only by the national or local authorities which were responsible to the public for police efficiency.

Part 2 Administrative law

---

9 Judicial review under Order 53

9.1 The nature of the inquiry under Order 53

R v Somerset County Council, *ex parte* Fewings (1995)
Facts: see 12.6 below.
Per Laws J:

> Although judicial review is an area of the law which is increasingly, and right-
> ly, exposed to a good deal of media publicity, one of its most important charac-
> teristics is not, I think, generally very clearly understood. It is that, in most
> cases, the judicial review court is not concerned with the merits of the decision
> under review. The court does not ask itself the question, 'Is this decision right
> or wrong?' Far less does the judge ask himself whether he would himself have
> arrived at the decision in question ... The only question for the judge is whether
> the decision taken by the body under review was one which it was legally
> permitted to take in the way that it did.

9.2   The availability of judicial review

9.2.1   The requirement of leave

Rules of the Supreme Court, Order 53, r 3(1)
3 – (1) No application for judicial review shall be made unless leave of the
court has been obtained in accordance with this rule.

Notes to the Rules of the Supreme Court, para 14/30
Leave to apply for judicial review – The application for leave to move for
judicial review must be made *ex parte* to a single judge, whether in term
time or vacation ...

The purpose of the requirement of leave is: (a) to eliminate at an early
stage any applications which are either frivolous, vexatious or hopeless,
and (b) to ensure that an applicant is only allowed to proceed to a

substantive hearing if the court is satisfied that there is a case fit for further consideration ...

R v Inland Revenue Commissioners, *ex parte* National Federation of Self-Employed and Small Businesses Ltd (1982) HL
Facts: see 11.1 below.
Per Lord Diplock:

> The need for leave to start proceedings in public law is not new. It applied previously to applications for prerogative orders, though not to civil actions for injunctions or declarations. Its purpose is to prevent the time of the court being wasted by busybodies with misguided or trivial complaints of administrative error, and to remove the uncertainty in which public officers and authorities might be left as to whether they could safely proceed with administrative action while proceedings for judicial review of it were actually pending even though misconceived.

9.2.2 Time limits governing applications for judicial review

Rules of the Supreme Court, Order 53, r 4
4 – (1) An application for judicial review shall be made promptly and in any event within three months from the date when grounds for the application first arose unless the court considers that there is good reason for extending the period within which the application shall be made.

(2) Where the relief sought is an order of *certiorari* in respect of any judgment, order, conviction or other proceeding, the date when grounds for the application first arose shall be taken to be the date of that judgment, order, conviction or proceeding.

(3) Paragraph (1) is without prejudice to any statutory provision which has the effect of limiting the time within which an application for judicial review may be made.

Notes to the Rules of the Supreme Court, para 14/31
Delay in applying for relief – Application for leave to move for judicial review must be made promptly, which in this context means as soon as practicable or as soon as the circumstances of the case will allow, and in any event such application must be made within three months from the date when grounds for the application first arose ... It is sometimes thought that an applicant for judicial review is always allowed three months in which to make his application for leave, and provided that he lodges it within that period leave cannot be refused on the grounds of delay. That is not so. The primary requirement laid down by the rules (r 4(1)) is that the application must be made 'promptly', followed by the secondary provision '... and in any event within three months ...'. Thus, there can be cases where, even though the application for leave was made within the three-month period, leave might be refused because, on the facts, the application had not been made promptly ...

R v Independent Television Commission, *ex parte* TV NI Ltd (1991) CA

The applicant, a regional television company, bid unsuccessfully for a licence to provide a television service. On 16 October, the ITC announced the names of the companies to which it would be granting licences. The applicant did not apply for leave to move for judicial review, because it was known that another disappointed bidder had so applied, and had been refused leave. On 4 December the ITC granted licences to the companies named earlier. The applicant now sought leave, was refused it at first instance, and renewed the application before the Court of Appeal.

Held, refusing leave, that after 4 December, the new licence holders were entitled to begin to invest in the setting up of the service which they had been chosen to provide, and it therefore became improper to put a licence in doubt by granting leave to question a competitor's failure to get it. Applicants in such matters, which could affect good administration through their impact on third party rights, had to act with the utmost promptitude. The present applicants had not done so.

R v Stratford-on-Avon District Council, *ex parte* Jackson (1985) CA

The applicant sought to challenge a planning decision of the local authority permitting construction of a supermarket. Planning permission was granted in August 1984, but the applicant failed to lodge her application for leave until May 1985. The delay was due to difficulties in obtaining legal aid, for which the applicant was not to blame. Leave to apply was granted, but subsequently set aside. The applicant renewed her application for leave to the Court of Appeal. The respondent argued that the three month period referred to in Order 53, r 4 limited the time in which the substantive application, and not merely the application for leave, should be made. The applicant submitted that when leave had been granted, it would no longer be open to the court at the substantive hearing to refuse a remedy on the ground of delay.

Held, granting leave, that the applicant's difficulties in obtaining legal aid constituted sufficient explanation for the delay. The applicant had not been to blame for it, and had shown a proper sense of urgency despite it. The court would use its discretion to extend the time period. Where delay was in question, the authorities relating to civil suits involving private law actions would not be in point since in judicial review proceedings there was no true *lis inter partes.* The period in which application was to be made referred to the application for leave; if it were otherwise, the applicant's ability to observe the time limit could depend on the state of the court lists. The grant of leave in a case of delay did not prevent the respondent from raising the matter at the substantive hearing, or fetter the judge's discretion to refuse a remedy on that ground. *Per* Ackner LJ:

The essential requirement of the rule is that the application must be made 'promptly'. The fact that an application has been made within three months from the date when the grounds for the application first arose does not necessarily mean that it has been made promptly. Thus there can well be cases where a court may have to consider whether or not to extend the time for making the application, even though the application has been made within the three-month period.

R v Dairy Produce Quota Tribunal for England and Wales, *ex parte* Caswell (1989) CA

The applicants challenged the decision of the Tribunal to fix their dairy produce quota pursuant to a misconstruction (as they alleged) of the relevant regulations. At the substantive hearing, the court accepted their arguments and granted a declaration, but refused substantive relief under s 31(6) of the Supreme Court Act 1981 on the grounds that the applicants' two year delay in applying amounted to undue delay, and the grant of relief in the circumstances would be prejudicial to good administration. The applicants appealed to the Court of Appeal.

Held, following *Jackson's* case (above), that the grant of leave to apply for judicial review where good reason for delay had been shown was without prejudice to the power of the court hearing the substantive application to refuse relief under s 31(6) of the Supreme Court Act 1981 on the basis that it would cause substantial hardship to, or substantially prejudice the rights of, any person or would be detrimental to good administration. The court did not find it possible or desirable to define detriment to good administration, but indicated that it would amount to positive harm, affirmatively established by or capable of being inferred from evidence, and that in determining whether the foreseen consequences would be harmful, it was permissible to look not only at the particular instance, but also at the effect of the particular instance on other potential applicants, and the consequence if their applications were successful. Here, there had been undue delay since the application had not been made in time, and there was a likelihood of detriment to good administration since the grant of relief to the applicants would either entail the re-opening of numerous other claims, or alternatively secure the applicants an unfair advantage over others who had been treated similarly. The appeal was dismissed.

9.2.3 The existence of other remedies

R v Epping and Harlow General Commissioners, *ex parte* Goldstraw (1983) CA

In the absence of income tax returns the applicant was assessed to tax, and appealed. The appeal was adjourned at the applicant's request, but at the re-listed date the applicant did not appear and was not represented. The appeal was determined by the commissioners in the applicant's absence, although on the basis of figures put forward by his accountant. Two months later, the applicant sought to re-open the appeal. The commissioners declined to allow this. The applicant sought judicial review of their decision, alleging that the commissioners had acted on advice given maliciously by their clerk to the effect that they had no power to do what the applicant asked.

Held, that the clerk's advice was correct, so that no question of his alleged malice was legally relevant. Furthermore, the applicant, after failing to attend the appeal hearing, could have applied within 30 days to the commissioners asking them to state a case for the opinion of the High Court, raising as a question of law the way in which the appeal had been conducted. He had not availed himself of that remedy. It was a cardinal principle that, save in the most exceptional circumstances, the residual supervisory jurisdiction of the court would not exercised where other remedies were available and had not been used.

Preston v Inland Revenue Commissioners (1985) HL

The appellant acquired and later sold shares in a company. An Inland Revenue inspector sought details of the share transactions. The appellant provided bare details, and subsequently sought and obtained the Revenue's assurance that in return for his abandoning claims to tax relief, no further inquiries would be made into the share transactions. At a later stage, when it had become too late for the appellant to make his tax relief claims, the Revenue sought further information about the transactions and in consequence of the information supplied by the appellant, it issued a notice cancelling a tax advantage gained in connection with the transactions. The appellant applied for judicial review of the Revenue's action and at first instance succeeded on the grounds that it had been unfair and unreasonable. The Revenue successfully appealed to the Court of Appeal, which held that its decision was merely managerial and therefore not open to review, and that it had not been unreasonable. The appellant appealed to the House of Lords.

Held, that the appeal would be dismissed on the ground that there had been no abuse of power by the Revenue. *Per* Lord Scarman:

... a remedy by way of judicial review is not to be made available where an alternative remedy exists. This is a proposition of great importance. Judicial review is a collateral challenge; it is not an appeal. Where Parliament has provided by statute appeal procedures, as in the taxing statutes, it will only be very rarely that the courts will allow the collateral process of judicial review to be used to attack an appealable decision ...

But cases for judicial review can arise even where appeal procedures are provided by Parliament. The present case illustrates the circumstances in which it would be appropriate to subject a decision of the commissioners to judicial review. I accept that the court cannot *in the absence of special circumstances* decide by way of judicial review to be unfair that which the commissioners by taking action against the taxpayer have determined to be fair. But circumstances can arise when it would be unjust, because it would be unfair to the taxpayer, even to initiate action under Pt XVII of the 1970 Act [to counteract a tax advantage]. For instance, as [Lord Templeman] points out, judicial review should in principle be available where the conduct of the commissioners in initiating such action would have been equivalent, had they not been a public authority, to a breach of contract or a breach of a representation giving rise to an estoppel. Such a decision would be an abuse of power; whether it was or not and whether in the circumstances the court would in its discretion intervene would, of course, be questions for the court to decide.

R v Chief Constable of the Merseyside Police, *ex parte* Calveley (1986) CA

The appellants were police officers against whom complaints had been made in consequence of their conduct during an arrest. An investigation into the complaints was instituted. The Police (Discipline) Regulations 1977 required officers subject to investigation to be informed 'as soon as is practicable' of the complaints or allegations made, and to be warned that statements made by them might be used in subsequent disciplinary proceedings. The appellants were not so informed for almost two and a half years. Their argument that the delay was so prejudicial as to render disciplinary proceedings against them unfair was rejected by the Chief Constable. They were found guilty of the charges brought against them. They gave notice of intention to appeal against the Chief Constable's decision under s 37 of the Police Act 1964, but before the hearing of the appeal they sought an order of *certiorari* by means of judicial review. The Divisional Court rejected their application on the ground that they had not yet exhausted the internal remedies available to them. The officers appealed to the Court of Appeal.

Held, that the appeal would be allowed. In deciding whether judicial review would be permitted where an alternative statutory remedy subsisted, it would be appropriate to contrast the speed of the respective procedures, and to consider whether the statutory remedy would resolve the question at issue fully and directly, and whether the appeal tribunal would be in a position to bring particular or technical knowledge to bear. The appeal procedure here was not speedy, and although the appeal tribunal had specialised expertise, it would be wrong to overlook the fact that a police officer's submission to police disciplinary procedures was not unconditional, and he was not to be put in peril of them unless there had been substantial compliance with police disciplinary regulations. Here there had been so serious a departure from them that the court would in its discretion grant judicial review.

9.3 Remedies available under Order 53

9.3.1 The Prerogative Orders

Certiorari

Notes to the Rules of the Supreme Court, Order 53, para 14/19
Certiorari – *Certiorari* is an order which brings up into the High Court a decision of an inferior court or tribunal or of a public authority for it to be quashed. Thus, where in judicial review proceedings the court concludes that a decision which has been made by an inferior court or tribunal or a public authority should be set aside, *certiorari* would normally be the appropriate form of order. Where the court quashes a decision, it has power to remit the matter to the court, tribunal or authority concerned with a direction to reconsider it and to reach a decision in accordance with the judgment given by the court in the judicial review proceedings ...

Attorney General for Hong Kong v Ng Yuen Shiu (1983) PC
Facts: see 15.4 below.
Held that the conditional order of prohibition made by the Court of Appeal would be replaced by an order of *certiorari* to quash the removal order which had been made against the respondent. *Per* Lord Fraser:

> That order of *certiorari* is of course entirely without prejudice to the making of a fresh removal order by the Director of Immigration after a fair inquiry has been held at which the respondent has been given an opportunity to make such representations as he may see fit as to why he should not be removed.

Prohibition

Notes to the Rules of the Supreme Court, Order 53, para 14/20
Prohibition – Prohibition is an order restraining an inferior court or tribunal or a public authority from acting outside its jurisdiction. Thus where, for example, a tribunal is proposing to adjudicate upon some matter which is not within its jurisdiction judicial review will lie and the court can make an order of prohibition.

R v Kent Police Authority *ex parte* Godden (1971) CA
The applicant, a police chief inspector, was placed on sick leave after the chief medical officer of the force, Dr Crosbie Brown, certified that he was unfit for police duty on the ground that he was suffering from mental disorder. The applicant's own doctor sent him to a consultant psychiatrist, who reported that he was in good mental and physical health. The police authority took steps compulsorily to retire the applicant, and notified him that they had selected Dr Crosbie Brown as their 'duly qualified practitioner' to determine whether the applicant was permanently disabled within the meaning of the Police Pensions Regulations 1971. The applicant sought orders of prohibition and *mandamus*.

Held, granting both orders, that the rule against bias disqualified Dr Crosbie Brown from acting. The doctor had already put his own medical opinion of the applicant on affidavit, and so had committed himself to his view. He would be disqualified either because he could not bring a completely impartial judgment to bear, or because it could not appear to the applicant that he could do so. *Per* Lord Denning MR:

> For that reason in my opinion the first request for prohibition should go 'to prohibit Dr Crosbie Brown from determining whether Chief Inspector Godden was permanently disabled within the police pension regulations for the time being in force'.

Mandamus

Notes to the Rules of the Supreme Court, Order 53, para 14/21

Mandamus – *Mandamus* is an order requiring an inferior court or tribunal or person or body of persons charged with a public duty to carry out its judicial or other public duty. An order of *mandamus* cannot be made against the Crown (s 40 of the Crown Proceedings Act 1947), but it will lie against an officer of the Crown who is obliged by statute to do some ministerial or administrative act which affects the rights or interests of the applicant.

R v Inland Revenue Commissioners, *ex parte* National Federation of Self-Employed and Small Businesses Ltd (1982) HL

Facts: see 11.1 below.

Per Lord Scarman:

> *Mandamus* is the most elusive of the prerogative writs and orders. The nature of the interest an applicant must show, the nature of the duty which it is available to enforce, and the persons or bodies to whom it may issue have varied from time to time in its development. It is, of course, a judicial remedy; it is equally clear that it is a remedy to compel performance of a public legal duty, that it does not go to the Crown itself and that it is only available if the applicant shows a sufficient interest.

Chief Constable of the North Wales Police v Evans (1982) HL

See 14.3.1 below.

9.3.2 Other remedies

Declaration

Dyson v Attorney General (1911) CA

The appellant brought an action for a declaration that he was not obliged to answer certain questions on a form issued to him by the Inland Revenue Commissioners. He proceeded against the Attorney General as a representative of the interest of the Crown. His action was disallowed at first instance on the ground that the only procedure available in such a case was the preferment of a petition of right.

Held, allowing the appeal, that the appellant might properly seek a declaration of his rights against the Attorney General as representative of the Crown. Cozens-Hardy MR gave the following account of the nature of declaratory relief:

> The power to make declaratory decrees was first granted to the Court of Chancery in 1852 by s 50 of 15 and 16 Vict c 86 ... The jurisdiction is, however, now enlarged, for by Order 25, r 5: 'No action or proceeding shall be open to objection, on the ground that a merely declaratory judgment or order is sought thereby, and the court may make binding declarations of right whether any consequential relief is or could be claimed or not.' I can see no reason why this section should not apply to an action in which the Attorney General, as representing the Crown, is a party. The court is not bound to make a mere declaratory judgment, and in the exercise of its discretion will have regard to all the circumstances of the case. I can, however, conceive many cases in which a declaratory judgment may be highly convenient ...

Q Are there any circumstances in which it might be in the interest of an applicant for judicial review to be granted merely declaratory relief?

O'Reilly v Mackman (1983) HL
Facts: see 9.3 below.
Per Lord Diplock:

> ... there may still be cases where it turns out in the course of proceedings to challenge a decision of a statutory authority that a declaration of rights rather than *certiorari* is the appropriate remedy. The *Pyx Granite* case (1959) provides an example of such a case. So Order 53 since 1977 has provided a procedure by which every type of remedy for infringement of rights of individuals that are entitled to protection in public law can be obtained in one and the same proceeding by way of an application for judicial review, and whichever remedy is found to be the most appropriate in the light of what has emerged on the hearing of the application, can be granted to him.

Equal Opportunities Commission and another v Secretary of State for Employment (1994) HL
Under the Employment Protection Consolidation Act 1978, full-time workers qualified for unfair dismissal and redundancy payments after two years, while part-time workers qualified only after five years. The majority of full-time workers in the UK were men; the majority of part-time workers were women. The Equal Opportunities Commission (EOC) considered that this situation resulted in indirect discrimination against women, contrary to the UK's obligations under European law. In a letter sent to the EOC, the Secretary of State declined to accept that this was the case. The EOC and a woman part-time worker made redundant after less

than five years' employment sought, *inter alia*, a declaration that the UK was in breach of its Treaty obligations. The Court of Appeal dismissed the individual applicant's claim on the grounds that it should have been brought in private law before an industrial tribunal. It held against the EOC on the grounds that the Secretary of State had made no 'decision' capable of review, that no justiciable issue had been raised, and that the EOC had no *locus standi* to seek judicial review against the Secretary of State. The EOC and the individual applicant appealed to the House of Lords.

Held, that the individual applicant's claim would be dismissed for the reasons given by the Court of Appeal. The differential provisions of the 1978 Act were incompatible with European law. There was no decision by the Secretary of State which could be the subject of a prerogative order of the court, but the EOC was not seeking to enforce the UK's Treaty obligations by order of the court; a declaration that the UK was in breach of them would be sufficient for the EOC's purposes, the court had jurisdiction to grant it, and would do so. The EOC did have *locus standi* to bring the proceedings (so held by a majority). On the question whether the court had jurisdiction to grant a declaration in circumstances in which it could not grant one of the prerogative orders, Lord Browne-Wilkinson noted that Order 53, r 1(2) did not say that declarations were available only in lieu of prerogative orders. The right to seek a declaratory judgment had previously been available in purely civil actions where there could be no question of the grant of a prerogative order. The institution of the Order 53 judicial review procedure was not to be taken to have restricted the availability of a declaration.

Injunction and damages
Rules of the Supreme Court, Order 53, rr 1 and 7

1 – (1) An application for:
    (b) an injunction under s 30 of the Supreme Court Act 1981 restraining a person from acting in any office in which he is not entitled to act, shall be made by way of an application for judicial review in accordance with the provisions of this Order.

(2) An application for ... an injunction (not being an injunction mentioned in para (1)(b)) may be made by way of an application for judicial review ...

7– (1) On an application for judicial review the court may, subject to para (2), award damages to the applicant if:
    (a) he has included in the statement in support of his application for leave under r 3 a claim for damages arising from any matter to which the application relates; and
    (b) the court is satisfied that, if the claim had been made in an action begun by the applicant at the time of making his application, he could have been awarded damages.

9.4 Public and private law

O'Reilly v Mackman (1983) HL

The appellants were prisoners who sought to challenge the validity of decisions of the Board of Visitors of Hull Prison to impose penalties on them following a prison riot. The appellants proceeded by writ, seeking a declaration that the decisions had been taken in breach of the rules of natural justice.

Held, dismissing the appeals, that the proceedings were an abuse of process. If the matters alleged in the appellants' statements of claim were true, then it was beyond dispute that they would have a public law remedy by way of judicial review under RSC, Order 53. However, the appellants had no private law rights against the Prison Board of Visitors. Although the remedy which they sought was equally available in private as it was in public law, and under Order 53, r 9(5) the court had power, in an application for judicial review, to order the proceedings to continue as if they had been begun by writ, the converse power did not exist. It would generally be wrong as a matter of principle to allow the vindication of public law rights by private action, since the new Order 53, as ratified by s 31 of the Supreme Court Act 1981, created procedural safeguards in public law for public authorities whose decisions were challenged in public law. Chief among these were the stringent time limits and the requirement of leave to apply for judicial review. Litigants should not be permitted to deprive public authorities of those safeguards. There might be exceptions to that general rule, particularly where the vindication of a public right arose as an issue strictly collateral to private litigation. The question whether there were other exceptions would be left to be developed on a case by case basis.

Cocks v Thanet District Council (1983) HL

The respondent was homeless. He instituted a private law proceeding in the county court claiming that the local housing authority had a duty to house him and was in breach of that duty, and sought a declaration to that effect, consequential mandatory injunctions and damages. It appeared that the authority had decided that the respondent had become homeless intentionally, so that he would be owed no more than a limited duty. In order to obtain the substantive relief sought, the respondent was obliged to impugn that decision. The question whether the respondent was entitled to a declaration against the decision by proceeding in private law was ordered to be tried as a preliminary issue, and was determined in his favour. The housing authority appealed to the House of Lords.

Held, allowing the appeal, that the respondent was not entitled to continue the proceedings or to seek any of the relief which he claimed otherwise than by an application for judicial review in public law. *O'Reilly v Mackman* had decided that as a general rule it would be contrary to public policy to permit a person seeking to establish that a decision of a public authority infringed rights to which he was entitled to protection under public law to proceed by way of an ordinary (private) action. The same general rule applied where the decision which the litigant wished to impugn was not alleged to infringe any existing right but was one which, being adverse to him, prevented him from establishing a necessary condition precedent to the statutory private law right which he wished to enforce.

Davy v Spelthorne Borough Council (1984) HL

The respondent alleged that he had agreed with the council not to exercise his right of appeal against an enforcement notice in return for a suspension of the notice for three years. He said he had entered into this agreement on the advice of council officers, and had refrained from appealing against the enforcement notice in pursuance of the agreement. His private law actions for an injunction to prevent enforcement of the notice and an order setting it aside were struck out by the Court of Appeal on the grounds that they could be pursued only by way of judicial review. He also issued a writ claiming damages for negligent advice from the council. The council appealed against the Court of Appeal's refusal to strike out that claim as an abuse of process.

Held, dismissing the appeal, that the claim in negligence was a straightforward private action in tort. Unlike the appellant in *Cocks v Thanet District Council* (1983) (above) the respondent was not seeking to impugn the enforcement notice; his entire case rested on the fact that he had lost the opportunity to impugn it. The expressions 'private law' and 'public law' were convenient expressions for descriptive purposes but, *per* Lord Wilberforce:

> We have not yet reached the point at which mere characterisation of a claim as a claim in public law is sufficient to exclude it from consideration by the ordinary courts: to permit this would be to create a dual system of law with the rigidity and procedural hardship for plaintiffs which it was the purpose of the recent reforms to remove.

Wandsworth London Borough Council v Winder (1985) HL

The respondent was a tenant of Wandsworth Council. The council raised his rent to a level which he claimed was unreasonable. He paid his original rent and added to it a sum representing a reasonable increase. The council sued the respondent for arrears of rent and for possession of his flat. The respondent's defence was that the decision to increase the rent was void for unreasonableness. The council argued that this challenge to the validity of its decision could be made only by way of public law under Order 53.

Held, dismissing the council's appeal, that the present case was distinguishable from *O'Reilly v Mackman* (1983) (above) on two grounds:

first, the present respondent could arguably claim an infringement of a contractual right in private law, and secondly, he had not himself initiated the action. The case could be distinguished on the same grounds from *Cocks v Thanet DC* (1983) (above). The new Order 53 had been a procedural reform, not intended to extend or diminish the substantive law. The respondent was seeking only to defend an action against him on the ground that he was not liable for the whole sum claimed, and should be entitled to do so.

Roy v Kensington and Chelsea Family Practitioner Committee (1992) HL

The respondent was a general medical practitioner. Under the Statement of Fees and Allowances made by the Secretary of State a practitioner was not eligible for the full rate of the basic practice allowance unless his local family practitioner committee considered that he was devoting a substantial amount of time to National Health Service practice. The committee decided on these grounds to reduce the respondent's allowance. The respondent brought an action claiming, *inter alia*, a declaration that the committee was in breach of its contract with him and payment of sums alleged to be due. The committee applied to strike out the claim as an abuse of process on the ground that challenge to its decision should have been brought by way of judicial review under Order 53, and not by writ.

Held, dismissing the appeal, that the respondent had private law rights against the committee. He was entitled to assert or to defend those rights by way of action brought by writ, even if that action could incidentally involve the examination of a public law issue. The respondent's private law rights dominated the proceedings, he could not obtain repayment of monies due by way of judicial review and his action should not be made dependent on the grant of leave or of remedies which were discretionary. *Per* Lord Lowry:

> ... unless the procedure adopted by the moving party is ill-suited to dispose of the question at issue, there is much to be said in favour of the proposition that a court having jurisdiction ought to let a case be heard rather than entertain a debate concerning the form of the proceedings.

9.5 Ouster clauses

9.5.1 Total ouster clauses

Anisminic v Foreign Compensation Commission (1969) HL

Facts: see 12.3 below.

The Foreign Compensation Act 1950, which established the statutory regime pursuant to which the commission was set up, provided, by s 4(4): 'The determination by the Commission of any application made to them under this Act shall not be called into question in any court of law.' The commission argued that the question whether its determination was *ultra vires* as a result of being based on an error of law was one which could be established only through legal proceedings, which were in terms prohibited by the Act.

Held, that s 4(4) of the Act did not preclude the court from quashing the commission's determination. It was not necessary or even reasonable to construe the word 'determination' to include everything which purported to be a determination but in fact was no determination at all. It should be taken that Parliament, if it had intended that result, would have used clear words to achieve it. *Per* Lord Reid:

> ... there are no degrees of nullity. There are a number of reasons why the law will hold a purported decision to be a nullity. I do not see how it could be said that a provision protects some kinds of nullity but not others: if that were intended it would be easy to say so.

Q Lord Reid bases his argument on an interpretation of the term 'determination'. Could the same result have been reached by considering the meaning of the words 'called into question'?

South East Asia Fire Bricks v Non-Metallic Mineral Products Manufacturing Employees Union (1980) (PC)
A strike by employees of the appellants gave rise to an industrial dispute concerning the legality of a lock-out. The Industrial Court of Malaysia adjudicated upon the matter, finding against the appellants. The High Court granted the appellants' application for an order of *certiorari* to quash the decision of the Industrial Court on the ground that it was vitiated by an error of law on the face of the record. The Federal Court of Malaysia reversed the decision, and on appeal to the Privy Council the question was whether the High Court had exceeded its powers by granting *certiorari* against the Industrial Court. Section 29(3)(a) of the Malaysian Industrial Relations Act 1967 provided that 'an award of the court shall be final and conclusive, and no award shall be challenged, appealed against, reviewed, quashed or called into question in any court of law'.

Held, dismissing the appeal, that the ouster was effective to exclude the grant of *certiorari* against a decision of the Industrial Court made within its jurisdiction.

9.5.2 Partial ouster clauses

R v Cornwall County Council, *ex parte* Huntington (1994)
The Wildlife and Countryside Act 1981 provided that any person aggrieved by a public right of way order made under the Act could apply to the High Court to question the order's validity provided such application was made within 42 days of the publication of the order. The Act further stated that 'Except as provided ... the validity of an order shall not be questioned in any legal proceedings whatsoever'. The respondent sought to have the

grant of leave to apply for judicial review set aside on the ground that a public local inquiry into the order was still pending. The time period specified by the Act had therefore not begun to run, and review outside the specified period was precluded by the terms of the Act.

Held, setting aside leave, that where legislation prescribed a conditional opportunity for legal challenge, that prescription was effective to preclude challenge which did not comply with the conditions stipulated. This was so irrespective of whether the decision sought to be challenged was fundamentally invalid and irrespective of the quasi-judicial or administrative character of the decision.

10 Who is subject to judicial review?

10.1 The jurisdiction as formerly defined

R v Electricity Commissioners, *ex parte* London Electricity Joint Committee Co (1924) CA
The committee sought orders of *certiorari* and prohibition against the Electricity Commissioners with reference to a scheme proposed by the commissioners for the improvement of the existing organisation of the supply of electricity in the London and Home Counties Electricity District. On appeal, the question arose whether the commissioners were a body against which the prerogative orders would lie.

Held (*per* Atkin LJ):

... the operation of the writs [of prohibition and *certiorari*] has extended to control the proceedings of bodies which do not claim to be, and would not be recognised as courts of justice. Wherever any body of persons having legal authority to determine questions affecting the rights of subjects, and having the duty to act judicially, act in excess of their legal authority, they are subject to the controlling jurisdiction of the King's Bench Division exercised in these writs.

10.2 Recent expansion of the jurisdiction

10.2.1 The source of the respondent's powers

Prerogative powers

R v Criminal Injuries Compensation Board, *ex parte* Lain (1967)
The Criminal Injuries Compensation Board was a non statutory body set up by the government in 1964 under prerogative powers. The applicant was the widow of a police constable who had applied to the board for compensation after sustaining serious injury. The Board decided that national insurance and police fund payments to the widow should be deducted from its award, and therefore made no payment. Counsel for the Board argued that it fell outside Atkin LJ's definition of the court's supervisory jurisdiction in *Ex parte London Electricity Joint Committee Co* (1925) (10.1 above) in that (i) the Board was not a body of persons having 'legal authority' in the sense of having statutory authority; and (ii) the Board did

not 'determine the rights of subjects', since its decisions gave rise to no enforceable rights. The applicant sought an order of *certiorari* to quash the Board's decision.

Held, refusing the application, that the Board's decision disclosed no error of law. The question which first arose was whether the Board's decisions were amenable to the court's supervisory jurisdiction. In answer to the Board's first argument (*per* Lord Parker CJ):

> ... the writ of *certiorari* has been issued not only to courts set up by statute but also to courts whose authority was derived, *inter alia*, from the prerogative. Once the jurisdiction is extended, as it clearly has been, to tribunals as opposed to courts, there is no reason why the remedy by way of *certiorari* cannot be invoked to a body of persons set up under the prerogative.

Further, the Board had been recognised by Parliament in debate, and received its funding from Parliament. Rejecting the Board's second argument, Lord Parker said that Atkin LJ had not intended to confine his principle to cases in which the determination affected rights in the sense of enforceable rights. He added:

> ... the exact limits of the ancient remedy of *certiorari* have never been, and ought not to be, specifically defined ... We have, as it seems to me, reached the position when the ambit of *certiorari* can be said to cover every case in which a body of persons, of a public as opposed to a purely private or domestic character, has to determine matters affecting subjects provided always that it has a duty to act judicially.

Self-conferred powers

R v Panel on Takeovers and Mergers, *ex parte* Datafin (1987) CA

The Panel was an institution in the City of London which devised and operated a code of conduct to be observed in the takeovers of listed public companies. It was a self-regulating, unincorporated association which had not been established by any recognised authority external to itself, and it performed its functions 'without visible means of legal support' (*per* Lord Donaldson MR). The applicants were engaged in a battle with a rival firm to take over a third company. They complained to the Panel that their rivals had been engaged in improper dealings with the third company. The Panel decided to reject their complaint. The applicants sought orders of *certiorari*, prohibition, *mandamus*, and an injunction. The Panel argued that the supervisory jurisdiction of the court was confined to bodies whose power derived solely from legislation or the exercise of the prerogative.

Held, that the Panel had made its decision properly and judicial review would therefore be refused. However, it was subject to the court's jurisdiction. Lord Donaldson MR approved the approach taken by the court in *Ex parte Lain* (10.2.1 above), and said:

In all the reports it is possible to find enumerations of factors giving rise to the jurisdiction, but it is a fatal error to regard the presence of all those factors as essential or as being exclusive of other factors. Possibly the only essential elements are what can be described as a public element, which can take many different forms, and the exclusion from the jurisdiction of bodies whose sole source of power is a consensual submission to its [sic] jurisdiction.

Regard was to be had not only to the source of the Panel's powers, but also to the fact that it operated as an integral part of a system which had a public law character and performed public law functions. The government had made the Panel the centrepiece of its legislation in the field of takeovers and mergers. Given that it remained self-regulating, it was more and not less appropriate that it should be subject to the supervisory jurisdiction of the court.

10.2.2 Bodies whose powers derive from contract

R v Lord Chancellor's Department, *ex parte* Nangle (1991)
The applicant held a clerical position in the civil service. His appointment was stated to be at the pleasure of the Crown, and was governed by the Civil Service Pay and Conditions of Service Code. The code stated that the relationship between civil servants was technically based not on contract but on the prerogative. The applicant was disciplined for misbehaviour by being transferred to another department, and losing salary increment rights. He applied for judicial review. The respondent department argued that the applicant had a contract of employment with the Crown.

Held, dismissing the application for judicial review, that all the incidents of a contract of employment were present in the applicant's relation with the Crown. There had been offer, acceptance, consideration and an intention to create legal relations at the inception of the applicant's employment. The Civil Service Code set out in detail the matters which would normally be covered by a contract of employment. The statement that the prerogative, rather than contract, was to govern the relationship did not suffice to make its conditions voluntary. It followed that the parties must have intended their relationship to be governed by private rather than public law. Accordingly, the applicant should have issued a writ claiming damages for breach of contract.

10.2.3 Bodies whose jurisdiction is exercised consensually

Law v National Greyhound Racing Club (1983)
The plaintiff was a greyhound trainer whose licence had been suspended because his greyhound had traces of prohibited substances in its tissues. The Club moved to strike out the plaintiff's action on the grounds that he was seeking public law remedies and should therefore have applied for judicial review under RSC Order 53.

Held, that the Club's argument was incorrect; the plaintiff was correct to proceed in private law. The plaintiff had a contract with the Club, and thus the Club's decision was made in private, not public, law. A stewards' inquiry under the Club's rules of racing concerned only those who voluntarily submitted themselves to the stewards' jurisdiction. Lawton LJ conceded that the public might well have an interest in the way in which the stewards' powers were exercised, and that the exercise of those powers might affect the rights of individuals. However, such consequences might equally flow from the decisions of many other domestic tribunals, and were insufficient to make a domestic, consensually appointed tribunal into a public body.

10.2.4 The potential governmental interest test

R v Advertising Standards Authority Ltd, *ex parte* The Insurance Service (1990)

The applicant, a motor insurance company, sought judicial review of the respondent Authority's decision to uphold a complaint about the accuracy of a promotional leaflet published by the applicant. The Authority was a company limited by guarantee which, by the first of the objects set down in its Memorandum of Association, undertook 'The promotion and enforcement throughout the United Kingdom of the highest standards of advertising in all media ...'. The Misleading Advertisements Regulations 1988, drawn up to implement an EC Directive, made the Director General of Fair Trading subject to a duty to consider complaints brought against advertisements. It appeared from the regulations that the Director General would use his powers only if satisfied that a complaint to the Authority had failed to produce a satisfactory result.

Held, that the Authority was subject to judicial review. Like the Panel on Takeovers and Mergers, the Authority had no powers granted to it by statute or at common law, nor any contractual relationship with the advertisers whom it controlled. Nevertheless, it was clearly exercising public law functions which, if the Authority did not exist, would undoubtedly be exercised by the Director General of Fair Trading. In the present case, the Authority had failed to take into account a material consideration in determining the applicant's case, and its decision would therefore be quashed.

R v Chief Rabbi, *ex parte* Wachmann (1992)

The applicant was the Orthodox rabbi of the Broughton Synagogue, Manchester. The synagogue was a member of the United Hebrew Congregations of Great Britain and the Commonwealth, the spiritual head of which was the Chief Rabbi. Allegations of conduct unbecoming a rabbi were made against the applicant and confirmed by a commission of inquiry appointed by the Chief Rabbi. The Chief Rabbi notified the president of the

Broughton Synagogue that he regarded the applicant as unfit to continue in office. In the light of the Chief Rabbi's decision the executive and council of the Broughton Synagogue terminated the applicant's employment. The applicant sought leave to move for judicial review of the Chief Rabbi's decision that he was unfit to hold office.

Held, that the Chief Rabbi was not subject to judicial review. To attract the court's supervisory jurisdiction, there had to be not merely a public but potentially a governmental interest in the respondent's decision-making power. The Chief Rabbi's functions were essentially intimate, spiritual and religious; there would be no intervention by Parliament, the government or the court in this area.

However, it was wrong to regard the applicant's submission to the jurisdiction of the Chief Rabbi as merely consensual. Rather, the applicant was pursuing a vocation in an area governed exclusively by the Chief Rabbi and therefore had no choice but to accept his jurisdiction.

R v Imam of Bury Park Jame Masjid, Luton, *ex parte* Sulaiman Ali and 304 others (1991)

The Imam of Bury Park Mosque, Luton, refused 305 Muslims the right to vote in the election of the mosque's executive committee. By the mosque's written constitution, rights of suffrage were limited to those who had paid £10 to the mosque. Those debarred from voting had, in the imam's determination, failed to pay that sum. Prior to the election of a new committee in 1988, a dispute over voting rights arose. On a motion in the Chancery Division, Mervyn Davies J ordered that further disputes were to be decided by the imam, whose decision was to be final. The applicants sought judicial review of the imam's decision on the ground that he had acted in breach of the rules of natural justice in that he was an employee of the committee and therefore not impartial, and that he bore malice towards the applicants.

Held, refusing the application, that the essential characteristic which made the exercise of a power amenable to judicial review was its public element. The fact that the power was not statutory or that it was exercised pursuant to a court order was not conclusive of the matter either way. In *R v Chief Rabbi, ex parte Wachmann* (1991) (above) the court had been influenced both by the absence of a potentially governmental interest in the power in question, and by its reluctance to become involved in matters intimate to a religious community. The same factors operated here to exclude review.

R v Disciplinary Committee of the Jockey Club, *ex parte* Aga Khan (1993) CA

The Jockey Club controlled and regulated horse racing in Great Britain. Owners who wished to race their horses entered into contractual relations with the Club, expressly submitting to the disciplinary jurisdiction of the committee. One of the applicant's horses failed a routine drugs test and was disqualified following an inquiry by the Committee. The applicant sought judicial review of the committee's decision. The Jockey Club contended that it was not subject to judicial review since it was independent of government in origin, constitution and function, and its relation with the applicant was essentially one of private law.

Held, that in the circumstances the committee's decision was not susceptible to judicial review. The issue was to be determined in the light of all the facts of the case; no single feature or test was decisive. Although the Jockey Club effectively regulated a significant national activity of which it had *de facto* control and exercised powers of a public character, it was not in origin a public body and its powers were not governmental in nature. Furthermore, the applicant's contractual relationship with the Club allowed him sufficient remedy against it in private law.

Q Applying the potential governmental intervention test, Farquharson LJ found nothing in the material before him to satisfy it. Sir Thomas Bingham MR took a contrary view. In light of this disagreement, does the test remain of any value?

R v Legal Aid Board, *ex parte* Donn & Co (1996)

The Legal Aid Board was established by the Legal Aid Act 1988. Section 4 of the Act empowered the Board to do anything which was calculated to facilitate the discharge of its functions. By s 4(4) this included entering into contracts, provided and solely to the extent that the Lord Chancellor directed. The applicants, a firm of solicitors, submitted a tender to an area office of the respondents seeking a contract to undertake multi-party litigation on behalf of hundreds of sufferers from 'Gulf War syndrome'. The respondent's office suspected that the presence of a Territorial Army officer among the applicant's advisers could give rise to a conflict of interest, and this was among the grounds on which a rival firm's tender was preferred. The applicants alleged that the respondents' investigation of the matter had been procedurally flawed and unfair, and submitted that the Board was judicially reviewable either because it was statutorily underpinned by the Act, or because the tendering process involved a sufficient public law element. At the invitation of Ognall J, the applicants developed only the second of their submissions on reviewability.

Held, that the question for the court was whether in the absence of statutory underpinning the Board might be subject to judicial review in administering the tendering process. In order to answer this question, it was appropriate to consider both the nature and purpose of the selection procedure, and the consequences to which the procedure would give rise. There could be no universal test of a sufficient public law element, and the answer would be one of impression and degree. In light of the amounts of public money being allocated by the Board on behalf of potential litigants who could afford no other means of vindicating their rights, the public interest in the proper outcome of the process was clear. Further, the Board was the sole and final arbiter of the tendering process. Even if some private law remedy were available to the applicants, the public dimensions of the matter were sufficient to render it justiciable in public law. On the facts, the applicants' complaints about the tendering process were made out, and the application accordingly succeeded.

11 The requirement of *locus standi*

11.1 The tests applied at the leave and at the substantive stages are not the same

R v Inland Revenue Commissioners, *ex parte* National Federation of Self-Employed and Small Businesses Ltd (1982) HL

In order to avoid tax, casual workers in the newspaper industry had been in the habit of giving false names when drawing their pay. The Inland Revenue Commissioners (IRC) decided to offer them an amnesty in respect of past tax avoidance in return for their co-operation in the future. The federation sought a declaration that the IRC's decision to grant the amnesty was unlawful, and *mandamus* to compel the IRC to assess and collect all arrears of tax. The IRC opposed the application on the ground, *inter alia*, that the federation did not have sufficient interest within the terms of RSC Order 53, r 3(5). The rule provided that 'The court shall not grant leave unless it considers that the applicant has a sufficient interest in the matter to which the application relates'. Leave to apply for judicial review was refused on these grounds by the Divisional Court but granted by a majority in the Court of Appeal. The IRC appealed to the House of Lords.

Held, allowing the appeal, that the rule required the applicant to show a sufficient interest *in the matter to which the application relates*. In all but the simplest cases, it was therefore necessary first to determine the nature of the matter in question at the substantive hearing and only then to judge the sufficiency of the applicant's interest in it. Where a favourable view of the applicant's *locus standi* had been taken at the leave stage, it might still alter as a result of the substantive hearing. *Per* Lord Diplock:

> My Lords, at the threshold stage, for the federation to make out a *prima facie* case of reasonable suspicion that the Board in showing a discriminatory leniency to a substantial class of taxpayers had done so for ulterior reasons extraneous to good management, and thereby deprived the national exchequer of considerable sums of money, constituted what was in my view reason enough for the Divisional Court to consider that the federation, or, for that matter, any taxpayer, had a sufficient interest to apply to have the question whether the Board were acting *ultra vires* reviewed by the court. The whole purpose of requiring that leave should first be obtained to make the application for judicial review would be defeated if the court were to go into the matter in any depth at that

stage. If, on a quick perusal of the material then available, the court thinks that it discloses what might on further consideration turn out to be an arguable case in favour of granting to the applicant the relief claimed, it ought, in the exercise of a judicial discretion, to give him leave to apply for that relief. The discretion which the court is exercising at this stage is not the same as that which it is called on to exercise when all the evidence is in and the matter has been fully argued at the hearing of the application.

The federation had no sufficient interest in the confidential affairs of another taxpayer (*per* Lord Wilberforce) and had failed to show any conduct that was *ultra vires* or unlawful (*per* Lord Diplock). Had it made out a case to the effect that the Inland Revenue had abused its managerial discretion, Lord Scarman would have held that it had shown a sufficient interest for the grant of leave to proceed further with its application.

Per Lord Wilberforce:

... the standing requirement may vary in strictness according to the remedy sought.

Q Do you agree that the words of r 3(5) discourage the treatment of sufficient interest as a preliminary point?

11.2 The test for *locus standi* may vary according to the remedy sought

R v Felixstowe Justices, *ex parte* Leigh (1987)

The applicant was a journalist who wanted to know the names of the individuals who had sat on the bench of a magistrates' court. He had not been involved in any capacity in the trial which he was seeking to report, nor had he been present at the proceedings. He sought a declaration that the justices had improperly decided that they should not disclose their names, and *mandamus* to compel them to disclose their names.

Held, that magistrates should not seek to carry out their functions anonymously. In view of the seriousness of this matter the applicant did have sufficient standing to obtain the declaration. However, he did not have sufficient standing to obtain *mandamus* to compel the magistrates on this bench to disclose their names.

11.3 Recent decisions on *locus standi*

R v Secretary of State for the Environment, *ex parte* Rose Theatre Trust Co (1990)

The remains of the Rose Theatre, which had seen the first performances of works by Shakespeare and Marlowe, were discovered during redevelopment works in the London Borough of Southwark. The applicant, whose members included distinguished archaeologists and actors, was formed in order to campaign for the protection of the remains. The applicant applied to the Secretary of State to protect the remains by scheduling them pursuant to powers granted to him by the Ancient Monuments and Archaeological Areas Act 1979. He refused. The applicant sought judicial review.

Held, that the applicant did not have a sufficient interest to apply for judicial review. Where individuals did not have sufficient interest, they did not obtain it by incorporating themselves into an association. Although the Secretary of State had corresponded with the applicant, that could not and should not afford the applicant sufficient interest to challenge the decision.

R v Secretary of State for Social Services, *ex parte* Child Poverty Action Group (1990) CA

The applicant contended that the provisions of ss 98 and 99 of the Social Security Act 1975 had been wrongly interpreted by the respondent, and that in accordance claims for supplementary benefit had not been handled in accordance with the intentions of the legislature. In view of the importance of the issue, the respondent did not dispute the applicant's *locus standi* in the Divisional Court, although it reserved its right to argue the point in analogous cases in the future. Counsel for the respondent wished to adopt the same approach before the Court of Appeal.

Held, that the applicant would be not be granted declaratory relief, and that the question of *locus standi* therefore did not arise. However, the respondent's reservation of its position on *locus standi* was inappropriate. *Locus standi* went to the jurisdiction of the court. The parties might not by agreement confer on the court a jurisdiction which it did not otherwise have.

Q What other reasons, besides the importance of the case, may discourage a respondent from contesting an application on *locus standi*?

R v Secretary of State for Foreign and Commonwealth Affairs, *ex parte* Rees-Mogg (1994)

The applicant sought a declaration that the UK could not lawfully ratify the Treaty of European Union signed at Maastricht on 7 February 1992.

Held, that the application for judicial review, assuming it to relate to a justiciable issue, would be dismissed on the merits. There was no dispute as to the applicant's *locus standi*, and therefore it was not appropriate to say anything more about it. The court did, however, accept 'without question that Lord Rees-Mogg brings the proceedings because of his sincere concern for constitutional issues'.

Q What are the consequences (if any) of this decision (a) for the law relating to *locus standi*; (b) for the principle that all are equal under the law?

R v HM Inspectorate of Pollution, *ex parte* Greenpeace (1994)

British Nuclear Fuels plc proposed to test its new thermal oxide reprocessing plant (THORP) in Cumbria before it became fully operational. To this end a variation of existing authorisations was obtained from the respondent. The applicant, an environmental protection organisation of international standing, was concerned about levels of radioactive emission from THORP. It sought an order of *certiorari* to quash the respondent's decision to vary the authorisations, and an injunction to stay the implementation of the authorisations and to prevent the testing. The respondent denied that the applicant had a sufficient interest in the matter.

Held, dismissing the substantive application, that the decision to vary the authorisations had been properly made. The applicant did have a sufficient interest. In deciding on *locus standi*, a court was to take into account the nature of the applicant, the extent of its interest in the issues raised, the remedy sought to be obtained, and the nature of the relief sought to be achieved. Here the applicant was an entirely responsible and respected body with a genuine concern for the environment. It had 2,500 members in the Cumbria region. If the applicant were denied *locus standi*, those it represented might not have an effective way to bring issues of concern to them before the court. *Per* Otton J:

> Consequently, a less well-informed challenge might be mounted which would stretch unnecessarily the court's resources and which would not afford the court the assistance it requires to do justice between the parties. Further, if the unsuccessful applicant had the benefit of legal aid, it might leave the respondent and BNFL without an effective remedy in costs.

The applicant was enabled by its expertise to mount a carefully selected, focused, relevant and well-argued challenge. The applicant was seeking *certiorari*, not *mandamus*: less stringent *locus standi* principles applied to the former remedy. The applicant had been treated as one of the consultees during the consultation process. However:

> ... it must not be assumed that Greenpeace (or any other interest group) will automatically be afforded standing in any subsequent application for judicial review ... This will have to be considered on a case by case basis at the leave stage and if the threshold is crossed again at the substantive hearing as a matter of discretion.

R v Secretary of State for Foreign Affairs, *ex parte* World Development Movement Ltd (1995)

The applicant sought judicial review of the Secretary of State's decision to make a grant to Malaysia under s 1(1) of the Overseas Development and Co-operation Act 1980. The grant was to be used for the funding of the Pergau Dam project. Section 1(1) confined the use of the power to the promoting of development. The applicant submitted that only sound development projects could lawfully be funded. The Secretary of State had received advice that the Pergau Dam project was not economically sound, had been motivated for purposes not permitted by the Act, and had taken into account irrelevant considerations in making his decision.

Held that the funding was not directed towards the promotion of development, and that it was therefore *ultra vires* the Act. On the issue of the applicant's *locus standi*, the court considered that there was nothing in *Ex parte National Federation of Self-Employed* (1982) (see 11.1 above) to deny standing. Further, an increasingly liberal approach to standing had been taken during the 12 years since that decision. The merits of the application were an important, if not a dominant factor when considering standing. Here the issue raised was of importance, the rule of law required to be vindicated, there was unlikely to be any other responsible challenger, and the court further took into account the nature of the breach of duty alleged against the Secretary of State, and the prominence of the applicants in their field. If the court had been able to accept in *Ex parte Rees-Mogg* (1994) (above) that the applicant there had standing in the light of his 'sincere concerns for constitutional issues', then *a fortiori* the present applicant had the expertise and interest to be granted standing.

Q Did the court in *Ex parte Rees-Mogg* (1994) accept that the applicant had standing *in the light of* his sincere concerns for constitutional issues? Must it now be taken to have done so?

12 The grounds for judicial review: illegality

12.1 General definition of illegality

Council of Civil Service Unions v Minister for the Civil Service (1985) HL
Facts: see 15.5.1 below.
Per Lord Diplock:

By 'illegality' as a ground for judicial review I mean that the decision-maker must understand correctly the law that regulates his decision-making power and must give effect to it. Whether he has or not is *par excellence* a justiciable question to be decided, in the event of dispute, by those persons, the judges, by whom the judicial power of the state is exercisable.

12.2 The *ultra vires* doctrine

12.2.1 The limited nature of public bodies' powers

R v Somerset County Council, *ex parte* Fewings (1995)
Facts: see 12.6 below.
Per Laws J:

Public bodies and private persons are both subject to the rule of law; nothing could be more elementary. But the principles which govern their relationships with the law are wholly different. For private persons, the rule is that you may do anything you choose which the law does not prohibit. It means that the freedoms of the private citizen are not conditional upon some distinct and affirmative justification for which he must burrow in the law books. Such a notion would be anathema to our English legal traditions. But for public bodies the rule is opposite, and so of another character altogether. It is that any action to be taken must be justified by positive law. A public body has no heritage of legal rights which it enjoys for their own sake; at every turn, all of its dealings constitute the fulfilment of duties which it owes to others; indeed, it exists for no other purpose.

Attorney General v Fulham Corporation (1921)

Under the Baths and Wash-houses Acts 1846–78 the corporation had power to establish baths, wash-houses and open bathing places. For many years it had operated a wash-house where residents could come and wash their clothes themselves. The corporation resolved to replace this by a system in which a customer bought a bag, filled it with washing, and left it to be washed by corporation employees. The washing would then be delivered to the customer, or could be collected by the customer. The Attorney General, at the relation of certain ratepayers of Fulham, alleged that the system operated by the corporation was *ultra vires* the enabling legislation.

Held, granting a declaration to that effect, that it was important that the doctrine of *ultra vires* should be maintained. It was for the corporation to show that it had authority to do the acts specified, or that it was doing merely what was reasonably incidental to or consequential upon what it was authorised to do. The corporation was authorised by statute to provide washing facilities. To wash customers' clothes for them was not incidental to or consequential upon that power.

Bromley London Borough Council v Greater London Council (1983) HL

In order to finance the manifesto policy of the controlling Labour group of reducing fares on London Transport by 25%, the Greater London Council (GLC) levied a supplementary rate. Bromley Council applied for an order of *certiorari* to quash the GLC's decision on the grounds, *inter alia*, that it was *ultra vires* the Transport (London) Act 1969. Under s 1 of the Act, the general duty of the GLC in relation to the provision of transport was to develop and encourage measures which would promote the provision of 'integrated, efficient and economic transport facilities and services for Greater London'.

Held, that the actions of the GLC were *ultra vires*. The statutory framework made it clear that the London Transport Executive was not to conduct its undertaking other than on economic lines. The Executive in making its proposals, and the GLC in accepting them, had no power totally to disregard any responsibility for seeking to ensure that outgoings were met by revenue.

12.2.2 The exercise of powers fairly incidental to those specifically granted

Attorney General v Crayford UDC (1962) CA

Section 111(1) of the Housing Act 1957 gave local authorities powers of 'general management' in connection with their stock of council houses. Claiming to use this power, Crayford UDC agreed to recommend to its tenants that they insure themselves on the favourable terms of a scheme negotiated by the council with the Municipal Mutual Insurance Ltd. The council acted as agent for the insurance company, using its rent collectors to receive insurance premiums and retaining a commission. A rival insurance company maintained that this scheme was *ultra vires* the powers granted by the 1957 Act. The question for the court was whether the operation of the scheme could be regarded as 'general management' within the terms of the 1957 Act.

Held that the scheme was either within, or fairly incidental to, the general management remit of the council. If the tenants did not insure themselves, and then suffered loss, they would be likely to default on their rent. It was the concern, if not the duty of the council, to insure that its tenants paid their rents. Lord Evershed MR approved the following words of Lord Selborne LC in *Attorney General v Great Eastern Railway Co* (1880) HL:

> I agree with James LJ that this doctrine ought to be reasonably and not unreasonably, understood and applied, and that whatever may fairly be regarded as incidental to, or consequential upon, those things which the legislature has authorised, ought not (unless expressly prohibited) to be held, by judicial construction, to be *ultra vires*.

12.3 The effect of a decision-maker's error of law

12.3.1 Errors of law not in the face of the record

Anisminic v Foreign Compensation Commission (1969) HL

Anisminic's property in Egypt was seized by the Egyptian Government at the time of the Suez crisis. Anisminic later sold its Egyptian business to an Egyptian company, but retained its right to claim compensation in respect of its earlier losses. In 1959 a treaty was concluded between the UK and Egyptian governments under which compensation was to be paid by the Egyptian government to the UK in respect of certain properties, including Anisminic's. The UK government set up the Foreign Compensation Commission in order to distribute the compensation.

Anisminic applied for to the commission for compensation. The commission considered that it was obliged to be satisfied that Ansiminic's successor in title to the property was or had been a British subject. It was not so satisfied, and accordingly rejected Anisminic's claim. Anisminic argued that the nationality of a successor in title was irrelevant where the claimant was the original owner of the property. The main question for the House of Lords was whether, on the assumption that the commission was mistaken in its interpretation of the legislative provisions, it had thereby exceeded its jurisdiction.

Held, allowing Anisminic's appeal (by a majority) that the commission's mistake had resulted in its deciding a question which it had no jurisdiction to decide, and its decision was therefore a nullity. *Per* Lord Reid:

... there are many cases where, although the tribunal had jurisdiction to enter on the inquiry, it has done or failed to do something in the course of the inquiry which is of such a nature that its decision is a nullity. It may have given its decision in bad faith. It may have made a decision which it had no power to make. It may have failed in the course of the inquiry to comply with the requirements of natural justice. It may in perfect good faith have misconstrued the provisions giving it power to act so that it failed to deal with the question remitted to it and decided some question which was not remitted to it. It may have refused to take into account something which it was required to take into account. Or it may have based its decision on some matter which, under the provisions setting it up, it had no right to take into account. I do not intend this list to be exhaustive. But if it decides a question remitted to it for decision without committing any of these errors it is as much entitled to decide that question wrongly as it is to decide it rightly.

Pearlman v Keepers and Governors of Harrow School (1979) CA

Under Schedule 8 of the Housing Act 1974 a county court judge had to determine whether the installation of central heating in a dwelling house amounted to 'structural alteration, extension or addition'. Without proffering a definition of the statutory words, the judge held that the work under consideration did not fall within them. The appellant sought an order of *certiorari* to quash the judge's decision, on the ground that it depended on an error of law and accordingly was beyond his jurisdiction.

Held (by a majority), that the judge's decision on the issue was such that he must be taken to have made an error of law in the interpretation of the statutory words. *Per* Lord Denning MR:

... the distinction between an error which entails *absence* of jurisdiction – and an error made within the jurisdiction – is very fine. So fine indeed that it is rapidly being eroded ... I would suggest that this distinction should now be discarded ... The way to get things right is to hold thus: no court or tribunal has any jurisdiction to make an error of law on which the decision of the case depends. If it makes such an error, it goes outside its jurisdiction and *certiorari* will lie to correct it.

Per Geoffrey Lane LJ (dissenting):

The judge is considering the words ... which he ought to consider. He is not embarking on some unauthorised or extraneous or irrelevant exercise. All he has done is to come to what appears to this court to be a wrong conclusion on a difficult question. It seems to me that, if this judge is acting outside his jurisdiction, so then is every judge who comes to a wrong decision on a point of law.

In re Racal Communications Ltd (1981) HL

Racal was suspected of defrauding the Ministry of Defence. The Director of Public Prosecutions made an application to court to examine Racal's documents under s 441(1) of the Companies Act 1948. The High Court judge at first instance refused to grant the order, holding that he had jurisdiction to do so only in respect of the internal management of a company's affairs, and that the matters alleged fell outside that area. Despite the provision in s 441(3) of the Act, that a decision of a judge of the High Court under the section should not be appealable, his decision was reversed by the Court of Appeal. The court considered that s 441(3) had no relevance to a case like the present in which an error of law had been made. Racal appealed to the House of Lords, arguing that the Court of Appeal had lacked jurisdiction to consider whether the judge's decision was right or wrong.

Held, allowing the appeal, that the Court of Appeal had been wrong to set up a distinction between mistakes of fact and mistakes of law. The jurisdiction of the Court of Appeal was exclusively statutory. It could be – and here it had been – excluded by statute whether in respect of alleged mistakes of fact or of law. Further, there was a distinction to be drawn between challenges to the decisions of administrative tribunals, and challenges to the decisions of courts of law. In the former case, where Parliament conferred power to decide questions defined by the Act conferring the power, there was a presumption that Parliament intended the tribunal only to answer questions as so defined. In the case of courts of law, there was no presumption that Parliament did not intend to give those bodies authority to decide questions of law. *Anisminic* was concerned only with the determination of an administrative tribunal. The decision of the majority in *Pearlman* was wrong, since the judge in that case as in this had had exclusive jurisdiction to construe the meaning of statutory words.

Page v Hull University Visitor (1993) HL

The appellant, a university lecturer, was dismissed from his post on the ground of redundancy. He petitioned the visitor of the university, contending that under the university's statutes it had no power to dismiss him for that reason. The visitor rejected the petition, and the appellant successfully sought judicial review. The Court of Appeal allowed the visitor's appeal, holding that the visitor had correctly understood the university's powers, but affirming the Divisional Court's determination that judicial review in principle lay against a decision of the visitor construing the university's statutes. The appellant appealed against the decision of the Court of Appeal, and the university and visitor cross-appealed from the determination that the visitor was amenable to judicial review for errors of construction.

Held, dismissing the appeal and allowing the cross-appeal (by a majority), that the question was whether the remedy of *certiorari* would lie against the visitor to quash his decision as being erroneous in point of law notwithstanding that the question of law arose under the domestic law of the university which the visitor had exclusive power to decide. Provided the visitor was within his jurisdiction in the narrow sense that he had power under the regulating documents to enter into the adjudication of the dispute the court could not intervene to quash his decision either for error of fact or of law. Judicial review would lie, however, where the visitor had acted outside his jurisdiction understood in that narrow sense, or where he had abused his powers or acted in breach of the rules of natural justice. In fact, the visitor had made no error of law in any event. Commenting on the effect of the decision in *Anisminic*, Lord Browne-Wilkinson said that it 'rendered obsolete the distinction between errors of law on the face of the record and other errors of law by extending the doctrine of *ultra vires*. Thenceforward, it was to be taken that Parliament had only conferred the decision-making power on the basis that it was to be exercised on the correct legal basis: a misdirection in law in making the decision therefore rendered the decision *ultra vires*'.

12.3.2 Errors of law on the face of the record

R v Northumberland Compensation Appeal Tribunal, *ex parte* Shaw (1952) CA

The applicant sought compensation under the National Health Service (Transfer of Officers and Compensation) Regulations 1948 for loss of employment. He appealed to the Tribunal against the quantum of compensation awarded by the local authority. The Tribunal upheld the award, and the applicant successfully obtained an order of *certiorari* from the Divisional Court. Here, and on the Tribunal's appeal to the Court of Appeal, it was common ground that the compensation decision was flawed. However, the Tribunal argued that the remedy of *certiorari* did not lie in respect of an error of law appearing on the face of the record where the decision-maker had not exceeded its jurisdiction, and further, that although there had been error here, it did not appear on the record.

Held, dismissing the appeal, that until some 100 years before the present case, the authorities showed that *certiorari* had regularly been used to challenge errors of law on the face of the record. In so far as it had fallen into disuse, that was because there had until recently been little occasion for its exercise, but with the advent of many new tribunals and the plain need for supervision over them, the remedy should be revived. It was unnecessary to discuss the types of error which respectively would or would not go to jurisdiction, because that question did not arise in the present case. Here the error did not distinctly appear on the face of the record, but that was because the record was incomplete; if complete, it would have disclosed the error. *Certiorari* would lie not only to quash an error of law on the face of the record, but also an error admitted openly in the face of the court. Denning LJ stated that the supervisory control of the Court of King's Bench 'extends not only to seeing that the inferior tribunals keep within their jurisdiction, but also to seeing that they observe the law. The control is exercised by means of a power to quash any determination which, on the face of it, offends against the law'.

R v Supplementary Benefits Commission, *ex parte* Singer (1973)
The applicant sought an order of *certiorari* to quash the Supplementary Benefits Commission's determination that he was ineligible for legal aid since his disposable income exceeded the statutory limit. As a basis for the assessment of income the Commission had taken into account loans and gifts to the applicant. However, this fact appeared only from a letter of explanation sent on behalf of the Commission in response to an inquiry by the applicant following the making of the determination. The applicant contended that this basis was erroneous, and that the letter formed part of the record of the Commission's decision.

Held, granting *certiorari* to quash the determination, that the applicant's arguments were both correct. *Per* Bridge J:

Counsel for the commission has taken the point that the letter of 29 June is not part of the record relating to the determination which is questioned; indeed that there is no such record available for the court to consider. We cannot accept this submission. It seems to us that whenever a statutory body, having made a decision of a kind which can be questioned in proceedings for an order of *certiorari*, has subsequently chosen to disclose the reasons for the decision, whether it could have been compelled to do so or not, and however informal the document embodying the reasons, the decision with the added reasons becomes a 'speaking order' and if an error of law appears in the reasons *certiorari* will lie to quash the decision.

R v Crown Court at Knightsbridge, *ex parte* International Sporting Club (London) Ltd (1981)
The applicant company, which had recently acquired three casinos, appealed to the Crown Court from the decision of magistrates to withdraw its gaming licences. The appeal was dismissed, and the dismissal was embodied in a formal order. The Crown Court judge also gave an oral judgment in which it was made clear that his decision rested on the way in which the casinos had been managed in the past, and took no account of the complete re-structuring of the applicant company since the withdrawal of the licences. The applicant submitted that this was an error of law, and that the record of the appeal hearing included the judge's oral judgment.

Held, granting *certiorari* to quash the decision of the Crown Court, that the applicant's submissions were both correct. Although there were passages in the older authorities which suggested that the court would not look at the reasons given by an inferior tribunal unless they were embodied in a formal order, they reflected a time when shorthand had only recently been invented and there was no electronic recording apparatus with which many courts were now equipped. Administrative law was in a phase of active development, and the judges would adapt the rules applying to the issue of the prerogative orders to protect the rule of law in a changing society.

12.3.3 Errors of fact/evidential insufficiency

Ashbridge Investments Ltd v Minister of Housing and Local Government (1965) CA

Upon the making of a compulsory purchase order in connection with a slum clearance scheme a local authority was bound to compensate the owners of habitable houses or other buildings to the value both of the site and of the building on it, but compensation in respect of uninhabitable houses was limited to the value of the site. A local inspector determined that two adjoining buildings within a terrace were uninhabitable. On the basis of the inspector's report, the Minister further considered that one of the buildings, which had undergone some structural alteration, was not to be regarded as a house. The owners of the buildings sought to quash the Minister's confirmation of the compulsory purchase order on the ground that neither building was a house, and invited the court to receive evidence afresh on this point. At first instance, Mocatta J held that the court should receive evidence of the facts and reach its own conclusion thereon.

Held, allowing the Minister's appeal, that the court could interfere with his decision only if the Minister had acted on no evidence, or unreasonably, or through misinterpreting the statute, or in consequence of some other error of law. Here, the Minister had acted on the local inspector's report. It was not for the court to substitute its own opinion for that of the Minister to whom Parliament had entrusted the decision.

Coleen Properties Ltd v Minister of Housing and Local Government (1971) CA

The appellants owned a modern building which had been included as added land within a slum clearance scheme. At a public local inquiry an inspector had concluded that the compulsory purchase of the appellants' building was not (as the Housing Act 1957 required it to be) 'reasonably necessary' for the satisfactory development or use of the cleared area. The Minister reversed the inspector's decision. His decision was upheld at first instance.

Held, allowing the appeal, that the fact of reasonable necessity had to be established as a condition precedent to the exercise of power to defeat the subject's proprietary rights by compulsory purchase. The question was not a matter of policy, and therefore the Minister could determine it only on the evidence before the inspector. Since no such evidence supported the Minister's decision, it was *ultra vires*.

Puhlhofer v Hillingdon London Borough Council (1986) HL

The local authority refused the appellants' application for accommodation under s 4(5) of the Housing (Homeless Persons) Act 1977 on the grounds that they were not 'homeless' within the meaning of the Act. Section 1 of the Act provided that a person was homeless if he had no accommodation. The appellants contended that the Act's reference to 'accommodation', although unqualified, was to be understood to mean 'appropriate accommodation', and that in the light of the conditions in which they were living they were not appropriately accommodated. The appellants succeeded at first instance, but the Court of Appeal allowed the local authority's appeal. The appellants appealed to the House of Lords.

Held, dismissing the appeal, that what was properly to be regarded as 'accommodation' was a question of fact for the local authority to determine. In determining that question, the circumstances of the occupants were relevant, but in the present case the council had been entitled to find that the applicants were not homeless for the purposes of the Act because they had accommodation within the ordinary meaning of that expression. *Per* Lord Brightman:

> Although the action or inaction of a local authority is clearly susceptible to review where they have misconstrued the Act, or abused their powers or otherwise acted perversely, I think that great restraint should be exercised in giving leave to proceed by judicial review … Where the existence or non-existence of a fact is left to the judgment and discretion of a public body and that fact involves a broad spectrum ranging from the obvious to the debatable to the just conceivable, it is the duty of the court to leave the decision of that fact to the public body to whom Parliament has entrusted the decision-making power save in a case where it is obvious that the public body, consciously or unconsciously, are acting perversely.

Zamir v Secretary of State for the Home Department (1980) HL

The appellant, whose parents had settled in the UK, applied for and received a certificate of entry to the UK. He was entitled to it under the Immigration Rules because at the time he was, among other qualifications, unmarried. He married in February 1976 and entered the UK alone the following month. He neither volunteered any information nor was asked any questions about his status, and was granted leave to enter for an indefinite period. It was later discovered that he had been married at the time of entry, whereupon he was detained as an illegal immigrant on the ground that the grant of leave to enter had been vitiated by his failure to disclose a change of circumstances which he knew or ought to have known would affect his qualification for entry. He applied unsuccessfully for a writ of habeas corpus to the Divisional Court and the Court of Appeal, and appealed to the House of Lords, arguing that the power to detain and remove him depended on the precedent establishment of the alleged deception as an objective fact.

Held, rejecting the appeal, that the nature and process of decision-making powers conferred on immigration officers by existing legislation was incompatible with any requirement for the establishment of precedent objective facts whose existence the court could verify. The court was not in a position to act, in effect, as a court of appeal as to the facts on which the immigration officer decided. The limit of the court's competence lay in ascertaining that there was evidence on which the immigration officer, acting reasonably, could decide as he had.

Khawaja v Secretary of State for the Home Department (1983) HL

The case involved conjoined appeals. In the first, the applicant had obtained leave to enter the UK for one month. He was already bigamously married to a woman settled in England. He said nothing about this marriage. He later applied for an extension of leave, informing the Home Office of the marriage (which had now been regularised). His application was refused and his detention pending removal was ordered on the ground that leave to enter had been obtained by deception. The facts of the second case were similar to those of *Zamir* (above). In both cases, the notification of removal provided to the applicant contained the statement of an immigration officer that there were 'reasonable grounds to conclude' that the applicant was an illegal entrant. On appeal to the House of Lords, the question arose, *inter alia*, whether the court was limited to determining whether the immigration officer had had reasonable grounds for that conclusion, or whether the court was required itself to decide whether the applicants were illegal entrants.

Held, that the appeal in the first case would be dismissed, and the second appeal allowed. In so deciding, the House itself determined the status of the appellants, finding the first clearly to have been guilty of procuring entry by deception, and finding the second innocent of deception on the evidence before the immigration officer. The construction of the Immigration Rules favoured in *Zamir* had limited judicial review in such a case to the *Wednesbury* heads of challenge comprising error of law, unreasonableness, and breach of natural justice. Thus limited, the court would not be competent to substitute its own view of the facts for that of the decision-making authority. However, that limitation was contrary to the development of the safeguards which the law provided to an individual whose liberty was vulnerable to the exercise of executive power. In such cases the courts would decide whether facts precedent to the availability of the power had been established. The standard of proof involved would be the civil standard applied with reference to the gravity of the issue at stake.

12.4 Delegation of powers

12.4.1 Permissible delegation

Carltona v Commissioners of Works (1943) CA

The appellants owned a food factory. In 1942 the factory was requisitioned by the Commissioners of Works under the Defence (General) Regulations 1939. The appellants claimed, *inter alia*, that the notice to requisition was invalid because the persons constituting the requisitioning authority had never brought their minds to bear on the question. The body known as the Commissioners of Works in fact never met; its functions were exercised by the Minister of Works and Planning who also held the office of First Commissioner. The notice issued to the appellants had been signed by his assistant secretary.

Held, dismissing the appeal, that the person acting for the First Commissioner in this matter was the assistant secretary, and that the question therefore was whether he had directed his mind to the decision in question. *Per* Lord Greene MR:

In the administration of government in this country the functions which are given to ministers (and constitutionally properly given to ministers because they are constitutionally responsible) are functions so multifarious that no Minister could ever personally attend to them. To take the example of the present case no doubt there have been thousands of requisitions in this country by individual ministries. It cannot be supposed that this regulation meant that, in each case, the Minister in person should direct his mind to the matter. The duties imposed upon ministers and the powers given to ministers are normally exercised under the authority of the ministers by responsible officials of the department. Public business could not be carried on if that were not the case. Constitutionally, the decision of such an official is, of course, the decision of the Minister. The Minister is responsible. It is he who must answer before Parliament ...

12.4.2 Impermissible delegation

Barnard v National Dock Labour Board (1953) CA

The National Dock Labour Board was set up by Parliament under the Dock Workers (Regulation of Employment) Order 1947. It was the duty of the national board to administer a scheme under which a number of functions, including disciplinary powers, were to be delegated to local dock labour boards. The London dock labour board further delegated its disciplinary powers to the London port manager. The port manager suspended a number of dockers in connection with an industrial dispute. The dockers applied for a declaration that their suspension was unlawful on the grounds that the local board had no power to delegate its disciplinary powers.

Held, allowing the appeal, that the disciplinary powers in question were of a judicial character, rather than merely administrative. *Per* Denning LJ:

> While an administrative function can often be delegated, a judicial function rarely can be ... It was suggested that it would be impracticable for the board to sit as a board to decide all these cases, but I see nothing impracticable in that. They have only to fix their quorum at two members and arrange for two members, one from each side, employers and workers, to be responsible for one week at a time.
>
> Next it was suggested that, even if the board could not delegate their functions, at any rate they could ratify the actions of the port manager, but, if the board have no power to delegate their functions to the port manager, they can have no power to ratify what he has already done.

12.5 The exercise of discretion

12.5.1 The fettering of discretion by the adoption of policy

R v Port of London Authority, *ex parte* Kynoch Ltd (1919) CA

The appellant owned land, and wished to use it for the construction of a deep-water wharf. For this a licence was required from the Port of London Authority. The authority declined to issue a licence, stating that the facility proposed was one which the authority itself had been charged by Parliament to provide. The appellant argued that the port authority had not properly heard and determined its licence application.

Held, dismissing the appeal, that the authority's affidavit made it clear that the merits of the application had been fully considered. However, even if they had not, the grounds specifically referred to by the authority for its refusal were rightly taken into consideration, and it was not wrong to apply them by policy. *Per* Bankes LJ:

> There are on the one hand cases where a tribunal in the honest exercise of its discretion has adopted a policy, and, without refusing to hear an applicant, intimates to him what its policy is, and that after hearing him it will in accordance with its policy decide against him, unless there is something exceptional in his case. I think counsel for the appellants would admit that, if the policy has been adopted for reasons which the tribunal may legitimately entertain, no objection could be taken to such a course. On the other hand, there are cases where a tribunal has passed a rule, or come to a determination, not to hear any application of a particular character by whomsoever made. There is a wide distinction between these two classes ...

Stringer v Minister for Housing (1971)

The applicant applied for and was refused planning permission for a residential development at Brereton Heath, four miles from the Nuffield

Radio Astronomy Laboratories which contained the Jodrell Bank Telescope. An agreement had been entered into by the local authorities with the operators of the telescope 'to discourage development within the limits of their powers at Brereton Heath until 1990'. Among the reasons given for the refusal of planning permission was the proximity of the proposed development to the radio telescope, and the likelihood of interference with the telescope's efficient running. The applicant appealed to the Minister. Following a local inquiry, the Minister upheld the refusal of planning permission on the ground, *inter alia*, that the proposed development would be contrary to the policy for the area around Jodrell Bank. The applicant argued, *inter alia*, that the Minister, in determining the appeal, had failed to discharge his duty to act fairly and judicially.

Held, dismissing the application, that the Minister had fairly considered the applicant's appeal. Cooke J quoted the passage from the judgment of Bankes LJ in *Kynoch's* case and continued:

> It seems to me that the general effect of the many relevant authorities is that a Minister charged with the duty of making individual administrative decisions in a fair and impartial manner may nevertheless have a general policy in regard to matters which are relevant to those decisions, provided that the existence of that general policy does not preclude him from fairly judging all the issues which are relevant to each individual case as it comes up for decision.

Q How does the use which the Minister is permitted to make of a policy in *Stringer's* case differ from the role of policy envisaged by Bankes LJ?

Lavender (H) & Son Ltd v Minister of Housing and Local Government (1970)
The applicants had applied for planning permission to extract sand, gravel and ballast from a site near Walton-on-Thames, designated as an area of high quality agricultural land. Planning permission was refused. There was evidence that the applicants would be able to restore the land to a high level of agricultural quality. The only substantial objection to the application was submitted by the Ministry of Agriculture, which wished to see the land maintained as agricultural land. No other reason for the refusal of planning permission was found by the planning authority. Appeal from the refusal of the application lay to the Minister of Housing and Local Government, who dismissed it on the grounds that it was his policy not to release land for mineral working unless there was no objection from the Minister for Agriculture. The applicants argued that the Minister of Housing and Local Government had fettered his own discretion by treating as decisive not his own view, but that of the Minister for Agriculture, and that he had thereby effectively delegated his discretion without authority.

Held, allowing the appeal, that the Minister of Housing and Local Government was entitled to have a policy, and to decide appeals in accordance with it. If, however, he had pre-empted himself from giving

111

any genuine consideration to the matter before him, he would have failed to carry out his statutory duties properly. There was nothing in the language of the Minister's decision to suggest that he had considered whether this might be an exceptional case which might have justified his departing from his policy. In the circumstances, it was not the authority made responsible by Parliament for the decision who had made it, but a different authority.

British Oxygen v Minister of Technology (1971) HL

British Oxygen had purchased a quantity of gas cylinders, each costing £20. The total purchase came to more than £4 million. British Oxygen applied to the Board of Trade for investment grants under the Industrial Development Act 1966 for a grant in respect of the purchase. The board refused to make any grant, giving as its reason, *inter alia*, that there was a lower limit of £25 of cost for single items eligible for grants. In addition to other remedies, British Oxygen sought a declaration that the board was not entitled to decline to make a grant on the grounds solely of its self-imposed lower price limit.

Held, refusing the declaration, that there was nothing in the Development Act 1966 which would guide the board as to the circumstances in which it should or should not pay grants. If the board considered that policy or good administration required the operation of some limiting rule, there was nothing to prevent its adoption. The most that could be said was that the absolute discretion conferred on the board should not be exercised in bad faith, or exercised so unreasonably as to show that there had been no real or genuine exercise of the discretion. Further (*per* Lord Reid):

> There may be cases where an officer or authority ought to listen to a substantial argument reasonably presented urging a change of policy. What the authority must not do is to refuse to listen at all. But a Ministry or large authority may have had to deal already with a multitude of similar applications and then they will almost certainly have evolved a policy so precise that it could well be called a rule. There can be no objection to that provided the authority is always ready to listen to anyone with something new to say ... In the present case, the Minister's officers have carefully considered all that the appellants have had to say and I have no doubt that they will continue to do so.

Bromley London Borough Council v Greater London Council (1982) HL

Facts: see 12.2.1 above.

Per Lord Diplock:

> I would also have held the decision and the precept to be void upon another ground ... the members of the majority party by whose votes the effective resolutions were passed acted upon an erroneous view ... that from first to last they regarded the GLC as irrevocably committed to carry out the reduction, whatever might be the additional cost to the ratepayers, because a reduction of

that amount had been pre-announced in the election manifesto issued by the political party whose candidates formed a majority of the members elected ...

R v Ministry of Agriculture, Fisheries and Food, *ex parte* Hamble (Offshore) Fisheries Ltd (1995)

The applicant acquired two fishing vessels with a view to transferring their beam trawl licences to a larger trawler (the *'Nellie'*) which it had earlier acquired for the purposes of the transfer. The Ministry's then policy permitted this licence transfer. In the meantime, the applicant transferred general licences to the *'Nellie'*. Following a change in policy and the introduction of a moratorium on the transfer of pressure stock licences onto beam trawlers, the Ministry wrote to the applicant informing it that the *'Nellie'* would not qualify for a beam trawl licence since she currently held a general licence and had no track record of beam trawling. The letter indicated that this changed policy was being applied in all similar cases, and that any deviation from it would be discriminatory. The applicant contended that it had a legitimate expectation that an exception to the policy would be made for those who had already acted with a view to a licence transfer, and further maintained that the application of the new policy without regard to the appropriateness of exception amounted to a failure to exercise discretion.

Held, that the applicant's arguments could not succeed. There had been no failure to exercise discretion, because the cases of those in the applicant's position had been taken into account in the framing of the policy. *Per* Sedley J:

> While the framer of a policy for the exercise of a governmental discretion must be prepared to consider making exceptions where these are merited, the inclusion of thought-out exceptions in the policy itself may well be exhaustive of the obligation. While any further candidates for exemption must be considered, it will always be a legitimate consideration that to make one such exception may well set up an unanswerable case of partiality or arbitrariness. The decision-maker must therefore balance the case for making no such exception against the case for generalising it. This, on the evidence, is what the respondent did.

12.5.2 The fettering of discretion by the giving of private undertakings

The general principle

Birkdale District Electric Supply Co Ltd v Southport Corporation (1926) HL
Facts: see 12.5.2 below.
Per the Earl of Birkenhead:

> ... [it is] a well established principle of law, that if a person or public body is entrusted by the Legislature with certain powers and duties expressly or

impliedly for public purposes, those persons or bodies cannot divest themselves of these powers and duties. They cannot enter into a contract or take any action incompatible with the due exercise of their powers or the discharge of their duties.

Applications of the principle

Ayr Harbour Trustees v Oswald (1883)

Harbour trustees had statutory powers and duties to acquire land to be used as need might arise for coastal or harbour works. On the compulsory purchase of a piece of land, they sought to save money by offering its owner a perpetual covenant not to carry out any works on the land acquired so as to cut off the land left to him from access to the harbour.

Held, that the covenant was *ultra vires*. Where the legislature conferred powers to take land compulsorily for a particular purpose, it had to be assumed that it was on the ground that the using of the land for that purpose would be to the public good. A contract seeking to bind the authority not to use those powers in any circumstances would be void.

Stourcliffe Estates Co Ltd v Bournemouth Corporation (1910) CA

The corporation purchased land from the plaintiff for use as a public park. It covenanted with the plaintiff not to build on the land except to erect 'such structures as summer houses, a band stand or shelters'. Section 85 of the Bournemouth Improvement Act 1892 gave the corporation power to build public conveniences in any of their public parks. The plaintiff sought and was granted an injunction to restrain the Corporation from erecting public conveniences on the land affected by the covenant. The Corporation argued that the covenant was *ultra vires*.

Held, that the plaintiff was entitled to the injunction. The Corporation's argument amounted to an assertion that it should be permitted to retain the land bought from the plaintiff while repudiating a part of the consideration. Further, the present case was distinguishable from *Ayr Harbour Trustees v Oswald* (1883) (see 12.5.2 above) because there the power granted by Parliament had been to purchase specific land; here the corporation might purchase where it pleased.

Ulterior purpose or improper motive

Birkdale District Electric Supply Co Ltd v Southport Corporation (1926) HL

Pursuant to electric lighting order made under statutory powers, the appellants took over the supplying of electricity from Birkdale Council. At the time of so doing, they covenanted not to charge private consumers more than was charged in the neighbouring borough of Southport by Southport Corporation. In 1911 Southport Corporation took over responsibility for the Birkdale area. From 1921 the appellants began to charge more for electricity than was charged by Southport Corporation. The

Corporation sought an injunction to restrain the appellants from exceeding the Southport price. The appellants argued that the initial agreement was *ultra vires* as a fetter on their power to fix their own prices (subject to certain statutory maximum charges). This was a power which they might in the future need to exercise in order to maintain the commercial conditions necessary to the performance of their statutory function. The Corporation replied that the initial agreement was a commercial arrangement which might have proved unwise for the appellants, but which was compatible with the performance of their statutory duty. The question of compatibility had to judged at the date of the agreement.

Held, dismissing the appeal, that the appellants' arguments depended on the proposition that it was one of the statutory objects of the electric lighting order that the appellants should make a profit. This was impossible to maintain; the order itself imposed a maximum price for the supply of electricity and so was logically capable of interfering with the appellants' freedom of charging in the same way as their initial agreement. *Per* Lord Sumner:

> It appears to me that no line can be drawn between the agreement now in question and any ordinary trading contract, if the appellants are right in testing the validity of the contract by its ultimate and theoretic possibility of bringing upon them a crippling loss. I do not think that a speculation as to the possible effect of what they have done is a legitimate ground for relieving them from their bargain ...

R v Hammersmith and Fulham London Borough Council, *ex parte* Beddowes (1987) CA

The council owned an estate of blocks of flats, Fulham Court, which was urgently in need of major repair. The Conservative majority on the council favoured dealing with the problem by selling the blocks of flats for development for owner-occupation. Labour councillors opposed the loss of council housing stock which this would entail. In 1986 the council resolved that one of the blocks should be sold to a private developer. In order to avoid being left in control of a single renovated block in the middle of an otherwise blighted estate, the developer required and obtained the council's covenant to continue its policy of selling the blocks for private development. The applicant, a resident of the estate, challenged the council's decision to sell the first block, arguing that the covenant obtained from the council constituted an unlawful fetter on its powers as a housing authority.

Held (by a majority), that the council's actions were not open to criticism. The council possessed overlapping or conflicting statutory powers; it had powers to create covenants restrictive of the use of the land it retained, and powers in relation to the use of the retained land for housing purposes. In these circumstances, it was necessary to ascertain for what primary purpose the retained land was held. That purpose was the provision of housing accommodation in the area. The provision of good accommodation at reasonable prices for owner-occupiers was no less within the purposes of the Housing Acts than the provision of rented housing. *Per* Sir Denys Buckley:

> ... if a statutory authority acting in good faith in the proper and reasonable exercise of its statutory powers undertakes some binding obligation, the fact that such obligation may thereafter preclude the authority from exercising some other statutory power, or from exercising its statutory powers in some other way, cannot constitute an impermissible fetter on its powers. Any other view would involve that the doctrine against fettering would itself involve a fetter on the authority's capacity to exercise its powers properly and reasonably as it thinks fit from time to time.

The decision in the instant case therefore depended primarily on the propriety and reasonableness of the council's actions.

Kerr LJ (dissenting) considered that the council's primary motivation was to ensure the continuance of its policy in the event of a political change in forthcoming elections. Accordingly its actions were designed to fetter future policies and were not motivated by any presently required contractual demands. His Lordship would have held the sale with covenants to have been unreasonable in the *Wednesbury* sense (*Associated Provincial Picture Houses Ltd v Wednesbury Corporation* (1948) see 13.1 below).

12.5.3 The availability of estoppel against a public authority

Lever (Finance) Ltd v Westminster Council (1971) CA

It was common practice for planning officers to accept minor modifications to plans sent with successful applications for planning permission. One of the defendant corporation's planning officers sanctioned a modification which (in the opinion of the Court of Appeal) was not minor, but required independent planning permission. When this was discovered, the Corporation suggested that the defendant apply for planning permission. Permission was refused. The plaintiff sought, and at first instance obtained, a declaration that there was valid planning permission in force which included the modification.

Held, that the declaration had been properly granted. Lord Denning MR referred to the authorities which set out the general rule that estoppel could not be pleaded against a public authority so as to prevent it performing its public duty, and went on:

> But those statements must now be taken with considerable reserve. There are many matters which public authorities can now delegate to their officers. If an officer, acting within the scope of his ostensible authority, makes a representation

on which another acts, then a public authority may be bound by it, just as much as a private concern would be.

Brooks and Burton Ltd v Secretary of State for the Environment (1976)
Per Lord Widgery CJ:

There has been some advance in recent years of this doctrine of estoppel as applied to local authorities through their officers, and the most advanced case is ... *Lever Finance Ltd v Westminster (City) London Borough Council.* I do not propose to read it. It is no doubt correct on its facts, but I would deprecate any attempt to expand this doctrine because it seems to me, as I said a few minutes ago, extremely important that local government officers should feel free to help applicants who come and ask them questions without all the time having the shadow of estoppel hanging over them and without the possibility of their immobilising their authorities by some careless remark which produces such an estoppel.

Laker Airways v Department of Trade (1977) CA
Facts: see 5.5.1 above.

Held, that estoppel could not be pleaded against a public authority. Whatever representations had been made to Laker Airways by the Secretary of State between 1972 and 1974, his successor necessarily remained free to go back on them provided he was satisfied that the public interest required him to do so. Estoppel could not be allowed to hinder the formation of government policy, even though Laker sustained loss as a result.

Western Fish Products Ltd v Penwith District Council (1981) CA
The company bought a disused factory which had been used for the production of fertiliser from fish and fishmeal. The company intended to use the factory to manufacture fishmeal, fish oil, and to prepare and package fresh fish for human consumption. The chairman of the company informed a representative of the council's chief planning officer that there existed an 'established user right' by virtue of the previous use of the factory which entitled the company to carry on their intended processes without the need for a new grant of planning permission. The officer said that if the company could satisfy him of the claimed right in writing, the council would do everything it could to facilitate the company's plans. In reply to information provided by the company, the officer confirmed that the claimed rights appeared to be established. On the strength of this reply and with the knowledge of the council, the company expended money modifying the factory premises. The council requested that the company seek planning permission, but explained that this was a formality only. Permission was refused. The company sought, *inter alia*, a declaration of its claimed rights. It was refused at first instance, and the company appealed to the Court of Appeal.

Held, dismissing the appeal, that the case did not fall within any exception to the general rule that a statutory body could not be estopped from performing its statutory duty. There were two exceptions to the rule. First, if a planning authority delegated power to its officers to determine specific questions, their decisions could not be revoked. *Lever (Finance) Ltd v Westminster Corporation* (above) was to be regarded as an example of this exception. Secondly, if a planning authority waived any procedural requirement relating to an application made to it for the exercise of its statutory powers, it might be estopped from relying on lack of formality as a ground for rejecting the application. Neither exception covered the present case, and the exceptions would not be broadened.

Q In terms of principle, why should the two situations referred to above be regarded as exceptions to the general rule?

12.6 Relevant and irrelevant considerations

Limitations on the principle

CREEDNZ v Governor General (1981) (New Zealand)
(The facts are not material)
Per Cooke J:

> What has to be emphasised is that it is only where the statute expressly or impliedly identifies considerations required to be taken into account by the authority as a matter of legal obligation that the court holds a decision invalid on the ground now invoked. It is not enough that a consideration is one which may properly be taken into account, nor even that it is one which many people, including the court itself, would have taken into account if they had to make the decision ... [However] there will be some matters so obviously material to a decision on a particular project that anything short of direct consideration of them ... would not be in accordance with the intention of the Act.

Q How many classes of consideration does this statement (approved by the House of Lords in *Findlay's* case) create?

Bolton Metropolitan District Council v Secretary of State for the Environment (1995) HL
The respondents to the appeal, a consortium of local authorities, property companies and other commercial organisations, objected to the Secretary of State's adoption of a planning inspector's recommendations regarding the grant of planning permission for one of a larger number of shopping centre developments in the Greater Manchester area. They alleged, *inter alia*, that the Secretary of State had failed to take certain material considerations into account, and in support of this contention they relied on the fact that his decision letter did not refer to all the material considerations. The Court of Appeal accepted that a planning decision letter had to refer to

each material consideration bearing on the decision. The Secretary of State appealed to the House of Lords.

Held, allowing the Secretary of State's appeal, that while he had to have regard to all material considerations before reaching his decision, he did not have to mention all of them in giving his reasons for it. *Per* Lord Lloyd of Berwick:

> There was nothing in the statutory language which required him, in stating his reasons, to deal specifically with every material consideration. Otherwise his task would never be done. The decision letter would be as long as the Inspector's report. He had to have regard to every material consideration; but he need not mention them all ... What the Secretary of State had to do was to state his reasons in sufficient detail to enable the reader to know what conclusion he had reached in the 'principal important controversial issues'. To require him to refer to every material consideration, however insignificant, and to deal with every argument, however peripheral, would be to impose an unjustifiable burden.

Roberts v Hopwood (1925) HL

Under s 62 of the Metropolis Management Act 1855, Poplar Borough Council had power to pay to its employees 'such salaries and wages ... as [the council] may think fit'. At a time when the cost of living was rising the council increased its minimum wage for men and women alike to 80 shillings a week. It maintained its minimum wage at that level despite later reductions in the cost of living. The District Auditor, who had made no objection when he first noticed the increase, found that the council's total wage bill substantially exceeded the amount which would have been paid if trade union rates had been applied. He heard representations from the Socialist majority on the council that they regarded themselves as bound to maintain these wage levels by a mandate of the electors. Claiming to act pursuant to his duty under s 247(7) of the Public Health Act 1875 to disallow unlawful items of expenditure and to surcharge the same on those making or authorising the payment, he disallowed £5,000 of expenditure on wages and surcharged it on the councillors concerned. The councillors sought an order of *certiorari* to quash the auditor's decision. The Court of Appeal allowed their appeal, and the auditor appealed to the House of Lords.

Held, allowing the auditor's appeal, that the council had ceased to regard the payments as wages due in proportion to work done, and had ceased to regard the purchasing power of the sums paid at a time of falling cost of living. The council stated that it had taken these matters into account, but it appeared to the court impossible to reconcile that assertion with setting of a flat rate of payment which (*per* Lord Buckmaster) 'standardised men and women not according to the duties which they performed, but according to the fact that they were adults'. The council had failed to have proper regard to the duty it owed to ratepayers to conduct administration in a fair and business-like manner with reasonable care, skill and caution. Since they had taken an arbitrary principle and fixed an arbitrary sum, they had not genuinely exercised the discretion imposed upon them by the Metropolis Management Act 1855.

Prescott v Birmingham Corporation (1955) CA

A ratepayer brought an action for a declaration that the Corporation had acted unlawfully in implementing a scheme for free bus travel for the elderly. The corporation had statutory power to charge 'such fares as they may think fit' on their public transport system.

Held, granting the declaration, that it was clearly implicit in the legislation that the transport undertaking was to be run as a business venture. Further, local authorities owed a fiduciary duty to their ratepayers in relation to the application of funds contributed by the latter. Concessions such as half-price travel for children were justifiable on business principles, and free travel for the disabled, if not strictly justifiable, was a minor act of elementary charity to which no reasonable ratepayer would be likely to object. The corporation had misapprehended the nature and scope of the discretion conferred on it.

Bromley London Borough Council v Greater London Council (1982) HL

Facts: see 12.2.1 above.

In addition to finding that the statutory framework imposed a duty on the London Transport Executive to run the transport system on economic lines, the House of Lords held that the GLC owed a fiduciary duty to ratepayers. That duty had to be balanced against its duty to provide for transport users. The GLC had power to make a grant to the London Transport Executive, but might only do so with proper regard to its fiduciary duty.

R v Somerset County Council, *ex parte* Fewings (1995) CA

The Council resolved to ban the hunting of deer with hounds on a common of which it was the owner. A paper circulated to councillors before the meeting at which the ban was imposed stated that a decision would have to be reached 'largely on the grounds of ethics, animal welfare and social considerations'. It was later agreed between the parties that the Council's powers of management were in fact to be found in s 120(1)(b) of the Local Government Act 1972, which permitted the council to acquire land for 'the benefit, improvement or development of their area'.

At first instance, Laws J quashed the hunting ban on the ground that the council had taken into account an irrelevant consideration by basing its decision chiefly on a freestanding distaste for the alleged cruelty of hunting. The council appealed to the Court of Appeal.

Held (Simon Brown LJ dissenting), that the judgment of Laws J would be upheld. There was a fundamental difference between the rights of private and public landowners; the former might do as they wished with-in the law, whereas the latter could act only with positive legal justifica-tion. The 'cruelty argument' was not necessarily an irrelevant considera-tion (Swinton Thomas LJ dissenting on this point), but the evidence showed that the limited scope of the council's powers of management had never been drawn to its attention. A relevant consideration had therefore been overlooked, and the council could not be said to have exercised its power to further the object prescribed by the statute.

Simon Brown LJ was of the opinion that s 120(1)(b) merely mirrored common law restraints on the council's powers, and he found no reason to conclude that the common law limits had not been present to the minds of the councillors. A relevant consideration had therefore not been over-looked. It was for the councillors to decide what weight to give to the cruelty argument; it was a relevant consideration, and might properly be treated as decisive. Had it not been considered, the council would have been open to criticism.

Q Sir Thomas Bingham MR declined to decide whether the hunting ban could have been imposed on proper grounds. Was that question material to the outcome of the case? See *R v Broadcasting Complaints Commission, ex parte Owen* (1985) (see 12.7.2 below).

12.7 The exercise of discretion for an improper purpose

12.7.1 Applications of the principle

Padfield v Minister of Agriculture, Fisheries and Food (1968) HL
The Agricultural Marketing Act 1958 provided that where complaints relating to the operation of a milk marketing scheme were made to the Minister, a committee of investigation should consider them and report on them to the Minister 'if the Minister in any case so directs'. The Minister received a complaint of unfair price differentials from the south-eastern producers, but declined to appoint a committee of investigation to consider it. The milk producers sought an order of *mandamus* to compel the Minister either to refer the complaint to a committee, or to deal effectively with the complaints on relevant consideration only to the exclusion of irrelevant considerations.

The Court of Appeal (by a majority), allowed the Minister's appeal, and the milk producers appealed to the House of Lords.

Held, allowing the appeal (by a majority) that the Minister was wrong to contend that the Agricultural Marketing Act 1958 gave him an unfettered discretion to choose whether or not to refer complaints. *Per* Lord Reid:

Parliament must have conferred the discretion with the intention that it should be used to promote the policy and objects of the Act; the policy and objects of the Act must be determined by construing the Act as a whole and construction is always a matter of law for the court ... if the Minister, by reason of his having misconstrued the Act or for any other reason, so uses his discretion as to thwart or run counter to the policy and objects of the Act, then our law would be very defective if persons aggrieved were not entitled to the protection of the court. So it is necessary first to construe the Act.

Lord Reid found that through the provision of the complaints procedure, the Act provided mechanisms calculated to safeguard those who were subject to its pricing machinery. The present complaint sought to activate those mechanisms, and it appeared to require investigation. By failing to refer it, the Minister was rendering nugatory a safeguard provided by the Act.

Congreve v Home Office (1976) CA

The Home Secretary decided to increase the cost of a television licence from £12 to £18 from 1 April 1975. Several licence holders renewed their existing licences prematurely in order to avoid paying the increased charge. Section 1 of the Wireless Telegraphy Act 1949 gave the Home Secretary power to issue licences 'subject to such terms, provisions and limitations as he may think fit'. It gave him an unfettered power to revoke licences. He threatened to revoke the licences prematurely renewed unless their holders paid the difference between the old and the new fees. Congreve, the holder of a prematurely renewed licence, sought a declaration that the threatened revocation would be unlawful.

Held, granting the declaration, that the Minister did indeed have a discretion as to the issue and revocation of licences. However, the revocation in this case was tainted by an illegal threat, and it was an improper use of a discretionary power to use a threat to exercise that power as a means of raising money which Parliament had given the executive no mandate to raise. *Per* Lord Denning MR:

> ... it is a discretion which must be exercised in accordance with the law, taking all relevant considerations into account, omitting irrelevant ones, and not being influenced by any ulterior motives ... The licence is granted for 12 months and cannot be revoked simply in order to enable the Minister to make more money. Want of money is no reason for revoking a licence. The real reason, of course, in this case was that the department did not like people taking out overlapping licences so as to save money. But there was nothing in the regulations to stop it. It was perfectly lawful; and the department's dislike of it cannot afford a good reason for revoking them.

Wheeler v Leicester City Council (1985) HL

The Council administered a recreation ground in trust to allow and promote its enjoyment by the public as an open space. It had the power to set aside pitches for the purpose of playing football. By s 56 of the Public Health Act 1925, the Council had the power to permit the use by any club of such a pitch, subject to such charges and conditions as the council thought fit. The Council passed a resolution banning Leicester [Rugby] Football Club from using the recreation ground because it considered that the club had done insufficient to discourage three of its members from participating in a sporting tour of South Africa. The council maintained that it was entitled to take into account its duty under s 71 of the Race Relations Act 1976, which read:

> ... it shall be the duty of every local authority to make appropriate arrangements with a view to securing that their various functions are carried out with due regard to the need ... to promote ... good relations, between different persons of different racial groups.

The club sought an order of *certiorari* to quash the council's decision. The Court of Appeal (by a majority) dismissed the club's appeal. The club appealed to the House of Lords.

Held, allowing the appeal, that the council had misused its statutory powers of management in order to punish the club. That this was the intention of the council was clear from the evidence. The club had done no wrong. Lord Templeman quoted from the judgment of Lord Denning MR in *Congreve v Home Office* (1976)(above), and continued:

> Similar considerations apply, in my opinion, to the present case. Of course this does not mean that the council is bound to allow its property to be used by a racist organisation or by any organisation which, by its actions or its words, infringes the letter or the spirit of the Race Relations Act 1976. But the attitude of the club and of the committee of the club was a perfectly proper attitude, caught as they were in a political controversy which was not of their making.

For Ackner LJ's and Lord Roskill's difference on the applicability of irrationality principles to the case, see 13.2 below.

The other Law Lords agreed with both Lord Templeman and Lord Roskill.

R v Derbyshire County Council, *ex parte* The Times Supplements Ltd (1990)

The Sunday Times published articles about Derbyshire County Council which led to the institution of libel proceedings by the Council's leader, Councillor David Bookbinder. The council resolved to remove all its advertising from newspapers owned by Rupert Murdoch and in consequence it appeared that its advertisements for teaching posts in particular would cost more and be seen by less of those at whom they were targeted. The applicant sought an order of *certiorari* to quash the decision.

Held, granting the order, that the majority Labour group on the Council had been motivated by bad faith or vindictiveness, despite claims in the affidavits before the court that educational considerations had prompted the transfer of the teaching post advertisements. The court would have been equally prepared to hold that the Council's decision was unreasonable in the *Wednesbury* sense (*Associated Provincial Picture Houses Ltd v*

Wednesbury Corporation (1947) see 13.1 below) as having no sensible or justifiable basis.

12.7.2 The co-existence of improper and legitimate purposes

Westminster Corporation v London and North-Western Railway Co (1905) HL

Under the Public Health (London) Act 1891, the corporation had power to construct public lavatories. The railway company owned a building on the east side of Parliament Street. The corporation built public lavatories underground below the middle of Parliament Street, with entrances on either side of the street. On various occasions the corporation and its predecessor, the Vestry of St Margaret's, Westminster, had referred to the intended works as a subway. The railway company sought an injunction to prevent the corporation's continued trespass on its premises and to obstruct the pavement opposite their premises, and damages. They argued that the Corporation's true purpose was to build a subway, and that it had therefore exceeded the powers given to it by the Act of 1891. The Court of Appeal considered that the Corporation had acted in bad faith.

Held (by a majority), that the Corporation had not acted in bad faith. After emphasising that the charge of want of good faith was a serious one, Lord MacNaghten continued:

> It is not enough to shew that the corporation contemplated that the public might use the subway as a means of crossing the street. That was an obvious possibility ... In order to make out a case of bad faith, it must be shown that the corporation constructed this subway as a means of crossing the street under colour and pretence of providing public conveniences which were not really wanted at that particular place.

Since the chairman of the works committee had declared on oath before the judge at first instance that the primary object of the committee was to provide the conveniences, and had been believed by the judge, his account should continue to prevail.

R v Inner London Education Authority, *ex parte* Westminster City Council (1986)

Under the Local Government Act 1972, the authority had power to incur expenditure on publishing within its area 'information on matters relating to local government'. In 1984 a sub-committee resolved to mount an advertising campaign costing £651,000 in order to inform the public about government education proposals, and to seek to persuade the public to share the authority's view of the proposals. The authority accepted that while the first of these objectives was lawful, the second was not. Westminster Council argued that the sub-committee's resolution was *ultra vires* the LGEA 1972 because the authority had an improper purpose and, because in allowing itself to be motivated by its desire to increase public opposition to government policy, it had taken into account an irrelevant consideration.

Held that the declaration sought by Westminster Council would be granted on both grounds. Glidewell J stated that the question for the court was whether a decision taken to achieve two purposes, one authorised by statute and the other unauthorised, was invalid. He cited the following passage from de Smith's *Judicial Review of Administrative Action*, 4th edn, 1980, pp 329–32:

> (1) What was the *true purpose* for which the power was exercised? If the actor has in truth used his power for the purposes for which it was conferred, it is immaterial that he was thus enabled to achieve a subsidiary object ...

> (5) Was any of the purposes pursued an unauthorised purpose? If so, and if the unauthorised purpose has materially influenced the actor's conduct, the power has been invalidly exercised because irrelevant considerations have been taken into account.

Glidewell J found as fact that the wish to persuade the public to adopt its own point of view was a (if not the) major purpose of the authority in making its decision. He further found that the authority had taken into account an irrelevant consideration, but declined to accept submissions that the authority had acted in disregard of its fiduciary duty to ratepayers, or that its decision was so unreasonable as to be perverse.

Q Glidewell J appears to regard the two tests in the passage quoted from de Smith as achieving 'much the same result'. Do they necessarily?

R v Broadcasting Complaints Commission, *ex parte* Owen (1985)

The applicant, Dr David Owen, was the leader of the Social Democratic Party, which had entered into an alliance with the Liberal Party. At the 1983 general election these two parties had obtained only slightly less votes than the Labour Party, but they had won far fewer seats in the Commons. The applicant wrote to the BBC complaining of unfair treatment in that the corporation had given more coverage to the views of the Labour Party than it had to those of the Alliance. The BBC replied that it had no jurisdiction to consider such a complaint, and that even if it had, it would have exercised its discretion under ss 54 and 55 of the Broadcasting Act 1981 not to consider it. The BBC gave a number of reasons for this stance. The applicant sought to persuade the court that the invalidity of one of any of the stated reasons would invalidate the BBC's decision.

Held, dismissing the application, that the BBC had been wrong to conclude that it did not have jurisdiction to consider the applicant's complaint, but that its exercise of its discretion would not be overturned. The third of the reasons given (that it would be burdensome to give fuller coverage to the Alliance's policies) was not a proper reason. In *R v Rochdale Metropolitan Borough Council, ex parte Cromer Ring Mill Ltd* (1982), Forbes J had held that academic and judicial authority established that the presence of an irrelevant consideration was sufficient to invalidate a decision even if its influence was not dominant; it was enough that it was substantial. However, the *Rochdale* case was one in which the reasons given were impossible to disentangle; in a case like the present where the reasons given were separate and alternative, and the decision was one which the authority would have reached even if it had not taken into account the improper consideration, the court would not intervene.

13 The grounds for judicial review: irrationality

13.1 General definitions of irrationality

Associated Provincial Picture Houses Ltd v Wednesbury Corporation (1948) CA

The Corporation, acting under the Sunday Entertainments Act 1932, gave permission to the appellants to open their cinema on Sundays, subject to the condition that 'No children under the age of 15 years shall be admitted to any entertainment, whether accompanied by an adult or not'. Counsel for the appellants argued that the imposition of the condition was unreasonable, and consequently *ultra vires* the corporation's powers.

Held, that the subject matter of the condition was one which could properly be considered by the corporation; the decision on what was reasonable was for the corporation and not for the court. However, Lord Greene MR added (*obiter*):

> It is true to say that, if a decision on a competent matter is so unreasonable that no reasonable authority could ever have come to it, then the courts can interfere. That, I think, is quite right; but to prove a case of that kind would require something overwhelming, and, in this case, the facts do not come anywhere near anything of that kind.

Council of Civil Service Unions v Minister for the Civil Service (1985) HL
Facts: see 15.5.1 below.
Per Lord Diplock:

> By 'irrationality' I mean what can now be succinctly referred to as 'Wednesbury unreasonableness' ... It applies to a decision which is so outrageous in its defiance of logic or of accepted moral standards that no sensible person who had applied his mind to the question to be decided could have arrived at it. Whether a decision falls within this category is a question that judges by their training and experience should be well equipped to answer, or else there would be something badly wrong with our judicial system. To justify the court's exercise of this role, resort I think is today no longer needed to Viscount Radcliffe's ingenious explanation in *Edwards v Bairstow* (1956) AC 14 of irrationality as a ground for a court's reversal of a decision by ascribing it to an inferred though unidentifiable mistake

of law by the decision-maker. 'Irrationality' by now can stand upon its own feet as an accepted ground on which a decision may be attacked by judicial review.

13.2 Applications of the principle

Wheeler v Leicester City Council (1985) CA and HL

Facts: see 12.7.1 above.

In the Court of Appeal, Ackner LJ considered whether the council's behaviour was irrational in the *Wednesbury* sense (see 13.1 above) in the following terms:

> Can it be said in the circumstances of this case that no reasonable local authority could properly conclude that temporarily banning from the use of their recreation ground an important local rugger club, which declined to condemn a South African tour and declined actively to discourage its members from participating therein, could promote good relations between persons of different racial groups? ... In my judgment, it would be quite wrong to categorise as perverse the Council's decision ...

In the House of Lords, Lord Roskill was of the opinion that the council's decision *was* unreasonable in the *Wednesbury* sense. It had gone beyond persuasion and applied illegitimate pressure coupled with a threat of sanctions. Lord Roskill would equally have been prepared to hold that the council's decision was unfair, within the meaning of the third of the principles stated by Lord Diplock in the *GCHQ* case (see 14.1 below).

Q Considering *Wednesbury* unreasonableness, Ackner LJ and Lord Roskill ask themselves the same question and reach diametrically opposed answers. Does the *Wednesbury* test appear diminished in value as a result?

Champion v Chief Constable of Gwent (1990) HL

The appellant, a police officer, was elected a school governor. He was refused permission by his chief constable to attend meetings of the appointments sub-committee in duty time, or to serve on the committee. The refusal of permission purported to be pursuant to paragraph 1 of Schedule 2 to the Police Regulations 1979, which required a member of a police force 'at all times [to] abstain from any activity which is likely to interfere with the impartial discharge of his duties or which is likely to give rise to the impression amongst members of the public that it may so interfere; and in particular a member of a police force shall not take any active part in politics'. The chief constable took the view that the appellant might have information about a candidate for appointment which he had obtained only because of his position as a police constable. He concluded first, that were this known to the candidate, the latter might suppose that the appellant had unfairly used this knowledge to prevent his appointment, and this would in turn give rise to an impression amongst members of the public that the appellant's activities as a member of the appointments sub-committee would interfere with the impartial discharge of his duties as a police officer. Second, the appellant might be embarrassed by his inability to pass such information to other members of the committee without the chief constable's permission. The chief constable indicated that permission would never be given. Further, he feared for the reputation of the police force were the appellant to become involved in controversial decision-making. The judge at first instance and the Court of Appeal refused the application for judicial review. The appellant appealed to the House of Lords.

Held (by a majority), that the appeal would be allowed. Lord Griffiths was of opinion that the chief constable had failed to give any weight to the use of the word 'likely' in the regulations, and so had relied on that prohibition for a purpose for which it had never been intended. Lord Ackner stated that he could find nothing irrational or perverse in the chief constable's decision. Lord Lowry concluded that the decision was so unreasonable that no reasonable chief constable could ever have come to it, but continued:

> The use of this stark language may be a salutary reminder of the heavy burden assumed by those who would attack administrative decisions, but I regret the identification which it implies of unreasonableness with the decision-maker as well as with the decision ... When the decision is made by a statutory authority or a public officer, I feel that it would be more becoming and more accurate to condemn (where that step must be taken) a decision 'so unreasonable that no statutory authority/public officer [to be specified] *acting reasonably* could ever have come to it', because it by no means follows that the authority or officer concerned has not in the past behaved or will not in future behave in the most reasonable way imaginable. The present case may be a case in point.

R v Ministry of Defence, ex parte Smith and others (1996) CA

The appellants were three servicemen and one service-woman, who had been discharged (towards the end of 1994) from the Armed Forces on the ground that they were homosexuals. Their discharge took place pursuant to a Ministry of Defence policy which stated 'Service personnel who are known to be homosexual or who engage in homosexual activity are administratively discharged from the Armed Forces'. The operation of the policy was thus non-discretionary. Together with all legislation affecting the Armed Forces it was reviewed every five years by a Select Committee of the House of Commons. The last review had taken place in 1991, when the Committee declined to recommend the policy's alteration. The appellants challenged the lawfulness of their discharge on the ground that it was irrational, contrary to the European Convention on Human Rights, and contrary to the EC directive on equal treatment of men and women (76/207). The Divisional Court refused their application, noting that when exercising its 'secondary' judgment on an irrationality challenge it was bound, even within a human rights context, to act with some reticence. There was 'still room for two views' on the merits of the policy, and it could not therefore be stigmatised as irrational. In the opinion of Simon Brown LJ the days of the policy were numbered; Curtis J disagreed, holding that the applications failed on their merits as well as in law. The appellant appealed to the Court of Appeal.

Held, dismissing the appeals, that the policy could not be stigmatised as irrational at the time when the appellants were discharged. Sir Thomas Bingham MR so stated despite finding the appellants' arguments of very considerable cogency. At the time of the discharge, the policy had support both from Parliament and from those to whom the Ministry of Defence looked for advice. The argument based on the European Convention was regarded, in the context of domestic law, as supporting the irrationality challenge, rather than as an independent ground for impugning an exercise of administrative discretion. The Equal Treatment Directive was not relevant, since it dealt with discrimination on the ground of gender, not sexual orientation. Sir Thomas Bingham MR approved the following test for irrationality, proposed by counsel for three of the applicants:

> The court may not interfere with the exercise of an administrative discretion on substantive grounds save where the court is satisfied that the decision is unreasonable in the sense that it is beyond the range of responses open to a reasonable decision-maker.

Q Where a discretion exists, does the law allow its exercise to be determined by a policy operated without regard to exceptional circumstances? Is there a distinction to be drawn between disciplinary and other policies?

13.3 The test as applied to decisions approved by the Commons

Nottinghamshire County Council v Secretary of State for the Environment (1986) HL

The Council sought judicial review of guidance on expenditure issued by the Secretary of State. The guidance was framed with reference to a notional standard expenditure known as 'grant-related expenditure' (GRE). The guidance differentiated between authorities which had budgeted at or below GRE in the preceding year, and those which had budgeted above the previous year's GRE. The Council claimed that the guidance did not comply with a requirement in the Local Government Planning and Land Act (LGPLA) 1980 in that it was not framed by reference to principles applicable to all local authorities. The Council further claimed that the guidance was unreasonable because it was disproportionately disadvantageous to certain authorities. Pursuant to s 60 of the LGPLA 1980 the guidance had been laid before the House of Commons and approved by a resolution of the House.

Held, holding for the Secretary of State on both arguments, that guidance might validly differentiate between different authorities on the basis of their past expenditure records. Giving his opinion on the Council's second submission, Lord Scarman refused to examine the detail of the guidance or its consequences. By the Commons approval procedure enacted in s 60 of the LGPLA 1980, Parliament had effectively made one of its Houses responsible for judging the guidance. The court's power of review was therefore diminished in so far as it overlapped with that function. *Per* Lord Scarman:

> Such an examination by the court would be justified only if a prima facie case were to be shown for holding that the Secretary of State has acted in bad faith, or for an improper motive, or that the consequences of his guidance were so absurd that he must have taken leave of his senses. The evidence comes nowhere near establishing any of these propositions.

Q Is Lord Scarman intending to restate the *Wednesbury* unreasonableness test when he refers to such absurdity that the decision maker must have taken leave of his senses, or is this formulation appropriate only in the particular circumstances of the case? See *Ex parte Hammersmith and Fulham LBC* (1991) below.

R v Secretary of State for the Environment, *ex parte* Hammersmith and Fulham London Borough Council (1991) HL

As a consequence of decisions by the Secretary of State under the Local Government Finance Act 1988 to impose budgetary restrictions on certain local authorities, each would be required to make proportionate reductions in the level of its community charge. The local authorities sought judicial review of the Secretary of State's decision on the grounds of illegality, irrationality, and procedural impropriety.

Held, rejecting the Councils' application on all grounds, that the restrictions placed on the scope of judicial review in the *Nottinghamshire* case were equally appropriate here. *Per* Lord Bridge:

> The restriction which the Nottinghamshire case ... imposes on the scope of judicial review operates only when the court has first determined that the ministerial action in question does not contravene the requirements of the statute, whether express or implied, and only then declares that, since the statute has conferred a power on the Secretary of State which involves the formulation and the implementation of national economic policy and which can only take effect with the approval of the House of Commons, it is not open to challenge on the grounds of irrationality short of the extremes of bad faith, improper motive or manifest absurdity. Both the constitutional propriety and the good sense of this restriction seem to me to be clear enough. The formulation and the implementation of national economic policy are matters depending essentially on political

judgment ... If the decisions have been taken in good faith within the four corners of the Act, the merits of the policy underlying the decisions are not susceptible to review by the courts and the courts would be exceeding their proper function if they presumed to condemn the policy as unreasonable.

14 The grounds for judicial review: procedural impropriety

14.1 General definition of the principle

Council of Civil Service Unions v Minister for the Civil Service (1985) HL
Facts: see 15.5.1 below.
Per Lord Diplock:

> I have described the third head [of judicial review] as 'procedural impropriety' rather than failure to observe basic rules of natural justice or failure to act with procedural fairness towards the person who will be affected by the decision. This is because susceptibility to judicial review under this head covers also failure by an administrative tribunal to observe procedural rules that are expressly laid down in the legislative instrument by which its jurisdiction is conferred, even where such failure does not involve any denial of natural justice.

14.2 Express procedural requirements

Howard v Bodington (1877)
Section 9 of the Public Worship Regulation Act 1874 provided that where a bishop received a complaint about any incumbent of his diocese, he should transmit a copy to the person complained of within 21 days of receiving it, unless satisfied that proceedings should be taken no further. The archbishop, acting on behalf of a bishop, received a complaint but failed to forward it as required by s 9.

Held, that the requirement was imperative (mandatory), and that the subsequent proceedings were therefore void.
Per Lord Penzance:

> I believe that as far as any rule is concerned, you cannot safely go further than that in each case you must look to the subject-matter; consider the importance of the provision that has been disregarded, and the relation of that provision to the general object intended to be secured by the Act; and upon a review of the case in that aspect decide whether the matter is what is called imperative or only directory.

14.2.1 Rigid and flexible approaches to mandatory and directory requirements

Bradbury v Enfield London Borough Council (1967) CA

By s 13 of the Education Act 1944, an education authority which planned to reorganise its schools had to give notice of its plans by posting details of them at or near the main gates of schools and by publishing them in the local press, 'and in such other manner as appears to be desirable for giving publicity to the notice'. The Council, which planned to reorganise its schools along comprehensive lines, failed to give notice of its intentions to the public. Local ratepayers obtained an injunction to prevent the Council implementing its plans until the statutory procedure had been followed.

Held, dismissing the Council's appeal, that the injunction had been properly granted despite the chaos which it would cause. The notice requirements were mandatory. *Per* Danckwerts J:

... in cases of this kind it is imperative that the procedure laid down in the relevant statute should be properly observed. The provisions of statutes in this respect are supposed to provide safeguards for Her Majesty's subjects. Public bodies and Ministers must be compelled to observe the law; and it is essential that the bureaucracy be kept in its place.

Coney v Choice (1975)

By s 13 of the Education Act 1944, an education authority which planned to reorganise its schools had to give notice of its plans by posting details of them at or near the main gates of schools and by publishing details of them in the local press, 'and in such other manner as appeared to be desirable for giving publicity to the notice'. The plans were not posted in the statutorily required way at two schools in the area.

Held, that the specific requirements were only directory. Templeman J construed the object of the legislative provisions to be that 'notice should be published in a manner designed to show a representative number of people what their rights are'. This object was mandatory. The notice provided had achieved substantial compliance with this object, so that no substantial prejudice would have been suffered by those for whose benefit the provisions had been made.

Q Do you consider that Templeman J gave expression to the intention of the legislature when he chose to regard its express requirements as merely directory, and his own construction of its objects as mandatory?

14.2.2 The gravity and relevance of the breach alleged

London & Clydeside Estates Ltd v Aberdeen District Council (1980) HL

By s 25 of the Land Compensation (Scotland) Act 1963 an authority which compulsorily purchased land was to provide a certificate at the request of its owner stating the uses for which planning permission might have been granted in respect of the land had it not been compulsorily acquired for a different purpose. The certificate was required to state that the owner had a right of appeal within one month to the Secretary of State. The Council issued a certificate to the company in which it stated that the grant of planning permission would have been limited to the purpose for which the land was in fact being compulsorily acquired. The certificate did not mention the right of appeal. The company's eventual appeal was rejected on the ground that it was out of time. It renewed its appeal to the House of Lords, and sought to impugn the validity of the certificate, arguing that the notice of appeal requirement was mandatory. The Council claimed that the requirement was merely directory, and fell either into the category of directory requirements with which substantial compliance was necessary, or into a secondary category of merely regulatory requirements.

Held, that the requirement was mandatory. *Per* Lord Hailsham:

When Parliament lays down a statutory requirement for the exercise of legal authority it expects its authority to be obeyed down to the minutest of details. But what the courts have to decide in a particular case is the legal consequence of non-compliance on the rights of the subject viewed in the light of a concrete state of facts and a continuing chain of events. It may be that what the courts are faced with is not so much a stark choice of alternatives but a spectrum of possibilities in which one compartment or description fades gradually into another. At one end of this spectrum there may be cases in which a fundamental obligation may have been so outrageously and flagrantly ignored or defied that the subject may safely ignore what has been done and treat it as having no legal consequences upon himself. In such a case, if the defaulting authority seeks to rely on its action it may be that the subject is entitled to use the defect in procedure simply as a shield or defence without having taken any positive action of his own. At the other end of the spectrum, the defect in procedure may be so nugatory or trivial that the authority can safely proceed without remedial action, confident that, if the subject is so misguided as to rely on the fault, the courts will decline to listen to his complaint. But in a very great number of cases, it may be in a majority of them, it may be necessary for a subject, in order to safeguard himself, to go to the court for declaration of his rights, the grant of which may well be discretionary, and by the like token it may be wise for an authority (as it certainly would have been here) to do everything in its power to remedy the fault in its procedure so as not to deprive the subject of his due or themselves of their power to act. In such cases, though language like 'mandatory', 'directory', 'void', 'voidable', 'nullity' and so forth may be helpful in argument, it may be misleading in effect if relied on to show that the courts, in deciding the consequences of a defect in the exercise of power, are necessarily bound to fit the facts of a particular case and a developing chain of events into rigid legal categories or to stretch or cramp them onto a bed of Procrustes invented by lawyers for the purposes of convenient exposition. As I have said, the case does not really arise here, since we are in the presence of total non-compliance with a requirement which I have held to be mandatory.

14.3 Natural justice

14.3.1 *Audi alteram partem* – the right to a fair hearing

The application of the principle

Cooper v Board of Works for the Wandsworth District (1863)
Statute provided that a person intending to build in Wandsworth should give seven days' notice to the board. Cooper gave insufficient notice, and the board sent workmen at night to demolish Cooper's half-built house. Cooper claimed damages for trespass, and argued that he should have been given notice of the board's intention to demolish his house, and the opportunity to argue against it.

Held, that the board had a discretion whether or not to demolish, and that Cooper should have been given the opportunity to excuse his apparent default and to persuade the board to look favourably on his case. Although there were no positive words in the statute which required this, it was founded on the plainest principles of justice.

Per Byles J:

... a long course of decisions, beginning with *Dr Bentley's* case (1723), and ending with some very recent cases, establish that, although there are no positive words in a statute requiring that the party shall be heard, yet the justice of the common law will supply the omission of the legislature.

The demise of a rigid distinction between judicial and administrative decisions

Ridge v Baldwin (1964) HL
Ridge, the Chief Constable of Brighton, was charged with conspiracy to obstruct the course of justice. The trial judge, directing his acquittal, suggested that the Brighton police force required new and better leadership. The local watch committee met and decided that Ridge should be dismissed. Ridge was not given notice of the meeting. His solicitor requested and was granted permission to address a later meeting of the committee which nevertheless resolved to adhere to the earlier decision. Ridge appealed on the grounds, *inter alia*, that the committee's decision was void for breach of the rules of natural justice. The Court of Appeal rejected his appeal on the ground that the decision to dismiss was an executive act, and that the committee was therefore not bound to hold an inquiry of a judicial or quasi-judicial nature.

Held, allowing the appeal, that a consistent line of authority would apply the requirement to observe the rules of natural justice to the present case. A tendency had more recently developed for the effect of those authorities to be limited. That was due in part to wartime circumstances in which the principles of natural justice had been neglected, and in part to a misunderstanding of a passage from the judgment of Atkin LJ in *R v Electricity Commissioners, ex parte London Electricity Joint Committee Co* (1924) (see 10.1 above). The duty to act judicially referred to in that case was in fact to be inferred from the nature of the decision-maker's power.

Chief Constable of the North Wales Police v Evans (1982) (HL)

The respondent, a probationary police constable, was informed by the Chief Constable of his force that if he did not resign, he would be discharged. The Chief Constable had decided to dispense with the respondent's services on the basis of rumours about his private life, but the respondent was at no stage told of the matters alleged against him, or given an opportunity to be heard in response to them. At first instance and in the Court of Appeal, the Chief Constable's decision was held to be in breach of natural justice. He appealed to the House of Lords, and the respondent cross-appealed, seeking substantive relief in the form of an order of *mandamus* to compel his reinstatement.

Held, dismissing the Chief Constable's appeal, that the treatment meted out to the respondent had been little short of outrageous. However, the grant of the order of *mandamus* sought would border on a usurpation of the Chief Constable's powers, and a declaration stating the rights of the respondent would be granted in its place. The statement of Lord Denning MR in the Court of Appeal, to the effect that the respondent was entitled not only to a fair hearing but also to a fair and reasonable decision by the Chief Constable was disapproved. *Per* Lord Hailsham LC:

> The function of the court is to see that lawful authority is not abused by unfair treatment and not to attempt itself the task entrusted to that authority by law ... I am not sure whether Lord Denning MR really intended his remarks to be construed in such a way as to permit the court to examine, as for instance in the present case, the reasoning of the subordinate authority with a view to substituting its own opinion. If so, I do not think this is a correct statement of principle. The purpose of judicial review is to ensure that the individual receives fair treatment, and not to ensure that the authority after according fair treatment, reaches on a matter which it is authorised or enjoined by law to decide for itself a conclusion which is correct in the eyes of the court.

The standard of the duty continues to vary according to the rights at stake

McInnes v Onslow-Fane (1978)

The plaintiff had held various licences in connection with boxing in the past, but all had been withdrawn, and he had since made several unsuccessful applications for a trainer's licence. The plaintiff applied again to the British Boxing Board of Control for a trainer's licence, and requested an oral hearing and advance notice of anything which might militate against a favourable outcome. The board refused his application without giving him a hearing, and gave him no reasons for the refusal of the licence. He sought, *inter alia*, a declaration that the board had acted in breach of natural justice and unfairly.

Held, dismissing the plaintiff's summons, that the requirements of natural justice or the duty to act fairly would vary according to the type of decision to be made. The present case did not involve the forfeiture of an existing right for some reason: in such cases there would be a right to an unbiased tribunal, a right to notice of the charges and a right to be heard in answer to them. The plaintiff had no legitimate expectation that his application would be granted. His case concerned the simple refusal of a benefit, without more. In fulfilment of its duty to act fairly in these circumstances, the board was under a duty only to reach an honest conclusion without bias, and not in pursuit of any capricious policy. In the absence of anything to suggest that the board's decision had been affected by any impropriety, there was no obligation on the board to give the plaintiff even the gist of its reasons for refusing his application.

Loss of common law procedural rights
The applicant's past conduct may disentitle him to be heard

Cinnamond v British Airports Authority (1980) CA
The authority had statutory power to make by-laws regulating the use of Heathrow Airport and the conduct of persons within the Airport. The appellants, who were minicab drivers, had regularly overcharged their customers, had convictions under the by-laws for offences of loitering, and had not paid fines imposed by the authority. The authority wrote to them informing them that they were banned until further notice from entering the airport save as bona fide passengers. The appellants sought to overturn the ban. They argued, *inter alia*, that they should have been given the opportunity to be heard before the ban was imposed.

Held, dismissing the appeal, that if the appellants had been of good character, fairness would have demanded that they be heard. However, it must have been apparent to them why the ban was ordered, and their record of persistent bad behaviour had disentitled them to a legitimate expectation of a hearing. *Per* Shaw LJ:

... it is clear on the history of this matter that the drivers put themselves so far outside the limits of tolerable conduct as to disentitle themselves to expect that any further representations on their part could have any influence or relevance.

The merits of the subject's substantive case go to the discretion of the court

Glynn v Keele University (1971)

A student was discovered sunbathing naked on university premises. Without being given any notice of the charges against him or any hearing, he was fined £10 by the vice-chancellor and excluded from the university for a year. The student learnt about the action taken against him only when he received a letter detailing the penalties imposed.

Held, that the vice-chancellor had been acting in a quasi-judicial capacity and that there had been a clear breach of the rules of natural justice. However, in the opinion of Pennycuick VC, the offence was a grave one, the penalties imposed were appropriate, and the student had put forward no specific justification for what he did. Had he been granted a hearing, he could only have put forward a plea in mitigation. The fact that he had been deprived of the opportunity to throw himself on the mercy of the vice-chancellor was not sufficient to justify setting aside a perfectly proper decision. A remedy would be refused in the exercise of the court's discretion.

Q Is this result capable of reconciliation with *Cooper v Board of Works for the Wandsworth District* (1863) 14.3.1 above?

Loss of procedural rights attributable to the failure of the subject's legal advisers

Al-Mehdawi v Secretary of State for the Home Department (1990) HL

The respondent, an Iraqi citizen, was notified in March 1985 that the Secretary of State had resolved to make a deportation order against him, following the expiry of his leave to remain in the UK and the refusal of his application for an extension of time. He instructed solicitors to appeal against the decision to an immigration adjudicator. Neither he nor his solicitors attended the hearing, and the adjudicator decided the appeal against him on the papers. He failed to lodge an appeal against the adjudicator's decision within time. Subsequently, it emerged that the solicitors had sent notice of the hearing date and of the adjudicator's decision to the wrong address. The respondent sought judicial review of the adjudicator's decision on the basis that he had been denied a hearing. The High Court and the Court of Appeal held for the respondent; the Secretary of State appealed to the House of Lords arguing that the rules of natural justice concerned only the propriety of the procedure adopted by the decision-maker.

Held, allowing the appeal, that in private law the litigant who had lost the opportunity to have his case heard through the default of his own advisers could not complain that he had been the victim of a procedural impropriety. No principle had been suggested which would lead to a different conclusion in the field of public law. The decision of the Court of

Appeal could only be supported at the cost of seriously undermining the principle of finality in decision-making.

Reduction in procedural rights in an emergency

R v Secretary of State for Transport, *ex parte* Pegasus Holdings (1988)
Facts: see 17.2 below.

Schiemann J declared that he was content to proceed on the basis that the rules of natural justice did apply, but that in the words of counsel for the respondent, in such an emergency as the present, with a provisional suspension being all that the court was concerned with, one was at the low end of the scale of duties of fairness. The Civil Aviation Authority had admittedly taken some time to refer the matter to the Secretary of State, but that delay would not lessen the appropriateness of the speedy action taken by the Secretary of State.

The inherent flexibility of procedural rights and the duty to act fairly in the circumstances

In re HK (An Infant) (1967)
Under the Commonwealth Immigrants Act 1962, the applicant's right to enter the country was dependent on his showing that he was less than 16 years old. It was argued on behalf of the applicant that the immigration officer was under a duty to conform to the rules of natural justice. Thus the applicant should have had the opportunity to persuade the immigration officer that he was under 16.

Held, dismissing the application, that an immigration officer was indeed under such a duty, but that it amounted to a duty to act fairly in the circumstances. It was not a duty to hold a full-scale inquiry, or to adopt judicial process and procedure. The applicant had known of what he had had to satisfy the authorities, and had been given ample opportunity to do so.

Specific aspects of the principle: the right to cross-examine witnesses

Bushell v Secretary of State for the Environment (1981) HL
Numerous parties objected to proposals to build stretches of motorway. The Secretary of State was statutorily obliged to hold an inquiry into the objections. The objectors sought to challenge statistical methods used by the Minister's department to predict future levels of traffic. The inspector who conducted the inquiry permitted the objectors to call expert witnesses to give evidence criticising the department's methodology, but he did not permit cross-examination of the departmental officials. The Secretary of State, acting on the basis of the inspector's report, approved the construction of the roads. The objectors exercised a statutory right of challenge to the decision on the grounds that the inspector had been wrong in law to disallow cross-examination. The Court of Appeal (by a majority) allowed their appeal. The Secretary of State appealed to the House of Lords.

Held, allowing the appeal (by a majority), that the question whether it was unfair to disallow cross-examination depended on all the circumstances of the inquiry. It could not be said to be unfair *per se* since it was not accorded in many legal systems, but was peculiar to the common law conception of procedure. A distinction was to be drawn between areas of government policy, with regard to which there was no discretion to allow cross-examination, and other matters, in regard to which there was a discretion. The choice of method used by the department to assess future traffic needs fell within a 'grey area' between the two categories, but was best regarded as a matter of policy which it was not appropriate to investigate on the limited facts of a single inquiry. Further, in the present case the matters on which the right to cross-examine was sought were very complicated. No one who was not an expert in the subject could form a useful judgment on it. The evidence of the expert witnesses called by the objectors was fully recorded for the consideration of the Secretary of State.

Per Lord Edmund-Davies (dissenting):

> The general law may, I think, be summarised in this way: (a) in holding an administrative inquiry (such as that presently being considered), the inspector was performing quasi judicial duties; (b) he must therefore discharge them in accordance with the rules of natural justice; (c) natural justice requires that objectors (no less than departmental representatives) be allowed to cross-examine witnesses called for the other side on all relevant matters, be they matters of fact or matters of expert opinion; (d) in the exercise of jurisdiction outside the field of criminal law, the only restrictions on cross-examination are those general and well-defined exclusionary rules which govern the admissibility of relevant evidence ... beyond those restrictions there is *no* discretion on the civil side to exclude cross-examination on relevant matters.

Specific aspects of the principle: the discretion to allow legal representation to prisoners

R v Secretary of State for the Home Department, *ex parte* Tarrant and another; R v Wormwood Scrubs Prison Board of Visitors, *ex parte* Anderson and others (1985)

The applicants were prisoners who were charged with grave offences against prison discipline. They sought legal representation at inquiries into the charges to be held by prison boards of visitors. In each case the request was refused. The applicants sought judicial review of the decisions to refuse legal representation on the grounds either that they were entitled to it or, alternatively, that the boards had a discretion to permit legal representation and should have exercised that discretion in the applicants' favour.

Held, allowing the application, that the court was bound by the authority of the Court of Appeal in *Fraser v Mudge* (1975) to hold that the applicants had no right to legal representation. However, a prison board of visitors had a discretion to permit legal representation. In deciding how to exercise that discretion, a board should take into account:

(1) the seriousness of the charge and of the potential penalty;
(2) whether any points of law were likely to arise in the proceedings;
(3) the prisoner's capacity in intellectual and educational terms to present his case;
(4) the prisoner's difficulties in contacting witnesses;
(5) the need for reasonable speed in making the adjudication; and
(6) the need for fairness as between prisoners or as between prisoners and prison officers.

The failure by the boards to consider the exercise of the discretion to allow legal representation was in all cases a substantial infringement of the applicants' rights, whether or not, if the discretion had been exercised, it would have been exercised in the applicants' favour.

Specific aspects of the principle: the right to an oral hearing

Lloyd v McMahon (1987)

The appellants were the majority group on Liverpool City Council. They purposely delayed setting a rate for the year 1985–86 in the hope of increasing the city's grant from central government. The district auditor notified the appellants that he proposed to consider whether to certify that the Council's loss should fall on them in consequence of their wilful default. The auditor's notice stated that the appellants could make written representations to him before he reached a decision. The appellants argued before the House of Lords that the auditor's decision to issue a certificate was vitiated by his failure to offer them an oral hearing.

Held, dismissing the appeal, that the auditor, like any other decision maker, was under a duty to act fairly. It was not unfair for the auditor to reach a decision on the basis of the written material submitted to him by the appellants. *Per* Lord Bridge:

... the so-called rules of natural justice are not engraved on tablets of stone. To use the phrase which better expresses the underlying concept, what the requirements of fairness demand when any body, domestic, administrative or judicial, has to make a decision which will affect the rights of individuals, depends on the character of the decision-making body, the kind of decision it has to make and the statutory or other framework in which it operates. In particular, it is well established that when a statute has conferred on any body the power to make decisions affecting individuals, the courts will not only require the procedure prescribed by the statute to be followed, but will readily imply so much and no more to be introduced by way of additional procedural safeguards as will ensure the attainment of fairness.

Specific aspects of the principle: the degree to which the applicant must be told the case against him

R v Gaming Board for Great Britain, *ex parte* Benaim and Khaida (1970) CA

The applicants, who were the joint managing directors of Crockfords Gaming Club, unsuccessfully applied to the Gaming Board for a licence to carry on their business. Under the Gaming Act 1968, the Board had to be satisfied of the applicants' willingness and ability to run the gaming in accordance with the provisions of the Act, and to do so fairly and properly and without disorder or disturbance. The applicants sought orders of *certiorari* to quash the decision to refuse the licence, and *mandamus* requiring the Board to provide them with sufficient information to enable them to answer the case against them.

Held, dismissing the application, that the Board had put before the applicants all the information which had led to their suitability being doubted, and had thereby discharged its duty to act fairly. It was not possible to lay down rigid rules as to when the principles of natural justice applied, nor as to their scope or extent. All depended on the subject matter of the decision in question. Here the Board was not depriving the applicants of an office, or depriving them of their property. In the circumstances, it was enough that the applicants be given notice in broad terms of the Board's opinion of their suitability and the opportunity to argue in their own favour. It was not necessary or desirable for the applicants to be told the sources of the Board's information.

14.4 *Nemo iudex in causa sua:* the rule against bias

14.4.1 The nature of the rule

R v Sussex Justices, *ex parte* McCarthy (1924)

A motorist appeared before a bench of magistrates on a charge of dangerous driving. A solicitor, as acting clerk to the justices, accompanied them when they retired to consider their decision. It was proved that the justices did not in fact consult the solicitor during their deliberations, and that the solicitor did not proffer any comments prejudicial to the accused. The same solicitor had however acted against the accused in an earlier civil case arising from the same motoring incident.

Held, that the conviction would be quashed, since the circumstances might have created a suspicion that there had been an improper interference with the course of justice. *Per* Lord Hewart CJ:

> It is not merely of importance, but of fundamental importance that justice should not only be done, but should manifestly and undoubtedly be seen to be done.

14.4.2 Pecuniary interest

Dimes v Grand Junction Canal Proprietors (1852) HL

Dimes, who claimed an interest in land through which the Grand Junction Canal passed, had for many years been involved in litigation with the canal proprietors. The case came before the Lord Chancellor, Lord Cottenham, who affirmed decrees made in favour of the proprietors. Dimes later discovered that the Lord Chancellor held shares in the canal company. He claimed that the Lord Chancellor had been judge in his own cause, and that his order was accordingly void.

Held, that the Lord Chancellor's order was not void but voidable, and would be set aside. No one could suppose that he could have been influenced by his interest in the company, but the rule that no man might be a judge in his own cause was of such importance that it should be seen to be upheld even in these circumstances.

The House of Lords then considered the substantive issue on its merits, and confirmed the decrees made by the Lord Chancellor.

Q If the order of the Lord Chancellor was tainted neither by bias or by the appearance of bias, was the court correct to set it aside?

14.4.3 Non-pecuniary interest

Metropolitan Properties v Lannon (1969) CA

Mr Lannon, a solicitor, sat as chairman of a rent assessment committee which fixed a 'fair rent' for flats in Oakwood Court, a block of flats in West Kensington. The rent fixed was unusually low. Mr Lannon lived with his father, who was the tenant of a flat in a similar block. The landlords of the two blocks of flats were companies associated in the same group. Mr Lannon had advised his father about a fair rent for his flat, and had advised other tenants in his father's block in connection with disputes with their landlord. The landlord of Oakwood Court alleged that since the determination of the rents for Oakwood Court would have an effect on the rents in the second block, Mr Lannon's decision was tainted by an appearance of bias. It was not alleged that he had actually been biased.

Held, granting *certiorari* to set aside the decision of the rent assessment committee, that Mr Lannon had effectively been acting against the landlords. Although, realistically, he could not be said to have a pecuniary interest in the subject matter of the committee's decision, he should not have sat on the committee. *Per* Lord Denning MR: '... there must appear to be a real likelihood of bias. Surmise or conjecture is not enough.'

Edmund-Davies LJ held that a reasonable suspicion of bias was enough to require that the decision be set aside.

R v Gough (1993) HL

The appellant appealed against conviction on the ground that there had been a serious irregularity in his trial. A juror had realised, after conviction and sentence, that she lived next door to the appellant's brother. The appellant argued that the test for bias was whether a reasonable and fair-minded person would reasonably suspect bias. The Crown argued that the test was whether there was a real likelihood of bias.

Held, that on the test applied by the Court of Appeal – namely, whether there had been a real danger of bias – the appeal failed and would be dismissed. The reference to a real danger should be taken to connote a possibility rather than a probability of bias, and if the 'real likelihood' test was to be understood as requiring proof of bias on a balance of probabilities, it was too rigorous. The real danger test should be applicable in all cases of apparent bias, whether concerned with justices or members of other inferior tribunals, or with jurors or with arbitrators. It was not necessary, in formulating the appropriate test, to require that the court should look at the matter through the eyes of a reasonable man, because the court in such cases personified the reasonable man.

Q Do you consider that the views of a court and of a reasonable man regarding the possibility of a decision-maker's bias would always coincide?

R v Inner West London Coroner, *ex parte* Dallaglio (1994) CA

During the adjournment of a coroner's inquests into the deaths of passengers on board the Thames launch '*Marchioness*', an application was made to the coroner for an exhumation order in respect of the body of one of the deceased. The application was unsuccessful, but attracted press attention. In the course of an attempt to defuse the situation, the coroner allegedly described the applicant as 'unhinged', and other relatives of the deceased as 'mentally unwell'. Another relative of one of the deceased now applied for judicial review of the coroner's decisions (a) not to remove himself on the grounds of apparent bias, and (b) not to resume the inquests. At first instance, the Divisional Court refused the application.

Held, allowing the appeal, that it was impossible to discount the possibility that the coroner had unconsciously allowed himself to be influenced against the applicant and other of the relatives by a feeling of hostility towards them. In the judgment of Sir Thomas Bingham MR, *R v Gough* recognised three classes of case in which bias might arise for consideration:

The first class comprises cases of actual bias. These are cases in which a decision-maker is shown, in fact and for whatever reason, to have been influenced in his decision-making by prejudice, predilection or personal interest. Such cases are very rare ... the law is very clear and very emphatic: where a decision is shown to have been tainted by actual bias it cannot stand.

The second class comprises cases in which the decision-maker has a direct pecuniary interest, however small, unless negligible, in the subject matter of the decision. In such cases it is irrelevant that the interest has had no effect on the decision in question. The nature of the interest is such that public confidence in the administration of justice requires that the decision should not stand ... It is rather as if, in such cases, the law presumes bias.

The third class comprises cases in which there is no actual bias and no direct pecuniary interest giving rise to a presumption of bias ... if despite the appearance of bias the court is able to examine all the relevant material and satisfy itself that that there was no danger of the alleged bias having in fact caused injustice, the impugned decision will be allowed to stand.

14.4.4 Decision-making power coexisting with policy or inalienable interests

R v Amber Valley District Council, *ex parte* Jackson (1985)
The applicant was a member of a local pressure group which opposed a proposed amusement park development. She sought an order of prohibition to prevent the respondent district Council from considering an application for planning permission on the ground that its decision was likely to be biased, unfair, and contrary to the duty imposed on it by s 29 of the Town and Country Planning Act 1971 to take into account all representations received relating to the application. The same political party had a majority both on the district and the county Councils, and its county group had already resolved to support the planning application. The Council stated in an affidavit that it would take into account all material considerations.

Held, dismissing the application, that the fact that the Council had a policy relating to the matter did not disqualify it from adjudicating on the planning application. The Council had an obligation to be fair and carefully to consider the evidence; in the light of the Council's affidavit the court was not prepared to doubt that it would discharge that duty. *Per* Woolf J:

The rules of fairness or natural justice cannot be regarded as being rigid. They must alter in accordance with the context. Thus in the case of highways, the department can be both the promoting authority and the determining authority. When this happens, of course any reasonable man would regard the department as being disposed towards the outcome of the inquiry. The department is under an obligation to be fair and to carefully consider the evidence given before the inquiry but the fact that it has a policy in the matter does not entitle the court to intervene. So in this case I do not consider that the fact that there is a declaration of policy by the majority group can disqualify a district Council from adjudicating on a planning application. It may mean that the outcome of the planning application is likely to be favourable to an applicant and therefore unfavourable to objectors. However, Parliament has seen fit to lay down that it is the local authority which have the power to make the decision ...

R v Sevenoaks District Council, *ex parte* Terry (1985)

The Council's planning sub-committee recommended acceptance of a developer's proposal to lease a site from the Council. The developer subsequently applied to the Council for planning permission and was granted it. The applicant, a local ratepayer, sought *certiorari* to quash the decision to grant permission on the grounds that the Council had regarded itself as committed to granting the permission, or because it would appear to a reasonable man that the Council had regarded itself as being so committed.

Held, dismissing the application, that the principle of *Metropolitan Properties v Lannon* (1969) (see 14.4.3 above) was not applicable to the case. *Per* Glidewell J:

> Of course, the Council must act honestly and fairly, but it is not uncommon for a local authority to be obliged to make a decision relating to land or other property in which it has an interest. In such a situation, the application of the rule designed to ensure that a judicial officer does not appear to be biased would, in my view, often produce an administrative impasse.

The question in cases of the present type was whether, before making its decision, the authority had acted in such a way that it was clear that it could not properly exercise its discretion. Here, the Council had not done so, and it was unnecessary for the court to go further to consider what the opinion of a reasonable man would be.

R v S of S for Environment, *ex parte* Kirkstall Valley Campaign (1996)

In its capacity as local planning authority, an urban development Corporation granted outline planning permission to a rugby club for a retail development on part of its land. The chairman of the corporation had an undeclared interest in other land which would materially increase in value if the club were able to move premises. This interest had not been declared. Other members of the Corporation were members, vice-presidents and the professional adviser of the club. The applicant was a community action group concerned with the interests of local residents in the development of the Kirkstall Valley. The respondent Minister, in his capacity as successor to the Corporation, argued that principles other than those laid down by the House of Lords in *R v Gough* (see 14.4.3 above) applied to non-judicial bodies. The proper test was not whether there was a real danger of bias on the part of any member of the tribunal, but whether the body as a whole could be shown to have gone beyond mere predisposition in favour of a particular course and to have predetermined it.

Held, dismissing the application, that although decisions taken in 1992 and 1993 had been vitiated by apparent bias, the decision challenged was the product of later processes which were so separate as to remain uncontaminated by the earlier flaws. Sedley J held that there was no authority to suggest that the principle in *R v Gough* was limited to judicial or quasi-judicial proceedings. It was appropriate that this should be so, given that in the modern State the interests of individuals or of the public might well be more radically affected by administrative than by judicial decisions. An individual with a personal, pecuniary or proprietory interest in the subject matter of a decision was to refrain from playing any part in its making. It was possible that the mere declaration of a disqualifying interest, followed by abstention from discussion or voting would not always be sufficient.

15 The doctrine of legitimate expectations

15.1 The emergence of the doctrine in English administrative law

Schmidt v Secretary of State for Home Affairs (1969) CA

The plaintiffs were Scientology students who had applied for an extension to their leave to remain in the UK. Their application was rejected. They sought a declaration that the refusal was *ultra vires* on the grounds that they had not been given an opportunity to be heard.

Held (*per* Lord Denning MR), that the question whether a hearing was required depended on whether the applicants had some right, interest or legitimate expectation of which it would not be fair to deprive them without hearing what they had to say. In respect of their entitlement to remain for the period originally limited they had; in respect of an extension to that period they had not.

15.2 Legitimate expectation as a means of establishing *locus standi*

O'Reilly v Mackman (1983) HL

Facts: see 9.3 above.

Per Lord Diplock:

> ... all that each applicant had was a legitimate expectation, based on his knowledge of what is the general practice, that he would be granted the maximum remission ... of one-third of his sentence if by that time no disciplinary award of forfeiture of remission had been made against him ... such legitimate expectation gave to each appellant a sufficient interest to challenge the legality of the adverse disciplinary award made against him by the board ...

15.3 The recognition of legitimate expectations

Findlay v Secretary of State for the Home Department (1984) HL

In October 1983, the Home Secretary announced his intention to abolish the joint Home Office/Parole Board committee which had formerly recommended when a life prisoner should first be considered by a local review committee for parole, and to determine that date himself in consultation with the judiciary. He further announced that prisoners sentenced for certain classes of offence would in future normally serve at least 20 years of their sentences. The appellants, who were affected by the changes in policy, sought, *inter alia*, an order of prohibition to prevent the Home Secretary from applying the new policy to them, arguing that the policy constituted a fettering of the Home Secretary's discretion and that they had a legitimate expectation of release at the date that would have been set under the previous policy.

Held, dismissing the appeals, that the adoption of the policy did not amount to a fettering of discretion since it did not preclude the consideration of individual cases, and that the expectation contended for by the appellants did not arise. *Per* Lord Scarman:

> They had good reason under the practice which had prevailed before the adoption of the new policy to expect release much earlier than became likely after its adoption ... It is said that the refusal to except them from the new policy was an unlawful act on the part of the Secretary of State in that his decision frustrated their expectation. But what was their *legitimate* expectation? Given the substance and purpose of the legislative provisions governing parole, the most that a convicted prisoner can legitimately expect is that his case will be examined individually in the light of whatever policy the Secretary of State sees fit to adopt, provided always that the adopted policy is a lawful exercise of the discretion conferred upon him by the statute.

R v Board of Inland Revenue, *ex parte* MFK Underwriting Agencies (1990)

With a view to offering an improved investment opportunity to the Lloyds market certain US banks proposed to issue index-linked US or Canadian dollar securities for the investment of US or Canadian premium income. The banks and their advisors approached the Revenue independently for confirmation that the index-linked element payable on redemption of the securities would be taxed as a capital gain, and not as income. The responses of Revenue officials indicated that they considered the index-linked element would be taxable as capital gain rather than income. The applicants purchased index-linked bonds on the basis that they would be so taxed. In fact the Revenue later decided to tax the index-linked element as income. The applicants sought judicial review of the Revenue's decision, contending that it breached their legitimate expectations, and was therefore unfair and amounted to an abuse of power.

Held, dismissing the application, that although the Revenue had informally promulgated guidelines and indicated its likely approach to the taxation question, several factors required to be proved before its responses could fetter performance of its public duty to collect taxes payable on a proper construction of the relevant law. The taxpayer would have had to have provided full details of the matter on which he sought the Revenue's ruling. He would have had to have made plain that a fully considered ruling was sought and to have specified the use to which he intended to put that ruling. The Revenue would be bound only by a ruling or statement which was clear, unambiguous and devoid of relevant qualification. In the judgment of Bingham LJ, it was one thing to ask an official of the Revenue whether he shared the taxpayer's view of a legislative provision, but quite another to ask whether the Revenue would forgo a claim to tax on any other basis.

R v Inland Revenue Commissioners, *ex parte* Unilever PLC (1996) CA

By s 393 of the Income and Corporation Taxes Act 1988, a taxpayer might make a claim for trading loss relief within two years from the end of the accounting period in which the loss was sustained 'or within such further period as the Board may allow'. For many years it had been the applicant's practice to offset trading loss against profits when submitting preliminary accounts. However, the offsetting of trading loss was expressly notified only after the finalisation of each year's accounts. As a result of the complexity of the applicant's tax affairs, this notification had fallen outside the statutory time period on thirty occasions. In respect of three recent accounting periods, the Revenue refused to allow the applicant loss relief on the ground that its claim was late. The applicant argued (a) that the preliminary accounts constituted notification of claim within the period, or (b) that in fairness the Revenue's past acquiescence debarred it from reversing its practice, and (c) that the Revenue should have exercised its statutory discretion in the applicant's favour. At first instance, the application succeeded on grounds (b) and (c).

Held, upholding the decision at first instance, that the claims had not been made within the two-year period. However, the Revenue's rejection of the applicant's claims without advance notice was so unfair as to amount to an abuse of power. It was true that the Revenue had made no clear, unambiguous and unqualified representation that it would accept late claims, nor could it be said to have acquiesced in or waived a non-compliance of which it had simply been unaware. However, the facts of the present case were unique. The entitlement to claim trading loss was a fundamental one. There was no useful purpose to be achieved by an insistence on the merely regulatory statutory time limit. The error with regard to the time limit was common to both parties, and the Revenue would presumably have alerted the applicant to its prejudicial consequences had it realised it. The tax now claimed was to be regarded as an adventitious windfall accruing to the revenue through the mistake of an honest and compliant taxpayer. In the circumstances that claim was so unfair as to amount to an abuse of power. Equally (and in the judgment of the Master of the Rolls this and the preceding point were substantially the same) the Revenue's failure to exercise its statutory discretion to extend the time limit was so unreasonable as to satisfy the public law test of irrationality.

R v Swale Borough Council and Medway Ports Authority, *ex parte* The Royal Society for the Protection of Birds (1991)

The applicant, a conservation charity with over half a million members, sought to challenge the grant of planning permission by the Council to the Authority for the 'land reclamation' of 125 acres of Lappel Bank, a site of recognised environmental importance under domestic and international law. The applicant argued, *inter alia*, that its officer Dr Clarke had received an assurance in the course of correspondence that he would be consulted on any application received, and that this legitimate expectation had been breached. The respondents contended that the assurance of consultation had been given only in the context of development proposals already received. It could not reasonably have been taken to extend to any application in the relevant location, and the absence of any immediate protest by the applicants when Dr Clarke was not consulted suggested further that he had in fact had no legitimate expectation of consultation.

Simon Brown J noted that Dr Clarke was as convinced that he had been entitled to be consulted as the respondent was that no such entitlement had arisen. The approach to such a misunderstanding being free from authority in public law, Simon Brown J adopted a contractual test; only if the reasonable bystander would regard the promise as being made in the sense contended for by the applicant would his expectation be regarded as not merely reasonable but legitimate also. On the application of this test to the facts, the applicants' contention was to be preferred. However, since they had unduly delayed so that the grant of relief would now be likely to cause substantial prejudice to third parties, their challenge was dismissed.

R v Secretary of State for the Home Department, *ex parte* Hargreaves (1996) CA

See 15.6.2 below.

15.4 Legitimate expectation as a means of securing procedural rights

Attorney General for Hong Kong v Ng Yuen Shiu (1983) PC

The government of Hong Kong announced that it was terminating its policy of not repatriating illegal immigrants from China who had reached the urban area of Hong Kong. The applicant and others, illegal immigrants of Chinese origin from Macau, sought to clarify their position. They were told by the Secretary for Security that they would be interviewed, and that each case would be treated on its own merits. A removal order was made against the applicant.

Held, that the removal order would be quashed. Although the applicant, as an illegal immigrant, had no general right to a fair hearing before a removal order was made against him, he had a legitimate expectation of a fair hearing based on what he had been told by the Secretary for Security. When a public authority had promised to follow a certain procedure, it was in the interest of good administration that it should act fairly and should implement its promise, so long as implementation did not interfere with its statutory duty. The quashing of the removal order was, however, entirely without prejudice to the making of a new order once the applicant had been heard.

15.5 Legitimate expectation as a means of securing substantive rights

R v Secretary of State for the Home Department, *ex parte* Khan (1984) CA

The applicant wished to adopt the child of a relative, living with its natural mother in Pakistan. Although the Immigration Rules did not permit a child's entry for these purposes, a Home Office circular stated that in exceptional circumstances the Secretary of State would permit entry if specified criteria were met. The criteria appeared to be satisfied in the Khans' case, but the Secretary of State applied different criteria and refused entry leave to the child. The applicant sought an order of *certiorari*.

Held, granting the order, that the Home Office circular gave the applicant a legitimate expectation that entry would be granted if the specified criteria were met. The Secretary of State was at liberty to change his policy, but before he did so *vis-à-vis* a recipient of the circular, he would be obliged to give full and serious consideration whether some overriding public interest justified the change.

R v Secretary of State for the Home Department, *ex parte* Ruddock (1987)

The applicant alleged that the Secretary of State had authorised the interception of her telephone calls in order to gain party political advantage. The criteria governing the issue of interception warrants had been published six times between 1952 and 1982, and adopted by the Secretary of State. The applicant argued that she had a legitimate expectation that the Secretary of State would abide by the criteria when deciding whether to intercept her calls, and that in her case the criteria were not met. Counsel for the Secretary of State contended that the doctrine of legitimate expectation related only to cases where an applicant's expectation was of being consulted or given the opportunity to make representations before a decision adverse to the applicant was taken. It had no relevance in the present circumstances, where the efficacy of the interception depended on the maintenance of secrecy.

Held, dismissing the application, that the applicant's evidence did not establish that the Secretary of State had acted for an improper purpose. However, the applicant did have a legitimate expectation. Although most of the cases on legitimate expectation were concerned with a right to be heard, the doctrine was not so confined. *Per* Taylor J: 'In a case where *ex hypothesi* there is no right to be heard, it may be thought the more important to fair dealing that a promise or undertaking given by a Minister as to how he will proceed should be kept.' Here the expectation arose both from an express promise given on behalf of a public authority, and from the existence of a regular practice which the applicant could reasonably expect to continue. The Secretary of State had adduced evidence that all decisions within his purview had been made in accordance with the criteria, and therefore the applicant's expectation had not been disappointed.

R v Ministry of Agriculture, Fisheries and Food, *ex parte* Hamble (Offshore) Fisheries Ltd (1995)
Facts: see 12.5.1 above.

Arguing against the substantive legitimate expectation claimed by the applicant, counsel for the respondent relied on a passage from the judgment of Laws J in *R v Secretary of Transport, ex parte Richmond upon Thames LBC* (1994) to establish that neither precedent nor principle permitted the vindication of substantive legitimate expectations. Disagreeing, Sedley J noted that *Ruddock's* case and *Findlay's* case [*obiter*] had recognised the possibility of substantive legitimate expectations, and continued:

> In my respectful view, principle as well as precedent points to these conclusions ... It is difficult to see why it is any less unfair to frustrate a legitimate expectation that something will or will not be done by the decision-maker than it it is to frustrate a legitimate expectation that the applicant will be listened to before the decision-maker decides whether to take a particular step. Such a doctrine does not risk fettering a public body in the discharge of public duties because no individual can legitimately expect the discharge of public duties to stand still or to be distorted because of that individual's peculiar position.

15.6 Considerations overriding legitimate expectations

15.6.1 National security

Council of the Civil Service Unions v Minister for the Civil Service (1985) HL
The Government Communications Headquarters (GCHQ) was responsible for the provision of intelligence to the government, and for the security of

military and official communications. Since the establishment of GCHQ in 1947, its staff had been permitted to belong to civil service trade unions, and GCHQ management had regularly consulted with the unions. Following industrial action at GCHQ, the Prime Minister (in her capacity as Minister for the Civil Service) sought to curtail staff rights of trade union membership by an instruction issued under prerogative powers for controlling the Civil Service. The CCSU sought a declaration that the Minister had acted unfairly in removing staff rights of trade union membership without consultation. The Minister argued that consultation would have provoked the very disruption and endangering of national security which her instruction was intended to terminate.

Held (proceeding on the basis that the exercise of delegated prerogative powers was justiciable), that although the staff had no legal right to prior consultation, they had a legitimate expectation to it. Such expectation might arise either from an express promise given by a public authority, or, as here, from a regular practice of consultation which the applicant could reasonably expect to continue. In the absence of evidence that an issue of national security was involved, it would have been proper to grant the declaration sought.

15.6.2 The need to preserve freedom of administrative action

R v Secretary of State for Health, *ex parte* United States Tobacco (1992)
The applicant manufactured oral snuff. In 1985, when the government was already aware of a link between oral snuff and cancer, the applicant received a government grant. At the same time the government obtained the applicant's agreement to place a health warning on its product, and not to market it to those aged less than 18 years. In 1988 the Department of Health announced that it intended to ban the manufacture of oral snuff. The applicant sought judicial review on two grounds: firstly, that the Secretary of State was in breach of a statutory duty to consult it as an affected party, and secondly, that it had a legitimate expectation that it would be permitted to continue to manufacture snuff as long as it kept to its agreement regarding marketing and the health warning.

Held that the applicant would succeed on the first ground and fail on the second. The applicant had no legitimate expectation. *Per* Taylor LJ: the Secretary of State's discretion to change his policy 'could not be fettered by moral obligations to the applicant deriving from the earlier favourable treatment of them'. *Per* Morland J: the applicant 'must have been aware that their expectations could never fetter the Secretary of State's public duty to promote and safeguard the health of the public'.

Q Instead of holding that the applicant's legitimate expectation is overridden here by the public interest in continuing governmental freedom of action, the court denies that a legitimate expectation arises in the first place. Is the distinction of any importance?

R v Ministry of Agriculture, Fisheries and Food, *ex parte* Hamble (Offshore) Fisheries (1995)
Facts: see 12.5.1 above.

The applicant's arguments based on legitimate expectation failed. Legitimacy, in the sense in which it applied to expectations in public law, was not absolute. Its presence was to be gauged by balancing the expectations induced by government and the policy considerations which militated against their fulfilment. Sedley J continued:

> The balance must in the first instance be for the policy-maker to strike; but if the outcome is challenged by way of judicial review, *I do not consider that the court's criterion is the bare rationality of the policy-maker's conclusion.* While policy is for the policy-maker alone, the fairness of his or her decision not to accommodate reasonable expectations which the policy will thwart remains the court's concern (as of course does the lawfulness of the policy). To postulate this is not to place the judge in the seat of the Minister ... [I]t is the court's task to recognise the constitutional importance of ministerial freedom to formulate and to reformulate policy; but it is equally the court's duty to protect the interests of those individuals whose expectation of different treatment has a legitimacy which *in fairness* outtops the policy choice which threatens to frustrate it ... legitimate expectation is now in effect a term of art, reserved for expectations which are not only reasonable but which will be sustained by the court in the face of changes of policy ... whether this point has been reached is determined by the court, whether on the grounds of rationality, of legality *or of fairness*, of all of which the court, not the decision-maker, is the arbiter.

(Emphasis supplied).

R v Secretary of State for the Home Department, *ex parte* Hargreaves (1996) CA
The applicants were three prisoners serving sentences at HMP Risley. Pursuant to rules made by the Secretary of State and in force at the beginning of their sentences, they would have been eligible to apply for periods of home leave after serving one-third of their terms of imprisonment. These rules were communicated to prisoners in the form of a notice and 'compact', setting out responsibilities undertaken by the prison, and requiring signed commitments to norms of good behaviour by the prisoners. In response to perceived public concern, the Secretary of State amended the rules by statutory instrument in 1995 with the result that eligibility to home leave accrued only on the completion of half the sentence to be served by a prisoner. The applicants claimed that the change denied them a legitimate expectation on the terms of the original rules. The Divisional Court dismissed the applications on the grounds: (a) that no clear and

unambiguous representations had been established, and (b) that the correct test by which to judge the Secretary of State's change of policy was not the balance of fairness and proportionality, but the public law test of irrationality.

Held, upholding the judgment of the Divisional Court, that the principle in *Findlay's* case (see 15.2 above) disposed of the present case. Although it was to be regretted that the compact and notice had insufficiently stressed the dependence of entitlement to home leave and other privileges upon the regime currently in force, those documents nevertheless suggested that this was the position, and certainly contained no contrary indications. Where procedural irregularity was alleged against a Minister, it was appropriate to inquire into the fairness of the procedure adopted by him, but where, as in the present case, a substantive defect was alleged, it fell to be judged by the far stricter irrationality test. The contrary suggestion by Sedley J in *Hamble's* case was inconsistent with authority and heretical.

Q Is a frustration of a legitimate expectation as to procedure *prima facie* to be regarded as a 'procedural irregularity' or as a 'substantive defect'?

16 The duty to give reasons

16.1 The consequences of failure to give reasons

Padfield v Minister for Agriculture, Fisheries and Food (1968) HL
Facts: see 12.7.1 above.
Per Lord Pearce:

> If all the *prima facie* reasons seem to point in favour of [the Minister] taking a certain course to carry out the intention of Parliament in respect of a power which it has given to him in that regard, and he gives no reason whatever for taking a contrary course, the court may infer that he has no good reason and that he is not using the power given by Parliament to carry out its intentions.

R v Secretary of State for Trade and Industry, *ex parte* Lonrho plc (1989) HL
Lonrho sought judicial review of, *inter alia*, the refusal of the Secretary of State to refer a rival company's acquisition of shares in House of Fraser to the Monopolies and Mergers Commission. Lonrho alleged that the refusal to refer was irrational, and submitted that the Secretary of State's failure to give reasons for his decision should lead to the conclusion that he had no proper reason for it.

Held, dismissing Lonrho's appeal on these and other grounds, that Lonrho had failed to establish that the Secretary of State had acted irrationally. *Per* Lord Keith:

> The absence of reasons for a decision where there is no duty to give them cannot of itself provide any support for the suggested irrationality of the decision. The only significance of the absence of reasons is that if all the other known facts and circumstances appear to point overwhelmingly in favour of a different decision, the decision-maker who has given no reasons cannot complain if the court draws the inference that he had no rational reason for his decision.

16.2 Circumstances in which the common law imposes a duty to give reasons

R v Civil Service Appeal Board, *ex parte* Cunningham (1991) CA
The applicant, a prisoner officer, was dismissed after accusations against him that he had assaulted a prisoner. As a civil servant, he had to seek compensation for unfair dismissal from the Civil Service Appeal Board,

rather than from an industrial tribunal. The board awarded him approximately one-third of the sum he could have expected to receive from an industrial tribunal, and gave no reasons for its decision.

Held, that in the circumstances the board was under a duty to give reasons for its decision. Leggatt LJ considered it obvious that for reasons of fairness the applicant should be entitled to know the reasons for the award, so that in the event of error he would be in a position to apply to court for judicial review to challenge it. He had 'a legitimate grievance, because it looks as though his compensation is less than it should be, and yet he has not been told the basis of the assessment'. The absence of reasons did not by itself entitle the court to hold that the award was not supportable. But the unexplained meagreness of the award did compel that inference.

In the view of McCowan LJ, not only had justice not been seen to be done, but there was no way, in the absence of reasons from the board, in which it could be judged whether in fact it had been done. McCowan LJ stated that he was influenced by the following factors:

(1) There is no appeal from the board's determination of the amount of compensation.
(2) In making that determination the board is carrying out a judicial function.
(3) The board is susceptible to judicial review.
(4) The procedure provided for by the code, that is to say the provision of a recommendation without reasons, is insufficient to achieve justice.
(5) There is no statute which requires the courts to tolerate that unfairness.
(6) The giving of short reasons would not frustrate the apparent purpose of the code.
(7) It is not a case where the giving of reasons would be harmful to the public interest.

Lord Donaldson MR considered that the board was a judicial body carrying out functions akin to those of an industrial tribunal. Fairness demanded that, just as an industrial tribunal would be under a duty to give reasons by virtue of the Tribunals and Inquiries Act 1958, so the board should give sufficient reasons for its decision to enable the parties to know the issues to which it addressed its mind and that it acted lawfully.

Doody v Secretary of State for the Home Department (1993) HL

Mandatory life sentences consisted of two periods of time – a fixed penal period, reflecting the requirements of retribution and deterrence, and the remaining 'risk period', at some time during which the prisoner might be released on licence. There were two inputs into the fixing of the penal period; recommendations made after trial by the trial judge, and a decision by the Home Secretary. The applicant argued that he was entitled to be told by the Home Secretary what penal period had been recommended by the judiciary and any departure by the Home Secretary from it. He further claimed that he should be told the reasons both for the judiciary's and the Home Secretary's views. In the Court of Appeal he succeeded in all but the last of his claims.

Held, that he should succeed in the final part of his claim as well. Lord Mustill began by reiterating the fact that the present law recognises no general duty to give reasons for an administrative decision, but added that in appropriate circumstances a duty might be implied. He explained the two approaches which led him to impose a duty in the present case. First, a refusal to give reasons was not fair to the prisoner. It was a matter of unparalleled importance to him. In the case of any other sentence, the prisoner would as a matter of course be told the reasons for it at the time of sentencing:

> Contrast this with the position of the prisoner sentenced for murder. He never sees the Home Secretary; he cannot fathom how his mind is working ... I therefore simply ask, is it fair that the mandatory life prisoner should be wholly deprived of the information which all other prisoners receive as a matter of course. I am clearly of opinion that it is not.

Lord Mustill added that he could have arrived at the same conclusion by the route taken in *Ex parte Cunningham* (1991) (above):

> I think it important that there should be an effective means of detecting the kind of error which would entitle the court to intervene, and in practice I regard it as necessary for this purpose that the reasoning of the Home Secretary should be disclosed.

R v Mayor, Commonalty and Citizens of London, *ex parte* Matson (1996) CA
The applicant sought to be elected an alderman of the Corporation of the City of London. The election process consisted of two stages. At the first, the common councilmen of a ward, meeting in a wardmote, voted whether or not to confirm a candidate as an alderman elect. The applicant received a substantial majority of the votes cast at this stage. At the second stage, the candidate was asked to complete a questionnaire, and was then interviewed in private by the court of aldermen. At this stage, the applicant's candidacy was rejected by an overwhelming majority. The applicant initially sought either an order of *certiorari* to quash the decision of the court of aldermen, or an order directing that court to reconsider its decision and reach a decision in accordance with the findings of the High Court or the Court of Appeal. On appeal from the rejection of his application by the High Court, the Court of Appeal found that the decision against the applicant could not in itself be impugned on the grounds either of irrationality or procedural unfairness.

Held, that the applicant's remaining submission that the court of aldermen was under a duty to give reasons for its decision was correct. The decision was not on its face aberrant, but fairness and natural justice required the giving of reasons. This was so because (amongst other considerations) it had been suggested to the applicant in the course of his interview that he had in the past acted in an inappropriate manner and he had been invited to explain himself; in the absence of reasons he had no way of knowing if the refusal of his candidacy arose despite the acceptance of his explanation or because of its rejection. Nor could he know whether to stand for election again, and if so, what further information to supply to the court of aldermen. In the circumstances, his rejection cast a shadow on his reputation. The giving of short reasons would not impede the working of the court of aldermen, but would enable it to ensure that its decisions in every case were sound and manifestly just and in the interests of the City.

R v Secretary of State for the Home Dept, *ex parte* Al Fayed (1997) CA
Section 44(2) of the British Nationality Act 1981 provides:

> The Secretary of State ... shall not be required to assign any reason for the grant or referral of any application under this Act the decision on which is at his discretion; and the discretion of the Secretary of State ... on any such application shall not be subject to appeal to, or review in, any court.

The applicants sought judicial review of the decision of the Secretary of State to reject their applications for naturalisation. The respondent accepted that s 44(2) did not oust the jurisdiction of the court to review a decision of the Secretary of State under any of the usual heads of judicial review.

Held (by a majority), that in the absence of s 44(2) a duty of fairness was owed to the applicants. The consequences of an adverse decision on naturalisation were of an importance which would give rise to a right to be informed of concerns which might lead to the refusal of the application, and a right to be heard in answer to such concerns. Properly understood, s 44(2) did not negate that duty which, in the instant case, would be met by requiring the Secretary of State to give the applicants sufficient information as to the subject matter of his decision to enable them to make such submissions as they wished. Were it not for s 44(2), the present case was such that reasons for the Secretary of State's refusal should have been given.

16.3 Rationales for the imposition of a duty to give reasons

R v Higher Education Funding Council, *ex parte* Institute of Dental Surgery (1994)
The Council had power to make grants for research to universities. Grant was awarded according to a rating system administered by the Council. The applicant institute, a university college, had previously been rated three on a scale out of five. In 1992 it was rated two out of five. Its grant was accordingly cut by £270,000. No reasons were given for the downgrading, and in correspondence, the Council refused to give reasons or to permit any

appeal. The institute sought judicial review, contending, *inter alia*, that the Council had acted unfairly in failing to give reasons, or alternatively, that in the absence of reasons its decision ought to be regarded as irrational.

Held, dismissing the application, that no duty would be imposed in the present case. Sedley J reviewed the arguments for and against the requiring of reasons in any given case as follows:

> The giving of reasons may among other things concentrate the decision maker's mind on the right questions; demonstrate to the recipient that this is so; show that the issues have been conscientiously addressed and how the result has been reached; or alternatively alert the recipient to a justiciable flaw in the process. On the other side of the argument, it may place an undue burden on decision makers; demand an appearance of unanimity where there is diversity; call for the articulation of sometimes inexpressible value judgments; and offer an invitation to the captious to comb the reasons for previously unsuspected grounds of challenge.

In *Doody's* case the nature and impact of the decision itself called for reasons as a routine aspect of procedural fairness. In *Cunningham's* case, there was a 'trigger factor'; the court could readily evaluate the difference between what the board had awarded and what an industrial tribunal would have awarded. The court was unable, in the present case, to judge whether the decision of the Council was extraordinary or not; it lacked the necessary academic expertise. In summary, Sedley J said:

(1) There is no general duty to give reasons for a decision, but there are classes of case where there is such a duty.

(2) One such class is where the subject matter is an interest so highly regarded by the law – for example personal liberty – that fairness requires that reasons, at least for particular decisions, should be given as of right.

(3)(a) Another such class is where the decision appears aberrant. Here fairness may require reasons so that the recipient may know whether the aberration is in the legal sense real (and so challengeable) or apparent.

(3)(b) It follows that this class does not include decisions which are themselves only challengeable by reference to the reasons for them. A pure exercise of academic judgment is such a decision.

17 Proportionality

17.1 Explicit discussion of disproportionality as a ground of review

17.1.1 The principle as an area for the future development of the common law

Council of Civil Service Unions v Minister for the Civil Service Unions (1985) HL

Facts: see 15.5.1 above.

Per Lord Diplock:

Judicial review has I think developed to a state today when, without reiterating any analysis of the steps by which the development has come about, one can conveniently classify under three heads the grounds on which administrative action is subject to control by judicial review. The first ground I would call 'illegality', the second 'irrationality' and the third 'procedural impropriety'. That is not to say that further development on a case-by-case basis may not in the course of time add further grounds. I have in mind particularly the possible adoption in future of the principle of 'proportionality' which is recognised in the administrative law of several of our fellow members of the European Economic Community.

17.1.2 Current judicial attitudes to the principle

R v Secretary of State for the Home Department *ex parte* Brind (1991) HL

In October 1988 the Secretary of State, acting under the Broadcasting Act 1981, issued directives to the BBC and the IBA prohibiting the broadcasting of 'words spoken' by members or apparent adherents of organisations proscribed under prevention of terrorism legislation. The appellants, who were journalists, alleged that the ban infringed their rights to freedom of expression, as guaranteed by the European Convention on Human Rights, and that it was disproportionate to the ends sought to be achieved.

Held, that proportionality was not yet a distinct ground of judicial review. Lord Lowry and Lord Ackner rejected it generally on the ground that it would inevitably involve consideration of the merits of the decision challenged – a matter entrusted to the decision-maker and not to courts of supervisory jurisdiction. Lord Lowry added that to accept it would be to encourage a rush of unmeritorious applications for judicial review. Lord Bridge and Lord Roskill accepted that proportionality might in time become an independent ground of review, but denied its application to the present case, Lord Bridge considering that review on the ground of irrationality would achieve a similar end. Lord Templeman, according similar importance to irrationality as a ground of review, noted that proportionality is required by the European Court of Human Rights, and held 'applying these principles' that the Secretary of State's decision was justifiable.

17.2 Implicit use of proportionality in judicial reasoning

R v Secretary of State for Transport, *ex parte* Pegasus Holdings (1988)

The applicants chartered aircraft and flying crews from the Romanian airline Tarom. Tarom held a permit from the Secretary of State for this purpose. Five of its pilots voluntarily took flying tests conducted by the British Civil Aviation Authority. Four of them failed for the reason that they displayed an inability to manoeuvre the aircraft. The Secretary of State provisionally withdrew Tarom's licence within a matter of hours of the results of the tests becoming known. This caused the applicant package holiday company great difficulties in transporting its customers. The applicant claimed that the Secretary of State had failed to grant it a fair hearing before withdrawing the licence.

Held, that on the facts there had been no breach of the rules of natural justice or of a duty of fairness. The requirements of fairness had to be considered in all the circumstances of the case. *Per* Schiemann J:

> One has in the context of fairness to bear in mind, on the one hand, the no doubt substantial economic damage to the applicants and perhaps the irritation and inconvenience that I do not doubt the passengers suffered. On the other hand one has to bear in mind the magnitude of the risk ...

18 The European Convention for the Protection of Human Rights and Fundamental Freedoms

18.1 The Convention and the UK courts

18.1.1 Statutory discretion need not be exercised in conformity with the Convention

R v Secretary of State for the Home Department, *ex parte* Brind (1991) HL
In addition to their claim that the consequences of the Secretary of State's decision were disproportionate to the end which he sought to achieve (see 17.1.2 above), the applicants argued that Article 10 of the European Convention on Human Rights was a relevant consideration to which the Secretary of State was bound to have proper regard. Section 29(3) of the Broadcasting Act 1981 conferred on the Secretary of State a discretion to prohibit broadcasting which was otherwise unfettered.

Held, that the acceptance of the applicants' submission would result in the effective incorporation of the Convention into English law, and that since Parliament had refused many opportunities to incorporate it by legislation, Parliament's intention must be deemed to be that the Convention should retain its current status. Lord Acker acknowledged that reference could be made to the Convention in order to resolve ambiguities in UK legislation, but denied that there was any ambiguity in s 29(3):

> The limit placed upon the discretion is simply that the power is to be used for the purposes for which it was granted by the legislation (the so-called *Padfield* doctrine) and that it must be exercised reasonably in the *Wednesbury* sense. No question of the construction of the words of s 29(3) arises ...

Accordingly, the authorities in which reference had been made to the Convention for the resolution of statutory ambiguity in accordance with the deemed intention of Parliament were insufficient to justify the applicants' submission that the Secretary of State should have had regard to it here. *Per* Lord Ackner:

> The fallacy of this submission is however plain. If the Secretary of State was obliged to have proper regard to the Convention, ie to conform with Article 10, this inevitably would result in incorporating the Convention into English domestic law by the back door. It would oblige the courts to police the operation of the Convention and to ask themselves in each case, where there was a challenge, whether the restrictions were 'necessary in a democratic society' ... applying the principles enunciated in the decisions of the European Court of Human Rights. The Treaty, not having been incorporated in English law, cannot be a source of rights and obligations and the question: 'Did the Secretary of State act in breach of Article 10?' does not therefore arise.

R v Morrisey, R v Staines (1997) CA

The appellants, who had been convicted of participation in a financial offence, appealed on the ground that answers given by them in the course of an investigation into the offences had rendered the proceedings unfair, and should have been excluded. The answers had been given to an inspector appointed under the Financial Services Act 1986, which provided (by s 177) that such answers should be admissible in evidence. The appellants' argument for exclusion rested on the discretion to exclude contained in s 78 of the Police and Criminal Evidence Act 1984, and on remarks made in *R v Saunders* (1996). In that case, the Court of Appeal had remarked that if the appellant were to appeal successfully to the European Court of Human Rights (which he later did), consideration would have to be given to implementing the effect of that decision in domestic law.

Held, dismissing the appeal, that s 177 raised a statutory presumption that the evidence in question was admissible. To exclude the evidence in deference to the decision in the European Court of Human Rights would amount to a purported judicial repeal of the domestic law. The European Convention on Human Rights, as interpreted by the Court of Human Rights, remained unenforceable in the English courts. Their Lordships were in express agreement with the appellants' submission that the resulting position was very unsatisfactory, but had no choice but to dismiss the appeal.

18.1.2 Circumstances justifying reference to the Convention as persuasive authority

Derbyshire County Council v Times Newspapers Ltd (1992–93) CA and HL

The County Council brought a libel action against the publishers, editor and two journalists of *The Sunday Times*. The newspapers had printed allegedly defamatory articles concerning the council's management of its superannuation fund. The defendants applied to strike out the statement of claim as disclosing no reasonable cause of action. For the claim to succeed, it was necessary for the plaintiffs to establish that a body corporate should be able to sue for libel. The defendants argued that it should not have that right, since it would be enabled thereby to suppress legitimate criticism of its activities. The defendants submitted that this would be contrary to Article 10 of the European Convention, and did not come within the derogation to Article 10. It was unnecessary in a democratic society for a body corporate to have the right to sue for libel since it could protect its reputation by suing for malicious falsehood, or by bringing a prosecution for criminal libel. At first instance the defendants' submissions were rejected. They appealed to the Court of Appeal.

Held, allowing the appeal, that a corporate public authority had no right in common law to sue for libel. In so holding, the court considered Article 10 of the Convention. On the admissibility of the Convention in English courts, Balcombe LJ remarked that although it had not been incorporated into domestic law, the authorities recognised its relevance in three situations:

(1) Article 10 may be used for the purpose of the resolution of an ambiguity in English primary or subordinate legislation (see *Brind's* case 17.1.2 above).

(2) Article 10 may be used when considering the principles upon which the court should act in exercising a discretion, eg whether or not to grant an interlocutory injunction (see *AG v Guardian Newspapers Ltd* (1987)).

(3) Article 10 may be used when the common law (by which I include the doctrines of equity) is uncertain. In *AG v Guardian Newspapers Ltd (No 2)* (1988) (see 22.1 below) the courts at all levels had regard to the provisions of Article 10 in considering the extent of the duty of confidence. They did not limit the application of Article 10 to the discretion of the court to grant or withhold an injunction to restrain a breach of confidence.

Even if the common law is certain, the courts will still, when appropriate, consider whether the UK is in breach of Article 10.

(As authority for this proposition, Balcombe LJ cited *Ex parte Choudhury* (1991). See 23.3.2 below.)

The plaintiffs appealed to the House of Lords.

Held, dismissing the appeal, that the judgment of the Court of Appeal would be upheld, but without reliance on the Convention. In the field of freedom of speech there was no difference in principle between English law and Article 10 of the Convention. Lord Keith added that he found it satisfactory to be able to conclude that the common law of England was consistent with the obligations assumed by the Crown under the treaty in this field.

18.2 Common law procedures for the vindication of fundamental rights

18.2.1 The intensity of judicial review of a decision may be increased proportionately to the importance of the rights which it determines

R v Secretary of State for the Home Department, *ex parte* Bugdaycay (1987) HL
The appellants obtained leave to enter the UK by false statements as to their purposes and as to the time for which they intended to stay. In fact they intended to seek asylum in the UK, and upon being granted entry, each unsuccessfully did so. Orders for their removal were made by the Secretary of State on the ground that the appellants were illegal entrants, since they had failed to disclose material facts when entering the UK. The appellants denied that the facts concealed by them were 'material', in that they were not facts which would have caused the immigration officer to refuse leave to enter. They further claimed that the court had jurisdiction to make a finding on their entitlement to asylum.

Held that the appeals would be dismissed on both grounds. *Per* Lord Bridge:

[the courts are entitled, within limits] to subject an administrative decision to the more rigorous examination, to ensure that it is in no way flawed, according to the gravity of the issue which the decision determines. The most fundamental of all human rights is the individual's right to life and when an administrative decision under challenge is said to be one which may put the applicant's life at risk, the basis of the decision must surely call for the most anxious scrutiny.

18.2.2 The decision-maker's failure to maintain a reasonable balance between human rights and competing interests may be subject to review on *Wednesbury* principles

R v Secretary of State for the Home Department, *ex parte* Brind (1991) HL
Facts: see 17.1.2 above.

With reference to his conclusion that in the absence of legislation incorporating the Convention into English law the Secretary of State's decision could not be impugned on the grounds that it did not properly take into consideration Article 10, Lord Bridge added:

But I do not accept that this conclusion means that the courts are powerless to prevent the exercise by the executive of administrative discretions, even when conferred, as in the instant case, in terms which are on their face unlimited, in a way which infringes fundamental human rights. Thus, Article 10(2) of the Convention spells out and categorises the competing public interests by reference to which the right to freedom of expression may have to be curtailed. In exercising the power of judicial review, we have neither the advantages or the disadvantages of any comparable code to which we may refer or by which we are bound. But again, this surely does not mean that in deciding whether the Secretary of State, in the exercise of his discretion, could reasonably impose the restriction he has imposed on the broadcasting organisations, we are not perfectly entitled to start from the premise that any restriction of the right to freedom of expression requires to be justified and that nothing less than an important competing public interest will be sufficient to justify it. The primary judgment as to whether the particular competing interest justifies the particular restriction imposed falls to be made by the Secretary of State to whom Parliament has entrusted the discretion. But we are entitled to exercise a secondary judgment by asking whether a reasonable Secretary of State, on the material before him, could reasonably make that primary judgment.

18.2.3 The common law requires a substantial public interest justification for the infringement of fundamental rights

R v Cambridge Area Health Authority, *ex parte* B (1995) Divisional Court and CA
The applicant, a girl aged 10 years, applied through her father as next friend for *certiorari* to quash the authority's decision to refuse her further medical treatment. She suffered from leukaemia, and was virtually certain to die in the very near future if the treatment were withheld. Her chances of recovery with the treatment were put at 10–20%.

Held (Laws J), granting the order and remitting the matter to the authority, that it had not taken into consideration the wishes of the father, and further, that it had taken a decision which interfered with the applicant's right to life. Respect for that and other fundamental human rights was not merely a matter of international obligation under the European Convention. It was of the same substance as the English common law. Decisions assaulting such rights could only be justified on substantial public interest grounds. The Authority had not sufficiently explained the priorities which had led it to deprive the applicant of her chance to life. On this (and other) grounds an order of *certiorari* would be granted.

Held, on appeal to the Court of Appeal, that the order would be discharged, since the legality of the Authority's decision could not be faulted. The court did not refer to the reasoning of Laws J summarised above.

R v Ministry of Defence, ex parte Smith and others (1995) CA
Facts: see 13.2 above.

The test for irrationality proposed by counsel for three of the appellants (and approved by the Court of Appeal) included a direction to take account of human rights issues:

The court may not interfere with the exercise of an administrative discretion on substantive grounds save where the court is satisfied that the decision is unreasonable in the sense that it is beyond the range of responses open to a reasonable decision-maker. But in judging whether the decision-maker has exceeded this margin of appreciation the human rights context is important. The more substantial the interference with human rights, the more the court will require by way of justification before it is satisfied that the decision is reasonable in the sense outlined above.

The Court of Appeal did not comment at length on the differential intensity of review made explicit by this approach. In the Divisional Court, however, Simon Brown LJ cited the authorities on judicial review in the human rights context, and stated that:

... they emphasise that within the limited scope of review open to it the court must be scrupulous to ensure that no recognised ground of challenge is in truth available to the applicant before rejecting his application. When the most fundamental human rights are threatened, the court will not, for example, be inclined to overlook some perhaps minor flaw in the decision-making process, or adopt a particularly benevolent view of the Minister's evidence, or exercise its discretion to withhold relief ... [However] even where fundamental human rights are being restricted, 'the threshold of unreasonableness' is not lowered. On the other hand, the Minister on judicial review will need to show that there is an important competing public interest which he could reasonably judge sufficient to justify the restriction and he must expect his reasons to be closely scrutinised. Even that approach, therefore, involves a more intensive review process and a greater readiness to intervene than would ordinarily characterise a judicial review challenge.

R v Secretary of State for Home Department, ex parte McQuillan (1995)

The applicant, a former member of the Irish Republican Socialist Party, sought review of the decision of the Secretary of State to refuse to revoke successive exclusion orders made against him under the Prevention of Terrorism (Temporary Provisions) Act 1989. He argued that the effect of the order, barring him from entering Great Britain, was to confine him to the one part of the UK where his life and his family's safety were most at risk.

Held, that if the court were possessed of the information held by the Secretary of State, its task would be to determine whether the Secretary of State's decision lay within the band of rational decisions available in a case which potentially called in question the right to life. Sedley J stated that rationality would be measured in this context by (among other things) asking whether in the light of its impact the exclusion order could reasonably be considered an expedient response by a Home Secretary who has given proper weight to the fundamental right thereby put at risk. However, this approach was not available in the present case, where the Crown's evidence had to be regarded in the light of authority as sufficient to invoke national security interests precluding further review.

The applicant had claimed rights under European law. Questions affecting the extent of those rights had already been referred to the European Court of Justice, and the present application would be stayed (without stay of the exclusion order) pending the outcome of those references.

Q In its reference to an 'expedient' response is the test suggested by Sedley J in fact a measure of rationality or proportionality?

18.3 The attitude of the European Court of Justice

Nold v Commission of the European Communities Case 4/73 (1974)

In 1969 the Commission authorised the merger of the mining companies of the Ruhr into a single company, Ruhrkohle. At a later date, the Commission promulgated new trading rules fixing the conditions required to be met for acquisition of the status of direct wholesaler of coal. Among the conditions was the requirement to buy at least 6,000 tonnes of coal from Ruhrkohle. Nold, a coal wholesaler and building merchant, complained that it could not attain this minimum quota. It claimed that it was the victim of discrimination since, unlike its competitors, it would now have to deal to its disadvantage through an intermediary. It further argued that its fundamental rights had been violated, namely the right to free development of the personality and the right to freedom of economic action. In the result, its very existence was endangered.

Held, that Nold had been treated no differently from any other undertakings, and that it had therefore not been the victim of discrimination. With regard to the matter of fundamental rights, Nold had no more than a commercial interest, the uncertainties of which were part of the very essence of economic activity. It was for Nold to acknowledge the changes which had taken place and to carry out the necessary adaptations. The action would be dismissed. The court included the following observations in the course of its judgment:

As the court had already stated, fundamental rights form an integral part of the general principles of law, the observance of which it ensures.

In safeguarding these rights, the court is bound to draw inspiration from constitutional traditions common to the Member States, and it cannot therefore uphold measures which are incompatible with fundamental rights recognised and protected by the constitutions of those States.

Similarly, international treaties for the protection of human rights on which the Member States have collaborated or to which they are signatories, can supply guidelines which should be followed within the framework of Community law.

19 Public assembly

19.1 Restriction for the avoidance of public disorder

Beatty v Gillbanks (1882)

The Salvation Army organised processions in the streets of Weston-Super-Mare. The processions were accompanied by another organised body called the Skeleton Army, which opposed itself to the Salvation Army. Factions supporting each of the two groups developed, and violent disorder broke out. After a major disturbance, a justices' notice requiring the cessation of assemblies to the disturbance of the public peace was posted in the town and served on the appellant organisers of the Salvation Army. The Salvation Army continued to march. They were met and stopped by the police, who told the appellants that they must obey the notice. The appellants refused, were arrested, and as a result of being charged with 'unlawfully and tumultuously assembling with others to the disturbance of the public peace, and against the peace of the Queen', were bound over to find sureties to keep the peace. They appealed to the Queen's Bench Divisional Court.

Held, allowing the appeal, that as regarded the appellants themselves, there was no disturbance of the peace. The appellants' aims were wholly lawful, if not indeed laudable. The disturbance which had taken place had been caused entirely by the unlawful and unjustifiable interference of the Skeleton Army. *Per* Field J:

I entirely concede that everyone must be taken to intend the natural consequences of his own acts, and it is clear to me that if this disturbance of the peace was the natural consequence of the acts of the appellants they would be liable, and the justices would have been right in binding them over. But the evidence set forth in the case does not support this contention; on the contrary, it shows that the disturbances were caused by other people antagonistic to the appellants, and that no acts of violence were committed by them ... The law relating to unlawful assemblies, as laid down in the books and the cases, affords no support to the view of the matter for which the learned counsel for the respondent was obliged to contend, *viz*, that persons acting lawfully are to be held responsible and punished merely because other persons are thereby induced to act unlawfully and create a disturbance.

Duncan v Jones (1936)

A meeting was to be held outside an unemployed training centre in Deptford to protest against the Incitement to Disaffection Bill. The appellant had addressed a meeting at the same location more than a year previously, and on that occasion there had been disturbances at the centre. The appellant, who intended to address the present meeting, was told by a police inspector that it could not be held at the intended venue, but could take place some 175 yards away in a different street. The appellant told the inspector that she was going to hold the meeting in any event, stepped onto a platform, and began to address the audience. The inspector then arrested her, to which she submitted without resistance. She was charged with obstructing the inspector in the execution of his duty contrary to s 12 of the Prevention of Crimes Act 1871. Upon conviction, she appealed to the London Quarter Sessions. The Deputy Chairman of Quarter Sessions held, dismissing the appeal:

(1) that in fact (if it be material) the appellant must have known of the probable consequence of her holding the meeting – namely a disturbance and possibly a breach of the peace – and was not unwilling that such consequences should ensue;

(2) that in fact the respondent reasonably apprehended a breach of the peace;

(3) that in law it thereupon became his duty to prevent the holding of the meeting; and

(4) that in fact, by attempting to hold the meeting, the appellant obstructed the respondent when in the execution of his duty.

The appellant appealed by way of case stated to the King's Bench Divisional Court.

Held, that the deputy chairman had been entitled to come to the conclusion to which he came on the facts which he had found. The case was a plain one. The *ratio* of *Beatty v Gillbanks* (1882) (above) was not in point, and the judgments in that case did not carry the matter any further. *Per* Lord Hewart CJ:

There have been moments during the argument in this case when it appeared to be suggested that the Court had to do with a grave case involving what is called the right of public meeting. I say 'called', because English law does not recognise any special right of public meeting for political or other purposes. The right of assembly, as Professor Dicey puts it (Dicey's *Law of the Constitution*, 8th edn, p 499), is nothing more than a view taken by the Court of the individual liberty of the subject. If I thought that the present case raised a question which has been held in suspense by more than one writer on constitutional law – namely whether an assembly can properly be held to be unlawful merely because the holding of it is expected to give rise to a breach of the peace on the part of persons who are opposed to those who are holding the meeting – I should wish to hear much more argument before I expressed an opinion. This case, however, does not even touch that important question.

Thomas v Sawkins (1935)

A public meeting to protest against the Incitement to Disaffection Bill was held on private premises. The organisers of the meeting had previously made it clear to the police that they were not welcome. Police officers nevertheless attended, and the appellant took hold of one of them in order to eject him. The officer resisted, and the appellant brought a private prosecution for assault. At first instance the case was dismissed, and the appellant appealed to the Divisional Court.

The question arose whether the police officers had been lawfully on the premises.

Held, that the decision to dismiss the case would be upheld. The police had been lawfully on the premises in the exercise of a power to enter and remain in order to deal with a breach of the peace or to prevent an anticipated breach of the peace. The court rejected the appellant's argument that no such power existed where a breach was merely expected by the police, and was not yet occurring. *Per* Avory J:

> I think it is very material in this particular case to observe that the meeting was described as a public meeting, that it was extensively advertised, and that the public was invited to attend. There can be no doubt that the police officers who attended the meeting were members of the public and were included in that sense in the invitation to attend. It is true that those who had hired the hall for the meeting might withdraw their invitation from any particular individual who was likely to commit a breach of the peace or some other offence, but it is quite a different proposition to say that they might withdraw the invitation from police officers who might be there for the express purpose of preventing a breach of the peace or the commission of an offence ...

> I am satisfied that the justices had before them material on which they could properly hold that the police officers in question had reasonable grounds for believing that, if they were not present, seditious speeches would be made and/or that a breach of the peace would take place. To prevent any such breach of the peace the police were entitled to enter and to remain on the premises.

Q In view of Avory J's opinion that the police had power to enter and remain in order to prevent an anticipated breach of the peace, was it 'very material to observe that the meeting was described as a public meeting'?

Jordan v Burgoyne (1963)

The respondent was a leader of the extreme right wing National Socialist movement. He addressed a rally in Trafalgar Square. A group of communists, Campaign for Nuclear Disarmament (CND) supporters and Jewish activists attended the rally, intending to prevent it taking place. Jordan used the following words:

> ... more and more people every day are opening their eyes and coming to say with us 'Hitler was right'. They are coming to say that our real enemies ... were

not Hitler and the National Socialists of Germany but world Jewry and its associates in this country.

At this point there was turmoil, and the police stopped the rally. Jordan was convicted of using insulting words whereby a breach of the peace was likely to be occasioned contrary to s 5 of the Public Order Act 1936. His appeal to quarter sessions was allowed on the ground that although his words had been insulting, they would not have been likely to lead ordinary, reasonable people to commit a breach of the peace. The prosecutor appealed to the Divisional Court.

Held, allowing the appeal, that it was difficult to imagine any reasonable person not being provoked beyond endurance by the respondent's words, but that there was no room for any test as to whether any member of the audience was a reasonable man or an ordinary citizen. *Per* Lord Parker CJ:

> This is ... a Public Order Act, and if in fact it is apparent that a body of persons are present – and let me assume in the defendant's favour that they are a body of hooligans – yet if words are used which threaten, abuse or insult them – all very strong words – then that person must take his audience as he finds them, and if those words to that audience are likely to provoke a breach of the peace, then the speaker is guilty of an offence.

19.2 Restriction in the interest of private right

Hubbard v Pitt (1975) CA

The defendants, who were opposed to property redevelopment in Islington, organised a campaign against the plaintiffs, a firm of local estate agents. They assembled outside the plaintiffs' offices with placards and leaflets stating that they would continue this picketing until the plaintiffs complied with their demands. The picketers were orderly and peaceful, co-operated with the police, and left sufficient room for pedestrians to pass along the pavement. The plaintiffs obtained an injunction to prevent the defendants from 'besetting' their offices, claiming that it was substantially interfering with their business. The defendants appealed.

Held (by a majority), that the appeal would be dismissed. The balance of convenience was in favour of maintaining the injunction until full trial. *Per* Lord Denning MR (dissenting):

> Finally, the real grievance of the plaintiffs is about the placards and leaflets. To restrain these by an interlocutory injunction would be contrary to the principle laid down by the court 85 years ago in *Bonnard v Perryman* and repeatedly applied ever since. That case spoke of the right of free speech. Here we have to consider the right to demonstrate and the right to protest on matters of public concern. These are rights which it is in the public interest that individuals should possess; and, indeed, that they should exercise without impediment as long as no wrongful act is done. It is often the only means by which grievances

can be brought to the knowledge of those in authority – at any rate with such impact as to gain a remedy ... As long as all is done peaceably and in good order without threats or incitement to violence or obstruction to traffic, it is not prohibited: see *Beatty v Gillbanks*. I stress the need for peace and good order. Only too often violence may break out: and then it should be firmly handled and severely punished. But, so long as good order is maintained, the right to demonstrate must be preserved. In his recent inquiry on the Red Lion Square disorders, Scarman LJ was asked to recommend 'that a positive right to demonstrate should be enacted'. He said that it was unnecessary:

'The right of course exists, subject only to limits required by the need for good order and the passage of traffic.'

19.3 Restriction in the interest of public right

Hirst and Agu v Chief Constable of West Yorkshire (1986)
The appellants, who were animal rights activists, carried on a protest outside a shop selling animal furs. They stood in various parts of the street outside the shop, holding a banner and handing out leaflets. The street was a spacious but busy pedestrian precinct. They were convicted of obstructing the highway contrary to s 137 of the Highways Act 1980 and appealed to the Divisional Court by way of case stated.

Held, allowing the appeal, that the Crown Court had been wrong to regard the appellants' activities as unlawful merely because they were not incidental to the lawful use of the highway to pass and re-pass. Where the activity on which the charge was based was not of itself contrary to law a court should consider: (a) whether a more than negligible obstruction had been caused; (b) whether the obstruction was deliberate; and (c) whether it was caused without lawful authority or excuse. In answering the third question, the court was to consider, as a question of fact, whether the activity was reasonable.

20 Public order

Brutus v Cozens (1973) HL

During a tennis match at Wimbledon which involved a South African player, the appellant stepped onto the court blowing a whistle, threw leaflets around, attempted to give one to a player and sat down on the court. Other protesters then made their way onto the court. Play was stopped. The appellant was charged with using insulting behaviour whereby a breach of the peace was likely to be caused, contrary to s 5 of the Public Order Act 1936. The magistrates held that the appellant's behaviour could not be described as 'insulting'. The prosecutor appealed to the Divisional Court, which defined the word 'insulting' and held that the evidence established that the appellant had used insulting behaviour. The appellant appealed to the House of Lords.

Held, allowing the appeal, that the meaning of the word 'insulting' was a matter of fact, not law, and that the question for the Divisional Court had therefore been whether the magistrates had acted unreasonably in holding that the appellant's behaviour was not insulting. They had not so acted. The Divisional Court had defined 'insulting' behaviour as that which affronted others and tended to evidence a disrespect or contempt for their rights. *Per* Lord Reid:

> I cannot agree with that. Parliament had to solve the difficult question of how far freedom of speech or behaviour must be limited in the general public interest. It would have been going much too far to prohibit all speech or conduct likely to occasion a breach of the peace because determined opponents may not shrink from organising or at least threatening a breach of the peace in order to silence a speaker whose views they detest.

R v Howell (1982) CA

In the course of attempting to disperse a group of people who had congregated on the street and were behaving in a disorderly manner, police arrested the appellant. During his arrest, the appellant struck a police officer in the face. He was convicted of an assault occasioning actual bodily harm. On appeal he argued that there had been no breach of the peace before the arrest, that the arrest was consequently unlawful, and that he had used reasonable force to prevent it.

Held, that the appeal would be dismissed. In so holding, Watkins LJ considered the definition of 'breach of the peace':

A comprehensive definition of the term 'breach of the peace' has very rarely been formulated ... The older cases are of considerable interest but they are not a sure guide to what the term is understood to mean today, since keeping the peace in this country in the latter half of the 20th century presents formidable problems which bear upon the evolving process of the development of this branch of the common law. Nevertheless, even in these days when affrays, riotous behaviour and other disturbances happen all too frequently, we cannot accept that there can be a breach of the peace unless there has been an act done or threatened to be done which actually harms a person, or in his presence his property, or is likely to cause such harm, or which puts someone in fear of such harm being done. There is nothing more likely to arouse resentment and anger in him, and a desire to take instant revenge, than attacks or threatened attacks upon a person's body or property ...

We are emboldened to say that there is a breach of the peace whenever harm is actually done or is likely to be done to a person or in his presence to his property or a person is in fear of being so harmed through an assault, an affray, a riot, unlawful assembly or other disturbance. It is for this breach of the peace when done in his presence or the reasonable apprehension of it taking place that a constable, or anyone else, may arrest an offender without a warrant ...

R v Chief Constable of Devon and Cornwall, *ex parte* CEGB (1982) CA

The Central Electricity Generating Board was obstructed by demonstrators in its attempts to exercise its statutory powers to survey land for suitability as a site for a nuclear power station. The police attended at the site, but refused to intervene on the grounds that there was no actual or threatened breach of the peace. The CEGB sought an order of *mandamus* to compel the police to remove or to assist in the removal of the demonstrators.

Held, that it would not be appropriate to order *mandamus*. Lord Denning MR, however, considered that there had been or was likely to be a breach of the peace. It might be constituted either by the physical steps taken by CEGB employees to prevent the obstruction, whether or not such reaction might be justified as a matter of self-help, or by the conduct of the demonstrators themselves. Lord Denning MR continued:

... the lifting up of a recumbent obstructor would be a battery unless justified as being done in the exercise of self-help. But in deciding whether there is a breach of the peace or the apprehension of it, the law does not go into the rights and wrongs of the matter – or whether it is justified by self-help or not. Suffice it that the peace is broken or is likely to be broken by one or another of those present. With the result that any citizen – and certainly any police officer – can intervene to stop the breach.

If I were wrong on this point, if there were here no breach of the peace nor apprehension of it, I would give a licence to every obstructor and every passive resister in the land. He would be able to cock a snook at the law as these groups have done. Public works of the greatest importance could be held up indefinitely. This cannot be. The rule of law must prevail.

Q May lawful behaviour constitute a breach of the peace, or would it be more accurate to say that lawful behaviour may give rise to a breach of the peace? Which formulation is suggested by Lord Denning's dictum?

The police as victims of public order offences

DPP v Orum (1989)

The Director of Public Prosecutions appealed to the Divisional Court by way of case stated from the dismissal of charges against the respondent for offences under s 5(1)(a) of the Public Order Act 1986 (causing harassment, alarm or distress) and s 51(1) of the Police Act 1964. The respondent had used threatening and abusive language to police constables who were intervening in an altercation between the respondent and his girlfriend, and he had later assaulted one of the constables. The only persons present had been the respondent, his girlfriend, and the two police constables.

Held, allowing the appeal, that the question requiring determination by the court was whether a police officer could be a person who was likely to be caused harassment, alarm or distress by the threatening, abusive or insulting words or behaviour of an accused. There was nothing in the Act to enforce the conclusion that as a matter of law he could not. As a matter of fact, words or behaviour which would have such an effect on an ordinary member of the public would often have little emotional impact on a police officer other than that of boredom. However, that was a question of fact for the magistrates to decide in the light of all the circumstances.

21 Protection of privacy

21.1 The absence of a general right to privacy at common law

Kaye v Robertson (1991) CA

The plaintiff, a well-known television actor, was seriously injured when debris fell on his car. He underwent head and brain surgery. As he was recovering in hospital, a journalist and photographer from the Sunday Sport entered his room, interviewed him and took photographs of his injuries. The plaintiff obtained an injunction against publication of the interview or the photographs, basing his application upon claims for libel, malicious falsehood, trespass to the person and the tort of passing off since the law recognised no general right to privacy. The defendants applied to the Court of Appeal for the discharge of the injunction.

Held, allowing the appeal in part, that the injunction had wrongly been granted on the basis of the claim of libel, though it would be upheld in modified form on the basis of the malicious falsehood claim. *Per* Leggatt LJ:

> We do not need a First Amendment to preserve the freedom of the press, but the abuse of that freedom can be ensured only by the enforcement of a right to privacy. This right has so long been disregarded here that it can be recognised now only by the legislature. Especially since there is available in the US a wealth of experience of the enforcement of this right both at common law and also under statute, it is to be hoped that the making good of this signal shortcoming in our law will not be long delayed.

21.2 Breach of confidence

21.2.1 The development of the equitable doctrine of breach of confidence

Albert v Strange (1849)

Queen Victoria and Prince Albert made etchings of their children. The Royal Family kept them privately, although a few copies were given to friends. The plates of the etchings were entrusted to a printer for further copies to be made. Without the printer's knowledge one of his employees made further copies. The defendant purchased them. He intended to exhibit them, and to prepare a catalogue listing and describing them. The plaintiff obtained an injunction to prevent the exhibition and the publication of the catalogue. In further proceedings, the defendant applied for the variation of the injunction to permit him to publish the catalogue, although he accepted that the exhibition should not be held. On appeal, counsel for the defendant contended that the injunction could be based only on breach of trust or on the property rights of the plaintiff.

Held, that a breach of trust, the protection of property rights, contract or a breach of confidence would justify the continuance of the injunction as originally made. The plaintiff undoubtedly had property rights in his own work. On the evidence adduced by the plaintiff and the absence of any explanation from the defendant, the court was bound to assume that the possession of the etchings by the defendant had been obtained in breach of trust, breach of an implied contract, or in breach of confidence.

21.2.2 The doctrine is independent of other legal rights

Duchess of Argyll v Duke of Argyll (1967)

Following the failure of his marriage to the plaintiff, the duke intended to publish in *The People* a series of articles relating to the couple's married life. The first two instalments were published, and the plaintiff sought injunctions against the duke and against the editor and publisher of *The People* to restrain further publication of 'secrets ... relating to her private life, personal affairs or private conduct, communicated to the first defendant in confidence during the subsistence of his marriage to the plaintiff and not hitherto made public property'.

Held, following a review of the authorities, that obligation of confidence could arise from property rights or from contract, but that these were not the only grounds on which a court could intervene. *Per* Ungoed-Thomas J:

These cases, in my view, indicate:
(1) that a contract or obligation of confidence need not be expressed but can be implied;
(2) that a breach of confidence or trust or faith can arise independently of any right of property or contract other, of course, that any contract which the imparting of the confidence in the relevant circumstances may itself create;
(3) that the court in the exercise of its equitable jurisdiction will restrain a breach of confidence independently of any right at law.

The confidential nature of a marital relationship was of its essence, and so obviously implicit in it that it did not need to be expressed. In the protection of that confidence:

... the court is not to be deterred merely because it is not already provided with fully developed principles, guides, tests, definitions and the full armament for judicial decision. It is sufficient that the court recognises that the communications are confidential, and their publication within the mischief which the law as its policy seeks to avoid, without further defining the scope and limits of the jurisdiction; and I have no hesitation in this case in concluding that publication of some of the passages complained of is in breach of marital confidence ...

21.2.3 Factors affecting the availability of the protection

Rights to confidentiality are incompatible with interests in publicity

Woodward v Hutchins (1977) CA

The plaintiffs were members of a well-known pop group. The defendant, their press relations agent, contracted with a national newspaper to write a series of articles about the group, giving details of its members' personal lives. The plaintiffs sued for libel, breach of contract and breach of confidence. At first instance, an injunction was granted to prevent breach of confidence, but not on the other two grounds. The defendants appealed to the Court of Appeal.

Held, that the injunction would be discharged. *Per* Lord Denning:

There is no doubt whatever that this pop group sought publicity. They wanted to have themselves presented to the public in a favourable light so that audiences would come to hear them and support them. Mr Hutchins was engaged so as to produce, or help to produce, this favourable image, not only of their public lives but of their private lives also. If a group of this kind seek publicity which is to their advantage, it seems to me that they cannot complain if a servant or employee of theirs afterwards discloses the truth about them. If the image which they fostered was not a true image, it is in the public interest that it should be corrected. In these cases of confidential information, it is a question of balancing the public interest in maintaining the confidence against the public interest in knowing the truth ...

Other considerations

Stephens v Avery (1988)

A man was convicted of manslaughter for the killing of his wife, whom he had found in a compromising position with another woman. The plaintiff told the defendant, expressly in confidence, that she had had a lesbian relationship with the wife. The defendant allegedly informed *The Mail on Sunday*, which then stated in print that the plaintiff was the woman who had been found with the wife. The plaintiff brought proceedings for breach of confidence, and the defendant applied for the claim to be struck out as disclosing no reasonable cause of action. The defendant argued (a) that the law did not protect information which related to grossly immoral behaviour; (b) that the law did not protect mere tittle-tattle or trivial gossip; (c) that information relating to sexual contact was inevitably known to both parties to it, and therefore not confidential; and (d) that in the absence of a legally enforceable contract or a pre-existing relationship such as that of employer and employee, doctor and patient or priest and penitent no legal duty of confidence arose. The master refused to strike out the claim, and the defendants appealed.

Held, that the appeal would be dismissed. It was correct to say that the law afforded no protection to information about grossly immoral conduct, but there was no longer any generally recognised code of sexual morality to which a judge would be justified in making reference. The triviality of the information sought to be protected went to the exercise of the court's discretion to afford an equitable remedy, and not to the nature of the plaintiff's right. Furthermore, the information in the present case either was not trivial or could not be judged to be so until trial. The mere fact that two people knew a secret did not deprive it of its quality of secrecy. *Attorney General v Guardian Newspapers (No 2)* (1988) (see 22.1 below) was authority for the proposition that information only ceased to be capable of protection as confidential when it was in fact known to a substantial number of people. No legally enforceable contract or pre-existing relationship was required by law. *Per* Sir Nicholas Browne-Wilkinson VC:

> The basis of equitable intervention to protect confidentiality is that it is unconscionable for a person who has received information on the basis that it is confidential subsequently to reveal that information. Although the relationship between the parties is often important in cases where it is said that there is an implied as opposed to express obligation of confidence, the relationship between the parties is not the determining factor. It is the acceptance of the information on the basis that it will be kept secret that affects the conscience of the recipient.

21.2.4 The defence of public interest compelling disclosure

Francome v Mirror Group Newspapers (1984) CA
The first plaintiff was a well-known jockey. He was approached by journalists who wished to confirm the authenticity of tapes of his telephone conversations. The tapes, which had been made by other unidentified persons, were said to reveal that he had breached the rules of racing. They had been made by the tapping of his telephone without his knowledge. The plaintiff brought proceedings against the journalists and the newspaper for which they wrote, claiming, *inter alia*, damages for breach of confidence. He obtained an interlocutory injunction to restrain publication based on the tapes until trial. On appeal, the defendants sought the discharge of the injunction. They argued in defence to breach of confidence that they had acted in the public interest in revealing the plaintiff's suspected wrongdoing.

Held, that an injunction had been properly granted, but would be upheld in amended terms. It was indeed in the public interest that the allegations against the plaintiff should be investigated by the proper authorities, and the injunction would be varied to permit the disclosure of the tapes to such authorities with the permission of the appropriate minister of the Crown. The editor of the *Daily Mirror* had asserted a right in the public interest to publish a story based on the tapes, although he admitted that publication would probably be an offence under s 5(b) of the Wireless and Telegraphy Act 1949. Sir John Donaldson MR regarded this as a claim to be bound by the law only in so far as it remained expedient in the public interest (as conceived by the editor) to be so bound, and rejected it in forceful terms. Reviewing the circumstances in which a subject might feel obliged to break the law, he added:

> ... I nevertheless recognise that, in very rare circumstances, a situation can arise in which a citizen is faced with a conflict between what is, [*sic*] in effect, two inconsistent laws. The first law is the law of the land. The second is a moral imperative, usually, but not always, religious in origin ... However, I cannot over-emphasise the rarity of the moral imperative. Furthermore, it is almost unheard of for compliance with the moral imperative to be in the financial or other best interests of the persons concerned ...

> The 'media', to use a term which comprises not only the newspapers, but also television and radio, are an essential foundation of any democracy. In exposing crime, antisocial behaviour and hypocrisy and in campaigning for reform and propagating the views of minorities, they perform an invaluable function. However, they are peculiarly vulnerable to the error of confusing the public interest with their own interest ... In the instant case, it is impossible to see what public interest would be served by publishing the contents of the tapes which would not equally be served by giving them to the police or to the Jockey Club.

21.2.5 Revelation of wrongdoing is not the only acceptable rationale for disclosure

Lion Laboratories Ltd v Evans (1985) CA

The plaintiffs were the manufacturers of the Lion Intoximeter 3,000, used by the police for measuring the blood alcohol levels of motorists suspected of drink-driving offences. Two former employees of the plaintiff passed company documents detailing the plaintiff's and the Home Office's doubts about the Intoximeter to the *Daily Express*. The plaintiff applied for and received an *ex parte* injunction to prevent publication of the documents, claiming breach of copyright or breach of confidence. The *Daily Express* subsequently published an article based on the documents. The defendants appealed the injunction.

Held, allowing the appeal and discharging the injunction, that the issue raised by the defendants was a serious question concerning the life and the liberty of an unascertainable number of Her Majesty's subjects. Although the information regarding the working of the Intoximeter was confidential and had been unlawfully taken in breach of confidence, the defendants would not be restrained from putting that information before the public.

In the evidence before the court, no misconduct was alleged against the plaintiffs. However, it was incorrect to assert that the publication of confidential information would be in the public interest only if it revealed wrongdoing on the part of the person to whom it was confidential. The revelation of wrongdoing was merely one instance of an occasion on which there might be just cause for breaching confidence.

Malone v Metropolitan Police Commissioner (No 2) (1979)

Facts: see 2.3.1 above.

Sir Robert Megarry VC addressed, *inter alia*, the contention that the tapping of the plaintiff's telephone had contravened his right of privacy. He observed that there was no general right of privacy recognised by English law, but added that if the existing rules, in combination with the requirements of justice and common sense, pointed to the existence of such a right, a court would not be deterred from acknowledging it. The creation of a wholly new right was a different matter, however, and a court would have to bear in mind that its function was judicial, not legislative. Further, the right claimed was broad in its scope:

> The wider and more indefinite the right claimed, the greater the undesirability of holding that such a right exists. Wide and indefinite rights, while conferring an advantage on those who have them, may well gravely impair the position of those who are subject to the rights. To create a right for one person, you have to impose a corresponding duty on another. In the present case, the alleged right to hold a telephone conversation in the privacy of one's own home without molestation is wide and indefinite in its scope ... In any case, why is the telephone to be subject to this special right of privacy when there is no general right?

Q What is the duty which corresponds to the right to hold a telephone conversation without molestation? Is it accurately described as a duty?

22 Freedom of expression

Schering Chemicals v Falkman Ltd (1982) CA

The plaintiff, the manufacturer of a pregnancy-testing drug, sought an injunction to prevent the broadcasting of a television documentary which concerned allegations that the drug had caused abnormalities in children born to women who had used it. The plaintiff claimed that the producer of the documentary, who was formerly its employee, had used material confidential to the plaintiff.

Held (by a majority), that the injunction granted to the plaintiff would be upheld. Although the material in question was said already to be in the public domain, its re-publication would cause further damage to the plaintiff. *Per* Lord Denning MR (dissenting):

> The freedom of the press is extolled as one of the great bulwarks of liberty. It is entrenched in the constitutions of the world. But it is often misunderstood. I will first say what it does *not* mean. It does not mean that the press is free to ruin a reputation or to break a confidence, or to pollute the course of justice or to do anything that is unlawful. I will next say what it *does* mean. It means that there is to be no censorship. No restraint should be placed on the press as to what they should publish ... The press is not to be restrained *in advance* from publishing whatever it thinks right to publish. It can publish whatever it chooses to publish. But it does so at its own risk. It can 'publish and be damned'. Afterwards – after the publication – if the press has done anything unlawful – it can be dealt with by the courts. If it should offend – by interfering with the course of justice – it can be punished in proceedings for contempt of court. If it should damage the reputation of innocent people, by telling untruths or making unfair comment, it may be made liable in damages. But always afterwards. Never beforehand. Never by previous restraint.

Attorney General v Guardian Newspapers (No 1) (1987) HL

Peter Wright, a former member of the British security service MI5, sought to publish a book in Australia giving an account of his experiences in the service. The Crown obtained an interim injunction in New South Wales against publication in Australia, and injunctions to prevent the publication of extracts from the book in British newspapers. Contempt of court proceedings were also prosecuted against newspapers which had published in disregard of the injunctions. Certain of the newspapers applied for the discharge of the injunctions, arguing that the contents of the book were now in the public domain. By the time the appeals reached the House of Lords the book had been published in its entirety in several countries, and no attempt was made to prevent individuals from freely importing copies into the UK.

Held (by a majority), that the injunctions would be upheld and broadened. *Per* Lord Bridge (dissenting):

... now that the original aim of preventing disclosure of secret material can no longer be attained, the deterrent argument can only carry minimal weight.

What of the other side of the coin and the encroachment on freedom of speech? Having no written constitution, we have no equivalent in our law to the First Amendment to the Constitution of the United States of America. Some think that puts freedom of speech on too lofty a pedestal. Perhaps they are right. We have not adopted as part of our law the European Convention for the Protection of Human Rights and Fundamental Freedoms to which this country is a signatory. Many think that we should. I have hitherto not been of that persuasion, in large part because I have had confidence in the capacity of the common law to safeguard the fundamental freedoms essential to a free society including the right to freedom of speech which is specifically safeguarded by Article 10 of the Convention. My confidence is seriously undermined by your Lordships' decision ...

Freedom of speech is always the first casualty under a totalitarian regime. Such a regime cannot afford to allow the free circulation of information and ideas among its citizens. Censorship is the indispensable tool to regulate what the public may and what they may not know. The present attempt to insulate the public in this country from information which is freely available elsewhere is a significant step down that very dangerous road.

22.1 Compatibility of English law and the Convention

Attorney General v Guardian Newspapers (No 2) (1990) HL

The Attorney General sought permanent injunctions to prevent the publication of material obtained directly or indirectly from Mr Wright, a general injunction against the future publication by certain newspapers of material derived from Mr Wright or other members of the security service, and an account of profits made by another newspaper which had begun to serialise the book.

Held (on the first issue by a majority only), that the permanent injunctions would not be granted because publication would not be contrary to the public interest. This was because the information in question was already in the public domain. The Crown was entitled to an account of the profits from that part of the serialisation which had already been published, but not with regard to future serialisation. The claim for general injunctions would be refused. In the course of his speech, Lord Goff considered the compatibility of the English law on confidentiality with Article 10 of the European Convention on Human Rights:

Finally, I wish to observe that I can see no inconsistency between English law on this subject and Article 10 of the European Convention on Human Rights. This is scarcely surprising, since we may pride ourselves on the fact that freedom of speech has existed in this country perhaps as long as, if not longer than, it has existed in any other country in the world. The only difference is that, whereas Article 10 of the Convention, in accordance with its avowed purpose, proceeds to state a fundamental right and then to qualify it, we in this country (where everybody is free to do anything, subject only to the provisions of the law) proceed rather upon an assumption of freedom of speech, and turn to our law to discover the established exceptions to it. In any event, I conceive it to be my duty, when I am free to do so, to interpret the law in accordance with the obligations of the Crown under this Treaty. The exercise of the right to freedom of expression under Article 10 may be subject to restrictions (as are prescribed by law and are necessary in a democratic society) in relation to certain prescribed matters, which include 'the interests of national security' and 'preventing the disclosure of information received in confidence'. It is established in the jurisprudence of the European Court of Human Rights that the word 'necessary' in this context implies the existence of a pressing social need, and that interference with freedom of expression should be no more than is proportionate to the legitimate aim pursued. I have no reason to believe that English law, as applied in the courts, leads to any different conclusion.

23 Freedom of religion

23.1 The definition of 'religion'

Barralet v Attorney General (1980)

The South Place Ethical Society had as its objects (i) 'the study and dissemination of ethical principles' and (ii) 'the cultivation of a rational religious sentiment'. In pursuit of both these objects the society had as its aim to rely on the methods of reason, rather than on instruction by supernatural revelation, and in the second of its objects the word 'religious' was used in a sense devoid of supernatural content. By an originating summons the society asked the court to declare whether or not its objects were charitable. The court considered whether the objects fell under the charitable heads of the advancement of religion, the advancement of education, or whether they were for purposes beneficial to the community.

Held, that the society's objects came under the latter two heads, but could not be brought under the first head. The society had contended that a sincere belief in ethical qualities was religious, because such qualities as truth, love and beauty were sacred, and the advancement of any such belief was the advancement of religion. Although it was true that such beliefs might occupy a place in the minds of their possessors parallel to that of religious beliefs, the two could not be equated. *Per* Dillon J:

> In a free country ... it is natural that the court should not desire to discriminate between beliefs deeply and sincerely held, whether they are beliefs in a god or in the excellence of man or in Platonism or some other scheme of philosophy. But I do not see that that warrants extending the meaning of the word 'religion' so as to embrace all other beliefs and philosophies. The two are not the same, and are not made the same by sincere inquiry into the question, what is God ... There is a further point. It seems to me that two of the essential attributes of religion are faith and worship.

23.2 The extent of the association between Christianity and the law

Bowman v Secular Society (1917) HL

The society's objects included the following: 'to promote ... the principle that human conduct should be based upon natural knowledge, and not upon super-natural belief, and that human welfare in this world is the proper end of all thought and action'. The appellants challenged the validity of a testamentary gift to the society on the grounds that acts done in pursuance of its objects were illegal.

Held (by a majority), dismissing the appeal, that such acts would not now be regarded as contrary to the law. Lord Sumner stated that the case gave rise to the question whether Christianity was part of the law of England, and if so, in what sense it was. While it was true that England was a Christian State, that the national religion was Christianity and that the English family was built on Christian ideals, the maxim that 'Christianity was part of the law of England' was rhetoric and not law. Lord Sumner continued:

> English law may well be called a Christian law, but we apply many of its rules and most of its principles, with equal justice and equally good government, in heathen communities, and its sanctions, even in courts of conscience, are material and not spiritual ... In the present day, reasonable men do not apprehend the dissolution or downfall of society because religion is publicly assailed by methods not scandalous. Whether it is possible that in the future irreligious attacks, designed to undermine fundamental institutions of our society, may come to be criminal in themselves, as constituting a public danger, is a matter that does not arise. The fact that opinion grounded on experience has moved one way does not in law preclude the possibility of its moving on fresh experience in the other; nor does it bind succeeding generations, when conditions have again changed.

23.3 The law of blasphemy

23.3.1 The protection of Christianity

Whitehouse v Lemon (1979) HL

The magazine *Gay News* published a poem entitled 'The Love that Dares to Speak its Name'. This, in the words of Lord Diplock, purported 'to describe in explicit detail acts of sodomy and fellatio with the body of Christ immediately after His death and to ascribe to Him during his lifetime promiscuous homosexual practices with the Apostles and with other men'. A private prosecution was brought against the magazine and its editor by Mary Whitehouse. Although the common law offence of blasphemous libel had been thought to have become a 'dead letter' (described thus by Lord Denning in *Freedom under the Law* (1949)), the defendants were convicted. They appealed to the House of Lords on the grounds that to sustain a conviction it was necessary to prove the accused's specific intent to shock believing Christians.

Held (by a majority), that the appeal would be dismissed. The Court of Appeal had correctly concluded that blasphemous libel was a crime of strict liability. It was sufficient to show an intent to publish the material in question; the motive for publication was irrelevant. Although the judge at first instance had stated that he would have been prepared if necessary to extend the protection of the law against blasphemous libel to other religions, the House made it clear that at present it applied exclusively to Christianity. It was not for the judiciary to broaden it. *Per* Lord Scarman:

> My Lords, I do not subscribe to the view that the common law offence of blasphemous libel serves no purpose in the modern law. On the contrary, I think that there is a case for legislation extending it to protect the religious beliefs and feelings of non-Christians. The offence belongs to a group of criminal offences designed to safeguard the internal tranquillity of the kingdom. In an increasingly plural society, it is necessary not only to protect the differing religious beliefs, feelings and practices of all but also to protect them from scurrility, vilification, ridicule and contempt.

23.3.2 The position of other religions

R v Chief Metropolitan Stipendiary Magistrate, *ex parte* Choudhury (1991)
The applicant sought judicial review of the Chief Magistrate's refusal to issue a summons alleging blasphemous libel and seditious libel against the publisher of Salman Rushdie's novel *The Satanic Verses*.

Held, refusing the application, that on the present state of the law the offence of blasphemous libel did not extend to protect any religion other than Christianity. If the law was to be changed in this respect, it was for Parliament and not the courts to change it. Were it open to the present court to change it, it would not in any event do so, since the extension of the protection would give rise to difficult questions of definition, and put the issue of the libel itself beyond the common understanding of a jury. Furthermore, in so far as the protection afforded by the common law of blasphemous libel was discriminatory, Watkins LJ (re-stating and apparently approving the submissions of counsel for the publisher) considered that state of affairs objectively justified:

> The offence of blasphemous libel is an offence of strict liability ... If the offence is extended to cover attacks upon religious doctrines, tenets, commandments, or practices of religions other than Christianity, the existence of such an extended law of blasphemy would encourage intolerance, divisiveness and unreasonable interference and interferences with freedom of expression. Fundamentalist Christians, Jews or Muslims could then seek to invoke the offence of blasphemy

against each other's religion, doctrines, tenets, commandments, or practices; for example denying the divinity of Jesus Christ; or for denying that the Messiah has yet to come; or for denying the divine inspiration of the Prophet Mohammed, and so on. An extended law of blasphemy which applied to all religions could be used as a weapon between Protestants and Roman Catholics in Northern Ireland, or by fringe religions, such as the Church of Scientology. The fact that the offence was committed only in cases of scurrilous attacks would mitigate, but would not eliminate, the resulting intolerance, divisiveness, and unreasonable interference with freedom of expression ...

Q Would it be preferable to maintain the *status quo*, or to abolish the offence of blasphemous libel, or to extend it to all religions, or to extend it and re-define its *mens rea* to require blameworthy motivation?

23.4 Religious discrimination and testamentary freedom

Blaythwayt v Baron Cawley (1976) HL

A testator who died in 1936 had settled property upon certain persons subject to a forfeiture clause providing that if any person who became entitled as tenant for life or tenant in tail male to possession of the estate should 'be or become a Roman Catholic ... the estate hereby limited to him shall cease and determine and be utterly void and my principal estate shall thereupon go to the person next entitled ...'. The question arose whether this clause was void for reasons of public policy.

Held, that it was not. Lord Wilberforce noted that the European Convention referred to freedom of religion and to enjoyment of that and other freedoms without discrimination on the ground of religion. He acknowledged that conceptions of public policy should move with the times, but was of the opinion that to introduce a rule of law avoiding the clause would be to uphold one freedom only at the cost of a substantial reduction in another – the freedom of testamentary disposition. The provision in question was a matter of choice, not of discrimination, and private choice was not a matter of public policy. *Per* Lord Cross of Chelsea:

Turning to the question of public policy, it is true that it is widely thought nowadays that it is wrong for government to treat some of its citizens less favourably than others because of differences in their religious beliefs; but it does not follow from that that it is against public policy for an adherent of one religion to distinguish in disposing of his property between adherents of his faith and those of another. So to hold would amount to saying that though it is in order for a man to have a mild preference for one religion as opposed to another it is disreputable for him to be convinced of the importance of holding true religious beliefs and the fact that his religious beliefs are the true ones.

Q Should a distinction be drawn in terms of public policy between a will which disentitles all but those of a given faith, and one which disentitles none but those of a given faith?

24 Freedom of movement

24.1 Freedom to travel abroad

Immigration Act 1971

1.– (1) All those who are in this Act expressed to have the right of abode in the UK shall be free to live in, and to come and go into and from, the UK without let or hindrance except such as may be required under and in accordance with this Act to enable their right to be established or as may be otherwise lawfully imposed on any person.

...

2.– (1) A person is under this Act to have the right of abode in the UK if:

(a) he is a British citizen ...

24.2 Exclusion orders: legal challenge

R v Secretary of State for the Home Department, *ex parte* Stitt (1987)
The applicant sought judicial review of the Secretary of State's refusal to revoke an exclusion order made under the Prevention of Terrorism (Temporary Provisions) Acts 1976 and 1984. Additionally, he applied to order the Secretary of State to give reasons for the making of the exclusion order.

Held, refusing the application, that the 1976 Act was comprehensive in its provision of rights to those against whom the legislation operated, and no such rights of the applicant had been breached. Further, the Secretary of State's refusal to give reasons was based on considerations of national security. Once there was *bona fide* evidence that security was involved, the court would not examine the strength of justification for the Secretary of State's actions.

24.3 Deportation

24.3.1 Considerations governing the discretion to make a deportation order after conviction

R v Nazari (1980) CA

Following their convictions for various offences, the three defendants, all of whom were immigrants, were recommended to be deported. The Court of Appeal laid down the following principles for general application in cases where there was jurisdiction to make a deportation order:

(1) The court was to consider whether the offender's continued presence in the UK would be to the country's detriment. The country had no use for criminals of other nationalities. The more serious the crime and the longer the offender's criminal record, the more obvious it was that a deportation order should be made;

(2) The court would not be concerned with the political systems operating in the country to which the offender would be deported. This was a matter for the Home Secretary to take into account at the end of the offender's sentence of imprisonment in this country;

(3) The court would consider the effect that an offender's deportation would have on innocent persons not before the court, such as the offender's family;

(4) Where an offender states his intention to return to his country voluntarily at the end of his sentence the court would be unwise to allow such a statement much weight;

(5) Where an offender is found to be an illegal immigrant, a deportation order should normally be made.

24.3.2 Legal challenge to the decision to deport

R v Governor of Brixton Prison, *ex parte* Soblen (1963) CA

Soblen was convicted of espionage in the USA. He absconded while on bail pending an appeal. During a flight returning him from Israel to the US, he inflicted wounds upon himself as the plane neared London, in order to force it to land. A deportation order was made against him by the Secretary of State, who let it be known that he intended Soblen to be placed on a flight to the US. Soblen sought a writ of habeas corpus on the ground, *inter alia*, that the deportation order was calculated to amount to extradition, and that the Secretary of State had accordingly acted for an improper purpose; no power to extradite in fact existed with respect to Soblen's offence. At first instance Soblen's application was refused.

Held, dismissing the appeal, that two principles were to be weighed together. First, the Crown had power to surrender a fugitive offender to another country only in so far as it might do so in accordance with the Extradition Acts. Secondly, the Secretary of State could deport an alien if he considered it to be conducive to the public good. It was necessary to enquire what the Secretary of State's purpose had been in making the order. If the deportation order was a mere sham, designed to achieve an unlawful extradition, then the court could overturn it. Here, however, there was no evidence that the Secretary of State had acted to achieve an improper purpose, and there were grounds on which he could genuinely have come to the conclusion that Soblen's deportation would be to the public good.

R v Secretary of State for the Home Department, *ex parte* Hosenball (1977) CA

The applicant, a US citizen, had been working in the UK as an investigative journalist. He was informed by the Secretary of State that he was to be deported on the ground of national security. The applicant sought further information from the Secretary of State, who considered the request but stated that it was to be refused in the interests of national security. By the terms of the Immigration Rules and of an undertaking given by the Secretary of State to the House of Commons, a person proposed to be deported was to be given a hearing and such particulars of the allegations against him as would not entail disclosure of sources of evidence. The applicant received a hearing, but was given no particulars of the case against him. He sought judicial review of the subsequent decision to issue a deportation order against him on the grounds that the Secretary of State was required either by the principles of natural justice or by the Rules or undertaking to distinguish between disclosable and non-disclosable allegations upon which the order was based.

The application was dismissed at first instance, and the applicant appealed to the Court of Appeal.

Held, dismissing the appeal, that the demands of national security could prevail over the requirements of natural justice. The balance between the demands of national security and natural justice was a matter for the Secretary of State. He had considered the applicant's request for further information, and he was entitled to refuse it. He would be answerable to Parliament, and not to the courts, for his judgment. *Per* Lord Denning MR:

> There is a conflict here between the interests of national security on the one hand and the freedom of the individual on the other. The balance between these two is not for a court of law. It is for the Home Secretary. He is the person entrusted by Parliament with the task. In some parts of the world national security has on occasions been used as an excuse for all kinds of infringements of individual liberty. But not in England.

R v Secretary of State for the Home Department, *ex parte* Cheblak (1991) CA

Shortly after the outbreak of hostilities in the Gulf in 1991, the applicant, a Lebanese citizen and a known pacifist, was arrested and served with a notice of the Home Secretary's intention to make a deportation order against him on the grounds of national security. The risk was later stated by the Home Department to arise from the applicant's association with an organisation which it was believed might indulge in terrorist activity in the UK. The Secretary of State subsequently stated in an affidavit that national security prevented the disclosure of further details of the case in favour of deportation. The applicant, arguing that the Secretary of State's decision was contrary to natural justice, irrational, and made in disregard of relevant considerations, sought judicial review and a writ of habeas corpus. Both applications were refused at first instance, and the applicant appealed to the Court of Appeal.

Held, dismissing the appeal, that the challenge failed on all three grounds. Concluding his judgment, Lord Donaldson MR noted that responsibility for decisions made on grounds of national security rested not with the courts, but with government; the courts would intervene if the Secretary of State were to be shown to have acted in bad faith or to have exceeded his statutory powers. Otherwise the court would accept that the Secretary of State had good grounds for his decision without requiring him to adduce evidence to that effect. Although it was true that tensions might arise between considerations of individual liberty and the requirements of national security, and that there would be cases where the latter would prevail over the former, it was relevant to remember that national security was in fact the foundation of all civil liberties.

24.3.3 Deportation and the rights of third parties

Singh v Immigration Appeals Tribunal (1986) HL
The applicant, a Sikh musician, overstayed his leave to remain in the UK by more than three years. He appealed unsuccessfully to an immigration adjudicator and thence to the Immigration Appeals Tribunal against a deportation order made against him by the Secretary of State. He then sought judicial review of the tribunal's decision. Before the House of Lords he contended that the damaging effect of his deportation on the Sikh community was either a compassionate circumstance or part of the relevant circumstances which the immigration authorities were bound by the 1982 Immigration Rules to take into account in considering an appeal against a deportation order.

Held, allowing the appeal, that the respondent tribunal had misdirected itself in law. The prejudice to third parties which would be caused by the applicant's deportation was a relevant factor under the Immigration Rules. Further, under principles of general law, it was a factor which the Secretary of State had been bound to consider by virtue of its bearing on the matter before him. It was therefore a matter which the tribunal should have directed itself to consider, since it was bound by s 19(1)(a) of the Immigration Act 1971 to decide whether the Secretary of State's decision was 'in accordance with the law'.

25 Prisoners' rights

25.1 Judicial review is available to vindicate the residual rights of prisoners

R v Board of Visitors of Hull Prison, *ex parte* **St Germain (No 1) (1979) CA**

As a result of their part in riots at Hull Prison, the applicants were subjected to various disciplinary penalties by the Board of Visitors. They sought orders of *certiorari* to quash the disciplinary awards on the grounds that the board had failed to observe the rules of natural justice. Their applications were refused by the Divisional Court on the preliminary ground that the determinations of the Board of Visitors in these circumstances could not be subject to judicial review, but concerned merely internal and domestic disciplinary matters. Further, recognition of the right of prisoners to apply for judicial review of decisions relating to prison discipline would render the position of the prison authorities intolerable. The applicants appealed to the Court of Appeal.

Held, allowing the appeals and remitting the case to the Divisional Court, that the supervisory jurisdiction of the High Court was in principle sufficiently broad for an order of *certiorari* to issue against the disciplinary award of a prison board of visitors. Shaw LJ cited provisions of the Prison Rules 1964, made under the Prison Act 1952, and concluded that '... despite the deprivation of his general liberty, a prisoner remains invested with residuary rights appertaining to the nature and conduct of his incarceration'. He continued:

> Now the rights of a citizen, however circumscribed by a penal sentence or otherwise, must always be the concern of the courts unless their jurisdiction is clearly excluded by some statutory provision. The courts are in general the ultimate custodians of the rights and liberties of the subject whatever his status and however attenuated those rights may be as the result of some punitive or other process ... Once it is acknowledged that such rights exist the courts have function and jurisdiction. It is irrelevant that the Secretary of State may afford redress where the rules have been infringed or their application has been irregular or unduly harsh. An essential characteristic of the right of a subject is that it carries with it a right of recourse to the courts unless some statute decrees otherwise.

R v Deputy Governor of Parkhurst Prison, *ex parte* Hague; Weldon v Home Office (1991) HL

The applicant in the first case sought judicial review of the prison governor's decision to transfer him between prisons and to segregate him from other prisoners, and included a claim for damages for false imprisonment. The Court of Appeal granted his application in part, but held that a claim for damages by a prisoner for breach of the Prison Rules did not lie, and a claim for false imprisonment would be maintainable only if the prisoner had been deprived of his residual liberty in bad faith, or the conditions of his imprisonment were 'intolerable'. In the second case a prisoner claimed damages against the Home Office for assault and battery, and for false imprisonment. The Home Office appealed to the House of Lords from the Court of Appeal's refusal to strike out the part of the claim relating to false imprisonment. The House heard the cases as conjoined appeals.

Held, dismissing the prisoner's appeal in the first case and allowing the Home Office's appeal in the second case, that a prisoner had no claim for damages arising from a breach of the Prison Rules, and could not maintain an action for false imprisonment on either of the grounds identified by the Court of Appeal. The second of these claims rested on the proposition that a prisoner had, despite his confinement, a residual liberty amounting to a right which the law would protect. That was incorrect. While it was true that the law would provide a remedy where the prisoner's conditions of detainment were intolerable, the remedy thus granted would be one which would not impugn the legality of the detainment.

Rejecting the concept of residual liberty, Lord Bridge said as follows:

> Can the prisoner then complain that his legal rights are infringed by a restraint which confines him at any particular time within a particular part of the prison? It seems to me that the reality of prison life demands a negative answer to this question. Certainly in the ordinarily closed prison the ordinary prisoner will at any time of day or night be in a particular part of the prison, not because that is where he chooses to be, but because that is where the prison regime requires him to be ... Thus the concept of the prisoner's 'residual liberty' as a species of freedom of movement within the prison enjoyed as a legal right which the prison authorities cannot lawfully restrain seems to me quite illusory. The prisoner is at all times lawfully restrained within closely defined bounds and if he is kept in a segregated cell, at a time when, if the rules had not been misapplied, he would be in the company of other prisoners at the workshop, at the dinner table or elsewhere, this is not the deprivation of his liberty of movement, which is the essence of the tort of false imprisonment, it is the substitution of one form of restraint for another.

25.2 Prisoners' rights of access to the courts

Raymond v Honey (1983) HL

Raymond, a prisoner, applied to commit the prison governor for contempt of court. The governor had intercepted and decided not to forward a letter written by Raymond to his solicitor which related not only to pending legal proceedings, but also contained allegations against an assistant governor. Raymond's application to commit the governor was also intercepted by him. Orders made under s 47 of the Prison Act (PA) 1952 permitted correspondence between a prisoner who was party to any legal proceedings and his solicitor, and gave the prison governor power to stop letters containing allegations against prison officers, requiring him to explain the correct complaints procedure to the prisoner. The Divisional Court held that the stopping of the first letter did not constitute contempt of court, but that the stopping of the second letter did. The governor appealed, and Raymond cross appealed.

Held, that both the appeal and the cross appeal would be dismissed. Two principles governed the case. The first was derived from *R v Gray* (1900). Any act calculated to obstruct or interfere with the course of justice, or the lawful process of the courts, was a contempt of court. The second principle, stated in *R v Board of Visitors of Hull Prison, ex parte St Germain (No 1)* (1979) (see 25.1 above), was that a convicted prisoner retained all civil rights which were not expressly or by necessary implication taken from him. The PA 1952 did not confer power to make regulations which would deny or interfere with a prisoner's right to have unimpeded access to a court. The orders made under s 47 of the PA 1952 would be interpreted narrowly in order to avoid ascribing to them that effect (which would have rendered them *ultra vires*). The governor had temporarily denied Raymond's access to the court, and had therefore committed a contempt.

26 The courts and police powers

26.1 Police duties and the nature of the citizen's duty to assist the police

Rice v Connolly (1966)

In the early hours of the morning, police constables were patrolling an area of Grimsby in which a number of burglaries had taken place the same night. The officers saw the appellant behaving suspiciously, and asked him where he was going, where he was coming from, and his name and address. The appellant gave only partial (although accurate) details and refused to provide more information. When he refused to accompany the constables to a police box to confirm his identity, he was then arrested on the grounds that he had wilfully obstructed a police constable in the exercise of his duty. The appellant was convicted, and appealed to the Divisional Court.

Held, that the appeal would be allowed. It was clear that the appellant had obstructed the police, and that the police had been acting throughout in accordance with their duty. It was part of the obligations and duties of a police constable (*per* Lord Parker CJ):

> ... to take all steps which appear to him necessary for keeping the peace, for preventing crime or for protecting property from criminal injury. There is no exhaustive definition of the powers and obligations of the police, but they are at least those, and they would further include the duty to detect crime and to bring an offender to justice.

However, it was necessary for the prosecution to prove that the obstruction was 'wilful', which in the context meant not merely 'intentional', but connoted something which was done without lawful excuse. Here the question was whether the appellant had a lawful excuse for failing to answer the questions which had been put to him. In the judgment of Lord Parker CJ he had; while every citizen had a moral or social duty to assist the police there was no legal duty to that effect, and the appellant was therefore within his rights to refuse to answer the questions put to him. *Per* Marshall J:

> In order to uphold this conviction it appears to me that one has to assent to the proposition that where a citizen is acting merely within his legal rights, he is thereby committing a criminal offence.

26.2 The requirement of legal justification for police action

R v Waterfield & Lynn (1964)

Per Ashworth J:

In the judgment of this court it would be difficult, and in the present case it is unnecessary, to reduce within specific limits the general terms in which the duties of police constables have been expressed. In most cases, it is probably more convenient to consider what the police constable was actually doing and in particular whether such conduct was *prima facie* an unlawful interference with a person's liberty or property. If so, it is then relevant to consider whether (a) such conduct falls within the general scope of any duty imposed by statute or recognised at common law and (b) whether such conduct, albeit within the general scope of such a duty, involved an unjustifiable use of powers associated with the duty.

26.3 The exercise of specific powers

26.3.1 Arrest

The meaning of 'reasonable suspicion'

Castorina v Chief Constable of Surrey (1988) CA

Section 2(4) of the Criminal Law Act (CLA) 1967 provided as follows: 'Where a constable, with reasonable cause, suspects that an arrestable offence has been committed, he may arrest without warrant anyone whom he, with reasonable cause, suspects to be guilty of the offence.' Detectives, who reasonably suspected that the burglary of a company's premises was an inside job, interviewed the respondent and arrested her. They had been informed that the documents taken by the burglar would have been useful to a person who had a grudge against the company. The respondent was detained at the police station for three and a quarter hours, interrogated, and released without charge. She claimed damages for wrongful arrest and detention. The court at first instance upheld her claim, holding that 'reasonable cause' required an 'honest belief founded on reasonable suspicion leading an ordinary cautious man to the conclusion that the person arrested was guilty of the offence'. It was further stated that an ordinary man would have sought more information from the suspect before arresting her, including an examination of whether she held any grudge against the company. The respondent was awarded £4,500. The Chief Constable appealed to the Court of Appeal.

Held, allowing the appeal, that in objective terms there was sufficient information available to the arresting officers to give them reasonable cause to suspect that the respondent was guilty of the burglary. The remaining question therefore was whether before arresting her the officers should have sought further information and explanation from her. Purchas LJ reviewed the authorities and concluded that they imposed no such requirement. Although the failure to follow an obvious course of questioning might in exceptional circumstances render the decision to arrest subject to challenge under the *Wednesbury* principle (*Associated Provincial Picture Houses Ltd v Wednesbury Corporation* (1948) (see 13.1 above)), the court should have been concerned in the present action only to establish whether the arresting officers had reasonable cause for suspicion, and not with any further inquiries which the officers might have carried out. The judge at first instance had not so confined himself, and had therefore directed himself wrongly in law in applying the provisions of the CLA 1967.

The requirement to inform the suspect of the grounds for his arrest

Christie v Leachinsky (1947) HL

The appellant was a rag merchant. He was arrested by two police officers of the Liverpool police force and charged under the Liverpool Corporation Act 1921 with the unlawful possession of a bale of cloth. He was detained in custody for a day, brought before a magistrate and twice remanded for periods of a week. At the hearing he was discharged, but was rearrested later the same day. The Leicester police then charged him with larceny and took him to Leicester in order to commit him for trial. The Leicester magistrates dismissed the charge. The appellant brought an action against the Liverpool police officers for false imprisonment and for trespass to the person.

Held, that under the Liverpool Corporation Act 1921 the police could arrest without a warrant in these circumstances only if the name and address of the suspect were unknown and could not be ascertained. That was not the case here, and the arrest was therefore unlawful. Further, the common law power of arrest was limited to arrest on a specific charge. Viscount Simon considered that the authorities established the following propositions:

(1) If a policeman arrests without warrant on a reasonable suspicion of felony, or of other crime of a sort which does not require a warrant, he must in ordinary circumstances inform the person arrested of the true ground of arrest. He is not entitled to keep the reason to himself or to give a reason which is not the true reason. In other words, a citizen is entitled to know on what charge or on suspicion of what charge he is seized.

(2) If the citizen is not so informed, but is nevertheless seized, the policeman, apart from certain exceptions, is liable for false imprisonment.

(3) The requirement that the person arrested should be informed of the reason why he is seized naturally does not exist if the circumstances are such that he must know the general nature of the alleged offence for which he is detained.

(4) The requirement that he should be so informed does not mean that technical or precise language need be used. The matter is a matter of substance, and turns on the elementary proposition that in this country a person is, *prima facie*, entitled to his freedom and is only required to submit to restraint on his freedom if he knows in substance the reason why it is claimed that this restraint should be imposed.

(5) The person arrested cannot complain that he has not been supplied with the above information as and when he should be, if he himself produces the situation which makes it practically impossible to inform him, eg by immediate counter attack or by running away.

An originally unlawful arrest may become lawful

Lewis and another v Chief Constable of the South Wales Constabulary (1991) CA

The appellants were arrested for burglary. They were not informed of the reason for the arrest until their arrival at the police station. This took place 10 minutes after arrest in the case of the first appellant and some 23 minutes after arrest in the case of the second appellant. Section 28(3) of the Police and Criminal Evidence Act (PACE) 1984 provided that 'no arrest is lawful unless the person arrested is informed of the ground for the arrest at the time of, or as soon as practicable after, the arrest'. The appellants brought an action against the Chief Constable for wrongful arrest and false imprisonment. The trial judge held that the arrest, although originally unlawful, was a continuing action and became lawful once the appellants were told the reasons for it. The jury awarded each appellant £200 in damages. The appellants argued on appeal that the arrest was a nullity, that an originally unlawful arrest could not later become lawful, and that they were accordingly entitled to damages in respect of the entire period of detention (some five hours).

Held, dismissing the appeal, that the authorities showed that arrest was to be regarded as an ordinary English word, and not a legal concept. Therefore the question whether a person had been arrested depended on the fact of deprivation of liberty, and not on the legitimacy of the arrest. The case of *Holgate-Mohammed v Duke* (1984) (see 26.3.1 below) showed that arrest was a continuing act, and remained good law in the light of the PACE 1984. There was nothing inconsistent with s 28(3) in holding that from the time the appellants had been informed of the reason for their arrest, the arrest became lawful.

Limits on restraint of suspects outside arrest

Kenlin v Gardiner (1967)

Two plain-clothes police officers became suspicious of the behaviour of two boys, who were visiting the homes of members of their school rugby team in order to remind them about a forthcoming match. One of the officers approached the boys, asked them what they were doing, and showed his warrant card. The boys nevertheless failed to realise that the men were police officers, and one of the boys attempted to run away. The officer took hold of the boy by the arm in order to prevent his escape. A struggle then took place, one of the officers was struck, and the boys ran away. They were charged under s 51(1) of the Police Act 1964, and appealed against conviction.

Held, that the appeal would be allowed. Winn LJ considered whether the officer had been entitled in law to take hold of the boy by the arm, and continued:

> I feel myself compelled to say that the answer to that question must be in the negative. This officer might or might not in the particular circumstances have possessed a power to arrest these boys. I leave that question open, saying no more than that I feel some doubt whether he would have had a power of arrest; but on the assumption that he had a power of arrest, it is to my mind perfectly plain that neither of these officers purported to arrest either of these boys. What was done was not done as an integral step in the process of arresting, but was done in order to secure an opportunity, by detaining the boys from escape, to put to them or to either of them the question which was regarded as the test question to satisfy the officers whether or not it would be right in the circumstances, and having regard to the answer obtained from that question, if any, to arrest them.

> I regret to say that I think there was a technical assault by the police officer ...

R v Inwood (1973) CA

The appellant was charged with assaulting a police constable in the exercise of his duty. He had attended voluntarily at a police station for questioning in connection with alleged thefts. During this procedure a detective constable had told the appellant that he proposed to charge him with theft and handling stolen goods, and had cautioned him. The police then carried out the formalities associated with arrest, including finger-printing the appellant. The appellant later attempted to leave the police station. The police sought to prevent his departure, and in the ensuing struggle two officers were injured. At trial, the judge directed the jury that the appellant had been legally arrested. The appellant was convicted.

Held, allowing the appeal, that the question whether it had been made clear to the appellant that he was under arrest was one of fact and should have been left to the jury. It would depend on the circumstances of individual cases whether enough had been done to demonstrate that a man had been arrested, and no particular formula would suit every case. Different procedures might have to be followed with different persons depending on their age, ethnic origin, knowledge of English, intellectual qualities or mental disabilities. In every case there would be an obligation to make it plain to the suspect by what was said and done that he was no longer a free man. Here, without the judge's direction the jury might or might not have found sufficient to have been done. The conviction would therefore be quashed.

Pedro v Diss (1981)

The appellant was charged with an assault on a police constable in the course of his duty, contrary to s 51(1) of the Police Act 1964. The officer had seen the appellant in the doorway of a house, and suspected that he might be in possession of house breaking implements or property stolen from the house. He searched the appellant. In response to further questioning, the appellant walked away. When the officer took the appellant by the arm and told him that he wanted him to return to the house, the appellant tried to pull away, swore at the officer, and hit him. At trial the appellant argued that the officer was acting unlawfully by detaining him without arresting him. The officer contended that s 66 of the Metropolitan Police Courts Act 1839 gave him power to detain. The appellant was convicted.

Held, allowing the appeal, that officer had not been acting in the course of his duty. There had been no arrest, and in order lawfully to detain the appellant under s 66, the officer should have communicated to him that he was no longer a free man, and the ground for the detention.

Challenge to the exercise of statutory powers of arrest

Holgate-Mohammed v Duke (1984) HL

A police officer suspected the appellant of the theft of jewellery, but considered that he needed further evidence in order to secure the appellant's conviction. Rather than interviewing the appellant under caution, the officer decided to arrest her and take her to a police station for questioning. The county court judge found the officer's intention was to subject the appellant 'to the greater stress and pressure involved in arrest and deprivation of liberty in the belief that if she was going to confess she would be more likely to do so in a state of arrest' (though it was not suggested that any impropriety took place). The judge awarded the appellant £1,000 damages for false imprisonment. The Court of Appeal allowed an appeal by the Chief Constable. The appellant appealed to the House of Lords.

Held, dismissing the appeal, that the powers under which the arrest had been made were not common law powers, but derived from s 2(4) of the Criminal Law Act 1967. Accordingly, the court was concerned with the exercise of a discretion conferred by statute. It could be challenged only by reference to the *Wednesbury* principles. Applying those principles, Lord Diplock noted that it had been found as fact by the county court judge that the officer had acted in good faith. The court therefore had only to determine whether the officer's exercise of his discretion had been reasonable. This depended on whether the officer's motivation constituted an irrelevant consideration. Lord Diplock was of opinion that it did not. Accordingly the arrest was lawful.

26.3.2 Other powers

A suspect's rights may not be infringed unless that necessity appears on the facts of the individual case

Lindley v Rutter (1981)

The appellant was arrested for disorderly behaviour while drunk. She was taken to a police station, where she refused to be searched. Two women police officers then forcibly searched her and removed her brassiere. In the course of the search, the appellant assaulted one of the officers. The officers believed that they were acting in accordance with standing orders of the chief constable which they understood to require them to search every female prisoner and remove her brassiere for her own protection. The appellant argued that the woman police officer had not been acting in the course of her duty when the appellant assaulted her.

Held, allowing the appeal, that the appellant's argument was correct, since the officer had exceeded her duty at the time of the assault. *Per* Donaldson LJ:

> It is the duty of the courts to be ever zealous to protect the personal freedom, privacy and dignity of all who live in these islands. Any claim to be entitled to take action which infringes these rights is to be examined with very great care. But such rights are not absolute. They have to be weighed against the rights and duties of police officers, acting on behalf of society as a whole. It is the duty of any constable who lawfully has a prisoner in his charge to take all reasonable measures to ensure that the prisoner does not escape or assist others to do so, does not injure himself or others, does not destroy or dispose of evidence and does not commit further crime such as, for example, malicious damage to property. This list is not exhaustive, but it is sufficient for present purposes. What measures are reasonable in the discharge of this duty will depend upon the likelihood that the particular prisoner will do any of these things unless prevented ... What can never be justified is the adoption of any particular measures without regard to all the circumstances of the particular case. This is not to say that there can be no standing instructions ... But the officer having custody of the prisoner must always consider, and be allowed and encouraged to consider, whether the special circumstances of the particular case justify or demand a departure from the standard procedure either by omitting what would otherwise be done or by taking additional measures. So far as searches are concerned, he should appreciate that they involve an affront to the dignity and privacy of the individual. Furthermore, there are degrees of affront involved in such a search. Clearly going through someone's pockets or handbag is less of an affront than a body search. In every case a police officer ordering a search or depriving a prisoner of property should have a very good reason for doing so.

A suspect must be informed of the reason for an infringement of his rights

Brazil v Chief Constable of Surrey (1983)

The appellant was asked but refused to leave a public house, and arrested by police officers for conducting herself in a way likely to cause a breach of the peace. Upon being taken to the police station she was informed by a woman police officer that everyone brought into the police station had to be searched for their own safety. The appellant then assaulted the officer. At this stage the police did not suspect the appellant of being in possession of controlled drugs. The officer in charge of the police station, Acting Inspector Martin, subsequently ordered the appellant to be searched by force. She then assaulted the woman police officer who was carrying out the search. Acting Inspector Martin did suspect the appellant of being in possession of controlled drugs, but he did not inform her that this was the reason for the search. The appellant contended that the first assault could not be an assault on a police officer in the execution of her duty because the justification given for the search was not a proper justification. With regard to the second search, the appellant argued, *inter alia*, that it was unlawful because she had not been informed of the reason for it.

Held, allowing the appeal and quashing the appellant's convictions, that both submissions were correct. In so holding, the court applied the reasoning of Donaldson LJ in *Lindley v Rutter* (1980) (see 26.3.2 above) in respect of the first search, and obtained guidance from *Christie v Leachinsky* (1947) (see 26.3.1 above) in respect of the second.

26.3.3 Protection of the subject through the exclusion of evidence

The considerations governing exercise of the common law discretion to exclude evidence

Jeffrey v Black (1978)

The respondent was arrested by members of the police drug squad for the theft of a sandwich from a public house. He was taken to a police station. Before he was charged, he was asked to give his consent to his flat being searched. The respondent accompanied the police to his flat and unlocked the door. In the course of the search, the police found cannabis and cannabis resin. The magistrates found as fact that the respondent had not given his consent to the search of his flat. They therefore exercised their common law discretion to exclude evidence found as a result of the search, and dismissed the charges. The prosecution appealed by way of case stated to the Divisional Court, asking, *inter alia*, 'were the justices right in ruling that the evidence of the finding of the articles was inadmissible if they found that the respondent had not given his consent to the search?'

Held, that there was no discretion to exclude relevant evidence solely on the ground stated, and the case would be sent back to be re-heard before a different bench. The test for the admissibility of evidence was whether the evidence was relevant to the matters in issue. The magistrates, in common with any other English court, had a general discretion to decline to allow any evidence to be called by the prosecution if they thought that it would be unfair or oppressive to allow that to be done. However, it would be appropriate to exercise the discretion only in exceptional circumstances. *Per* Lord Widgery CJ:

> ... if the case is exceptional, if the case is such that not only have the police officers entered without authority, but they have been guilty of trickery or they have misled someone, or they have been oppressive or they have been unfair, or in other respects they have behaved in a manner which is morally reprehensible, then it is open to the justices to apply their discretion and decline to allow the particular evidence to be let in as part of the trial.

There is no discretion to exclude evidence on the ground that it was obtained by entrapment

R v Sang (1980) HL

In the course of the appellant's trial on charges of conspiracy in connection with counterfeit bank notes, his counsel sought to persuade the judge to rule against the admissibility of the prosecution's evidence on the ground that it related to offences which the appellant would not have committed unless he had been induced to do so by police officers acting as *agents provocateurs*. The judge ruled that he had no discretion to exclude evidence on this ground, and therefore refused to hear the evidence by which the entrapment was intended to be established. The appellant then changed his plea to one of guilty. His appeal against the judge's ruling was dismissed by the Court of Appeal. He renewed it before the House of Lords.

Held, dismissing the appeal, that the judge's ruling had been correct. The court was concerned not with how evidence was gathered, but rather with the use made of it at the trial. To allow the exclusion of evidence on the basis for which the appellant contended would effectively be to introduce into English law a defence of entrapment. No such defence existed. *Per* Lord Diplock:

> ... the function of a judge at a criminal trial as respects the admission of evidence is to ensure that the accused has a fair trial according to the law. It is no part of a judge's function to exercise disciplinary powers over the police or prosecution as respects the way in which evidence to be used at the trial is obtained by them. If it was obtained illegally there will be a remedy in civil law; if it was obtained legally but in breach of the rules of conduct for the police, this is a matter for the appropriate disciplinary authority to deal with ...

Statutory exclusion of evidence

R v Keenan (1989) CA

Police officers stopped the appellant's car, arrested the appellant for taking and driving the car away without authority, and searched the car in the appellant's absence. They found a home-made spear in it. The appellant was charged with driving offences, and with possession of an offensive weapon. After his committal, at which the only evidence relating to the spear was provided by the officers who had found it, further evidence was served in which two other officers alleged that the appellant had been asked about the spear. They stated that he had admitted that he knew it was in the car, but denied it was his. In breach of provisions of the Code of Practice for the Detention, Treatment and Questioning of Persons by Police Officers issued under s 66 of the Police and Criminal Evidence Act 1984, the alleged interview had not been properly recorded or documented by the police. The appellant maintained that it had never taken place. He was convicted, and appealed on the ground that evidence of the alleged interview should not have been admitted.

Held, allowing the appeal and quashing the conviction, that the breaches of the code had been serious and substantial. To admit the evidence was to penalise the appellant if he intended to exercise his right to remain silent at the trial, or to force him to challenge it and thereby open his past record to cross examination or to put him at a disadvantage since there was no contemporaneous record of the interview. The evidence should therefore have been excluded under s 78 of the 1984 Act. *Per* Hodgson J:

> The provisions [of the 1984 Act and the Codes of Practice issued under it] will only be workable if and when compliance with them becomes the habitual practice of the police ... It is to be hoped that in future no police officer will display the ignorance of even the important provisions in issue in this case as these officers did ... We think that in cases where there have been 'significant and substantial' breaches of the 'verballing' provisions of the code, the evidence so obtained will frequently be excluded. We do not think that any injustice will be caused by this. It is clear that not every breach or combination of breaches of the code will justify the exclusion of interview evidence under s 76 or s 78: see *R v Hallett* (7 March 1989, unreported). They must be significant and substantial. If this were not the case, the courts would be undertaking a task which is no part of their duty; as Lord Lane CJ said in *R v Delaney* (at 341): 'It is no part of the duty of the court to rule a statement inadmissible simply in order to punish the police for failure to observe the codes of practice.'

27 Glossary

Act of State – an action authorised or adopted by the executive in the conduct of its relations with another State or its subjects.

Applicant – the party which applies to court for judicial review of a public authority's decision or action.

Attorney General – the government's principal legal advisor and representative, responsible for the supervision of criminal justice and competent in all cases to vindicate public rights.

Caution – a statement required to be made to a person suspected by the police of an offence, indicating that his answers or silence in response to questioning may be given in evidence in a criminal prosecution.

Certiorari – a remedy available in judicial review proceedings, bringing up and quashing the decision which is subject to challenge.

Collective ministerial responsibility – the convention that government ministers should not disagree publicly with government policy.

Common law – (as contrasted with statute): the entire corpus of binding judicial decisions and the legal principles to which it gives rise.

Constitutionalism – the principle that the legal power of government should derive from and be limited by a higher form of law.

Constitutionality – the conformity of actions, practices, decisions or legislation with a formal constitution.

Conventions – non-legal rules derived from practice, serving to define the constitutionally proper exercise of power.

Declaration – a non-coercive remedy available in judicial review proceedings, consisting of a formal statement of the law as it applies to the facts before the court.

Delegated legislation – see subordinate legislation.

Entrenchment – the conditional or absolute protection of a legislative measure from subsequent repeal.

Exclusion Order – an order made pursuant to ss 5, 6 or 7 of the Prevention of Terrorism (Temporary Provisions) Act 1989, normally used to remove a person of Northern Irish origin from Great Britain.

Fairness – the term preferred in the modern law to express the procedural duty to apply the requirements of natural justice as they vary in the circumstances of individual cases.

Habeas Corpus – a writ requiring that a person detained be brought before a court, and that a justification be given for the detention.

Hansard – the official report of debates in each House of Parliament

Incorporation – the legislative action of Parliament by which a treaty of the Crown becomes part of UK domestic law.

Individual Ministerial Responsibility – the convention that a minister is politically responsible to Parliament for failure within his or her Department.

Injunction – a court order granted in equity, frequently sought during or at the outset of litigation (an interlocutory injunction), requiring or prohibiting defined actions.

Locus Standi – the requirement (imposed by s 31(4) of the Supreme Court Act 1981 and the Rules of the Supreme Court Order 53 r 3(7)) that an applicant for judicial review should have 'a sufficient interest in the matter to which the application relates'.

Judicial Review – the form of High Court legal challenge to the decisions or actions of public authorities, established by s 31 of the Supreme Court Act 1981 and Order 53 of the Rules of the Supreme Court.

Legitimate Expectation – the presumption that a representation given by a public authority as to its future action will be honoured unless the public interest requires otherwise.

Malice – (in the law of defamation): the maker's lack of belief in the truth of a statement, or its making for an improper purpose.

Margin of appreciation – a principle found chiefly in the jurisprudence of the European Court of Human Rights, allowing signatory states a measure of discretion in their treatment of certain Treaty rights.

Mandamus – a remedy available in judicial review proceedings, compelling a public authority to perform its legal duty.

Natural Justice – the principles of fair adjudication developed in the supervisory jurisdiction of the High Court, permitting challenge to a decision vitiated by bias or the appearance of bias or failure to consider both sides of the question.

Ouster clause – a legislative provision accompanying the grant of a power, calculated either to deny or to restrict legal challenge to the manner of the power's exercise.

Parliamentary privilege – the rights and immunities claimed by each House of Parliament and/or its members, and acknowledged by the courts.

Parliamentary Roll – the register onto which the Clerk of Parliament formerly transcribed Acts which had received the Royal Assent. Today, the official copies of Acts of Parliament are those deposited in the House of Lords library and the Public Records office.

Parliamentary sovereignty – see Parliamentary supremacy.

Parliamentary supremacy – the principle that the courts recognise the authority of the Queen in Parliament to legislate on any matter whatsoever and the absence of any higher legislative authority (outside the context of European law).

Privilege – see Parliamentary Privilege, Qualified Privilege.

Prerogative – see Royal Prerogative.

Prerogative orders – the remedies of *certiorari*, *mandamus* and prohibition, applied for by an application for judicial review.

Prohibition – a remedy available in judicial review proceedings, forbidding a public authority from acting contrary to law.

Proportionality – the doctrine (not accepted as a formal principle of English public law) that the legitimacy of administrative action depends in part upon the maintenance of a reasonable balance between its express objective and its collateral consequences.

Purposive interpretation – a principle of statutory construction whereby a literal interpretation of the wording of legislation is rejected in favour of an interpretation which better realises the presumed legislative intention in the circumstances of the case.

Qualified privilege – a defence to a defamation suit, defeasible by proof that the defendant acted with actual malice.

Ratification – the procedure whereby the legislation gives its assent to an international agreement made by the executive.

Respondent – (1) the party against whose decision an applicant seeks judicial review; (2) the party defending an appeal.

Royal Assent – the final stage in the passing of a Bill into law, symbolising the agreement of the monarch to the terms of the legislation.

Royal prerogative – residual non-statutory powers exercisable by the Crown and its servants and recognised by the courts.

Rule of Law – the principles that all should be subject to the law, that government should be according to law, and that legislation should be guided by open, stable and general rules.

Rules of the Supreme Court – subordinate legislation governing the conduct of proceedings in the higher courts.

Separation of powers – the theory that the avoidance of absolutism requires the vesting of executive, legislative and judicial power respectively in separate agencies of the State.

Subordinate legislation – rules promulgated by the executive pursuant to power delegated by Act of Parliament.

Supervisory jurisdiction – the power of the High Court, derived from common law, to adjudicate upon the legality of the actions and decisions of public authorities.

Weight – the extent to which a consideration should properly influence the making of an administrative decision.

Index